Strong Gurney

Early landmarks of Syracuse

Strong Gurney

Early landmarks of Syracuse

ISBN/EAN: 9783337111175

Printed in Europe, USA, Canada, Australia, Japan

Cover: Foto ©Andreas Hilbeck / pixelio.de

More available books at **www.hansebooks.com**

OF

SYRACUSE

— — — —

BY

GURNEY S. STRONG

City Editor of The Sunday Times

With an Introduction by

GEORGE J. GARDNER

Long a prominent member of the Onondaga Historical Association

— — — — — — —

SYRACUSE, N. Y.

Printed and Illustrated by

THE TIMES PUBLISHING COMPANY

1894

PREFACE

In order that valuable material, almost lost by neglect, might be rescued from obscurity; and that those who once played a prominent part in the early history of Syracuse, even though their descendants might not have been publicly distinguished, should have the story of their services to the city recorded and preserved for the city's future historian; and lastly, that a work might be presented within the reach of the most modest purse, the author has undertaken the compilation of the following historical sketches. No attempt has been made to unduly praise the men prominent in the early history of this city, nor to detract from any one the credit that is rightly due.

In compiling this material—valuable to the student, to the historian, and to every one who is interested in the city's continued prosperity, whether descendants of the early settlers or coming hither in later years—the author has availed himself of the books already written.

It is a singular fact that "Clark's Onondaga,"

(iii)

written by Joshua V. H. Clark in 1849, and the
"Memorial History of Syracuse," edited by Dwight
H. Bruce and published in 1891, are very rare and expensive books, exceedingly difficult to obtain. Aside
from recourse to those books, assistance has been
obtained from M. C. Hand's "From a Forest to a City."

The author would extend his special acknowledgments to George J. Gardner, whose mind is a storehouse of historical information and whose library
contains many pamphlets and papers very rare and
priceless; to ex-Lieut-Gov. Thomas G. Alvord, whose
retentive memory has supplied many names and dates
and events; to Gen. Dwight H. Bruce, whose encour-
agement and advice have been of great assistance;
and he is none the less under obligations to the many
others who have kindly aided in this undertaking by
furnishing facts and suggestions.

The records in the County Clerk's office have been
critically examined; and for aid in the prosecution of
this part of the work acknowledgments are due to
County Clerk De Forest Settle and the search clerks,
Jonathan B. White, James Butler and James B.
Hitchcock. The old newspaper files have also been
consulted, valuable aid having been rendered in this
labor by the Rev. Ezekiel W. Mundy, Librarian of
the Central Library.

In writing the chapter on the Onondaga Academy,
the author has been greatly aided by the historical

address of John T. Roberts, prepared for the reunion of the graduates of the academy, June 19, 1885. And the chapter on the "Jerry Rescue" was compiled from a paper written by Charles Russell Bardeen as a special report in United States history in Harvard University, April 13, 1893.

For reasons well understood in this community, it is deemed proper to state that not one of the illustrations has been or will be paid for by anyone excepting the author, who alone bears the entire expense of this publication.

The county is about to celebrate the centennial of its existence; and the matter has been brought to the attention of the public and county authorities by the well directed endeavors of the Onondaga Historical Association. If the present volume shall prove of any advantage or contribute in any degree to the proper and worthy observance of the occasion, this publication will perhaps not be deemed inopportune at the present time.

THE AUTHOR.

Syracuse, N. Y., January, 1894.

INTRODUCTION

" Breathes there the man, with soul so dead,
Who never to himself hath said,
    This is my own, my native land!
Whose heart hath ne'er within him burned,
As home his footsteps he hath turned
    From wandering on a foreign strand?
If such there breathe, go, mark him well;
For him no minstrel raptures swell:
High though his titles, proud his name,
Boundless his wealth as wish can claim,—
Despite those titles, power, and pelf,
The wretch, concentred all in self,
Living, shall forfeit fair renown,
And, doubly dying, shall go down
To the vile dust, from whence he sprung,
Unwept, unhonored and unsung."

Thus sang the great Scottish Bard—a sentiment which should find an echo in every patriotic breast.

A writer has said that three most tender and touching words in the English language are Mother—Home—Heaven. A man who does not love his country—who will not labor for its interests—who smothers the fire of patriotism which naturally

(vii)

smoulders in every heart, is fit only "for treason, stratagem and spoils." No man can truly be called a good citizen, who will not cheerfully do what lies in his power and use his best endeavors to rescue from oblivion the fast decaying evidences of a past age. It thrills the heart of every true lover of his country to call to mind the efforts used and the results attained during the last decade, in the many centennial celebrations which have been held all over our land—patriotic, civic and personal in character, yet all of a somewhat, though varied, historical nature.

We, of this county, stand on the threshold of the second century of our civil existence as an integral portion of the great Empire State. The residents of and actors in the earlier period of our history have all passed away. Here and there may occasionally be seen a patriarch nonagenarian or octogenarian, but "like angels' visits, they are few and far between." If found, their memories are so clouded—their descriptive powers so weakened, or their backward vision so hazy, that but little reliable information can be gleaned from them. Well may we ask in the language of Scripture,—"The fathers—where are they? and the prophets—do they live forever?"

This geographical section is rich in archaeological treasures, and the explorer will be amply rewarded for his labors if he will work diligently in the rubbish of the past. Many of our Indian historical traditions

ante-date the birth of our county, and have been
preserved and handed down to posterity through the
indefatigable efforts and perseverance of our well
known and justly styled authentic writer and histori-
ographer, Joshua V. H. Clark.

Imbued with the same spirit, the writer and compiler of this volume has endeavored to place before the
reader the results of his investigation, so far as our own
immediate municipal locality is concerned, covering
the period of our babyhood as a village and our more
mature years as a populous city, embracing a period
of over half a century of our rural and city life.
Existing landmarks have been visited—individuals
have been consulted—records have been searched—
musty and time-worn documents have been examined,
and every authority, written or verbal, has been sought
whereby information could be obtained, or any data
or incident, connected with the object sought, procured,
regardless of expenditure of time or means in the
pursuit of the knowledge necessary to make the work
a faithful record of the object described.

Many local landmarks, whether now existing or
those passed away, have been minutely and accurately
described, and many relics historical or otherwise
which have been preserved or destroyed by the tooth
of time, have been resurrected from the past and
placed in the historic archives, where the historian of
the future can have ready access to them.

The enterprise has been a laudable one—we trust that aside from the pleasure experienced in compilation, the pecuniary recompense will be adequate for the undertaking.

GEORGE J. GARDNER.

Syracuse, N. Y., January, 1894.

CONTENTS

CHAPTER I

CHAPTER II

CHAPTER III

(xi)

CHAPTER VII

CHAPTER VIII

CHAPTER IX

CHAPTER XIX

CHAPTER XX

LIST OF ILLUSTRATIONS

THE HOME OF HARVEY BALDWIN.—From a recent photograph

CHAPTER I

THE FIRST MAYOR OF SYRACUSE

The large old-fashioned wooden dwelling on the northwesterly corner of West Onondaga and West streets, now occupied by the widow of George Everson, was once the centre of the most fashionable society in this city, being occupied by one of the most noted families between New York and Chicago. Whenever a distinguished man visited this city in the early days, and many men of national reputation visited Syracuse, the hospitable owner of that mansion, Harvey Baldwin, was chosen as by natural right to be the host and entertainer. Mr. Baldwin was a gentleman of rare intelligence, courtesy and refinement; and he was distinguished for his enterprise, public spirit, zeal and benevolence in good works. His family was a large one, consisting of his accomplished and beautiful wife, the daughter of Col. William I. Dodge, and several children, the daughters being remarkably beautiful and the belles of the city. The children were highly educated;

and as the daughters were able to play on different
musical instruments and all the children could sing
admirably, the many guests were accorded a delightful entertainment. The grounds which surrounded
that old homestead, consisting of several acres, were
beautified by fine gardens and driveways, with several high mounds nicely turfed, and containing
many natural forest trees. They were so large as to
afford abundant room for picnics and other festival
gatherings, besides containing a park where several
deer roamed at their pleasure.

The property was sold March 9, 1839, by David S.
Colvin to Horace White, a prominent banker, for
$800, and it is described as "commencing where the
road leading towards the Stone Mill (now known as
West street) joins the Cinder road" (now known as
West Onondaga street). Mr. White built his residence on the property ; but as he considered that it
was too far into the country and away from his office
he sold it in 1841 to James L. Voorhees, formerly the
owner of the Empire House block, for $4,000, the
deed being acknowledged January 12, 1842.   Mr.
Voorhees sold the property to Harvey Baldwin for
$5,000, May 18, 1844. Mr. Baldwin enlarged the
house and greatly improved the grounds. And he
continued to live there till his death, August 22, 1863,
at the age of 67 years. He was buried in his family
vault in Rose Hill cemetery, the first cemetery vault

built in this city, which was erected in 1844. His second wife, Ann Sarah Dodge, who was born September 28, 1816, and died December 20, 1886, is also buried there. His first wife was the daughter of James Geddes, the founder of the village of Geddes.

Harvey Baldwin was the second son of Dr. Jonas C. Baldwin, a wealthy gentleman who founded the village of Baldwinsville and who was the second son of Captain Samuel Baldwin, a soldier in the revolutionary war. According to the inscription on the family vault, Harvey was born in 1796. He enlisted in the war of 1812. During the winter of 1816, which is memorable throughout the country as "the cold year," he was adopted by the Oneida Indians, many of whom were provided for that winter by his father, and given the name of "Cohongoronto," signifying a boat having a sharp prow constructed for the navigation of rapid waters, and intended as emblematical of the profession of law, in the study of which he was then engaged. The old homestead on the old Cinder road has been the scene of many entertainments given to the Indians by Cohongoronto. Mr. Baldwin studied law in the office of Elisha Williams and Judge Miller of Oneida county and of Thaddeus M. Wood of Onondaga Valley. He was admitted to the bar February 28, 1820. He practiced law at Onondaga Valley till 1826, when, in company with his law partner, Schuyler Strong, he removed to

Syracuse, opening an office in the east wing of the
Syracuse House.   The remarkable foresight which
distinguished Mr. Baldwin is shown in this removal
from Onondaga Valley, at that time considered of
far more importance than the village of Syracuse.
But the grand canal celebration, given in honor of
Governor Clinton and suite on their first passage
down the canal, Nov. 1, 1825, convinced the young
man that Syracuse was destined to become the principal city.   And he was soon followed by Elias W.
Leavenworth, B. Davis Noxon, James R. Lawrence
and other men prominent among the early settlers,
some of whom came with the removal of the Court
House in 1829.

The event in Harvey Baldwin's life which will
always keep his memory green was his celebrated
"hanging-garden speech," which made him the first
mayor of Syracuse.   This speech—the most sanguine,
hopeful, confident, regarding the future of Syracuse
that was ever delivered—subjected its author to unbounded ridicule and caused him to be looked upon
as a fool.   But subsequent events have proven that
the man, who had traveled extensively through
Europe and this country, was wiser than his day and
generation.   The speech was delivered in 1846, when
Syracuse had so wonderfully increased in size and
population that the subject of securing for it a city
charter began seriously to be discussed.   There was

considerable difference of opinion among the inhabitants as to the extent of territory that should be embraced. Some were for including the whole original Salt Springs Reservation, while others advocated only the village of Syracuse. The matter finally resulted in the grant of a charter in 1848 including the villages of Syracuse and Salina, with the name of Syracuse. In the following year the census showed that the city's population was 16,000.

An attempt was made when Mr. Baldwin was the Democratic candidate for Congress to stem this tide of ridicule by saying: "The description of the destiny of Syracuse, whether reality or vision, is a proud dream. To some extent it may be visionary; but it is no more visionary than would have been twenty years ago a description of Syracuse as she now really is. He came here when there were but five or six hundred inhabitants settled down in the midst of a swamp.". The speech is in part as follows:

"Were we permitted to indulge in visions of the future, I would present a view of our village or city, as it is to appear hereafter, when all of us who are now on the busy stage of life shall be slumbering with our fathers. It is a remarkable fact that everybody away from our village, foreign travelers and all, predict for us a higher destiny than we claim for ourselves. It is universally conceded that we are to become the great inland town of the State, and next

in size and importance to New York and Buffalo—
that we are to go on by rapid strides, increasing in
population, until we shall number from 100,000 to
200,000. If past experience will throw any light upon
the subject, then may we fairly claim that the short
space of fifty years will give us a population of more
than 100,000 souls. Let us, sir, for a moment contemplate the city of Syracuse as she will then appear.
Immense structures of compact buildings will in every
direction cover this delightful plain, and every hill,
knoll and swell of ground be occupied by some stately
mansion or neat cottage.

"All bordering territory will have been brought
into a high and perfect state of cultivation, and our
beautiful lake, on all its beautiful shores and borders,
will present a view of one continuous villa, ornamented
with its shady groves and hanging gardens, and connected by a wide and splendid avenue that shall
encircle its entire waters, and furnish a delightful
drive to the gay and prosperous citizens of the town,
who will, toward the close of each summer's day,
throng it for pleasure, relaxation or the improvement
of health. In every salt manufactory that studs its
shores will be seen the ponderous steam engine,
breathing forth its heated vapor, and by the same
power drawing rich treasure from the bowels of the
earth, and converting it into an article indispensable
to the human family ; while it drives a thousand

wheels and propels cotton, woolen and flouring mills, and all the varied machinery known to man or that may be by man's ingenuity designed and adopted to his necessities and wants.

"Then, too, will be seen the magnificent steamers of the ocean and of our inland seas arriving and departing or lying at our extended wharves, receiving and discharging their heavy and well assorted cargoes; and everywhere will be heard the hum of its busy, thrifty and happy people. On yonder hill will be seen the gilded dome of the stately and massive capitol ; and pinnacles and spires towering from the plain in every direction, pointing their tall shafts towards heaven, as emblems of those who worship beneath. What a beautiful view will here burst upon the delighted traveler as he treads the lofty deck of the ocean or lake steamer just emerging from the slackened water and deepened channel of the Oswego into our beautiful lake, or as he is whirled with locomotive power and speed along the numerous railways that on the east and west, the north and south, approach the town. The extended city, with its hundred spires, pinnacles and domes, its ascending smoke, vapor and dust, lies before him. On the east and west, the sloping hills, which, by an easy and gentle gradation from the south, drop here to the level of the valley, are studded with splendid mansions and neat cottages ; and southward still, rising in magnificent gradation, are seen in the dim distance the blue and folding hills of Onondaga, Lafayette and Pompey, whose sides and summits are chequered by neat farms, carved out from the forest, and these again chequered and colored by all the various crops of the husbandman, with innumerable flocks and herds feeding upon their green and rich pastures, or basking in the genial rays of the sun that warms its fertile soil—while at the north our beautiful lake lies like a gem in the lap of the extended valley, which, unbroken, sweeps away towards the mighty Ontario, whose waters wash the northern shores of our Republic, and whose centre channel defines our northern boundary.

"In short, sir, everything is clustered here calculated to invite and gladden the heart of man—everything which the lover of the world, the man of pleasure or business, the Christian, the philanthropist or the admirer of nature can desire, and which, collectively, make up the beautiful landscape. Deem me not extravagant, sir. I speak of things that are and are to be. This is not a fancy sketch, but a slight pencilling, an imperfect and dim shadowing forth of the future."

It is needless to say that Mr. Baldwin advocated the measure—indeed, he made the motion—to include not only Geddes and Liverpool, but the entire reservation. And his unbounded faith in the future

prosperity of the town took a substantial form. He
purchased property in every part of the city; so that a
railroad could not pass through the city nor a manufacturing concern locate here without coming to him
for the purchase of land. And he was a strong
public spirited citizen. He took a prominent and
active part in the construction of plank roads and
bridges and in the organization of every railroad constructed in the early days. The very first winter that
he came to Syracuse he organized a Mechanics'
Library ; he started a Lyceum ; he was one of the
originators of an Association Library ; he contributed aid liberally to the building of every church in
the city; he was one of the fathers of the State Agricultural Society, the sole founder of the Onondaga
County Agricultural Society and one of the originators of the present common school system; a fast
friend of the free school system, and active in the internal improvement of both the city and the county ;
and acting in all merely as a private citizen. He
brought into the county and distributed a great variety
of foreign and other valuable seed, and was the first
to introduce the Durham and Berkshire stock and
good breeds of sheep. He was at one time Chief of
the old Volunteer Fire Department. He was the
counsel and legal adviser in the organization of the
old Onondaga County Bank, the first institution of
the kind in the county, and continued its attorney

for many years. He was appointed not only the
agent, but the legal adviser of the Syracuse Company,
which formerly owned almost all of Syracuse. He
was the principal originator and the first President of
the Syracuse Savings Institution, which was the first
of the kind in this section of the State.

The bar of Onondaga County paid a fitting tribute
to his memory at the time of his death, saying that
"the high and extensive culture, polished manners,
great integrity and persuasive eloquence which he
brought to the performance of his professional duties,
rendered him justly eminent among the lawyers of
this county." The Common Council also passed resolutions, saying : "Mr. Baldwin has been foremost
in promoting all measures of public utility, and in
advancing by his personal efforts and by pecuniary
sacrifices the interests of the community in which he
lived."

The last will of Harvey Baldwin, dated May 27,
1863, contains this eccentric clause : "And regarding
the use of tobacco in any form whatever as an un-
gentlemanly, filthy and pernicious practice, and
wishing to express my dislike and abhorrence of it, I
hereby declare that any of my children who shall
offend in the premises after the publication of this,
my last will and testament, and before the distribution and final settlement of my estate, shall have his
or her share as the case may be, charged with the sum

of $1,000, to be deducted from such share or shares, and the amount thereof shall be distributed equally among the surviving children who shall not so offend." When Mr. Baldwin died his estate possessed considerable property in Syracuse and Onondaga county, besides very large tracts of land in Louisiana and Texas.

An account of the life of Harvey Baldwin would be incomplete without some mention being made of his accomplished children. At the time of his death his minor children were Cora, Grace, Sarah, Burnet T., and Irving D. His other children who were living at that time were Laura, who married Washington Morton, of New York, and whose wedding was the first one in this city to which tickets of admission were issued—this being made necessary on account of the numerous friends of the family ; Harvey ; Julia ; and Mary, who married Edward Renshaw Jones, a wealthy gentleman of New York city, now deceased. The daughters were considered the most beautiful and accomplished young ladies in the city, and they were the recipients of much favorable attention in the best social circles of Europe, to which their father's social standing admitted them. The surviving children are living in or near New York city.

CHAPTER II

A FAMOUS COFFEE HOUSE

The coffee house which formerly stood on the corner of Washington and Warren streets, where the Vanderbilt House now stands, was a very famous eating house in its day, being favorably known throughout the entire State and exceedingly popular with the people who then resided in Syracuse. The erection of the building, as a two-story wooden dwelling house, was begun in 1824 by Gen. Jonas Mann, who moved in his family the next season and during the summer finished the work. After a couple of years the house was occupied by Col. Elijah Phillips, who was for many years agent of the great line of stages of Thorpe & Sprague from Albany to Buffalo. The wife of Col. Phillips was the daughter of Asa Danforth, jr., the first white child born in Onondaga county and the mother of Mrs. Peter Outwater, who was the mother-in-law of Andrew D. White, Ex-President of Cornell University.

In later years the place was rented by Andrew

(30)

COOK'S COFFEE HOUSE. - From an old stereoscopic view.

Leinhart as a German tavern and boarding house.
The place was afterwards run as a saloon by a German named Seigle. The bar was made very attractive by means of mirrors and bird cages. And among the many birds there was an old and wicked parrot, well informed in bar-room etiquette, who would call in the most deliberate manner for the different kinds of drinks. The place was fitted up in a better style than was usual for those days, and it was a popular place of resort, especially among the Germans. But that which distinguished it most was in being the scene of one of the greatest riots that ever occurred in the village of Syracuse.

On the night of the first of January, 1844, while a New Year's ball was in progress in that house, several roughs from Salt Point, as Salina was then called, entered the bar room. William Blake, who had been celebrating the day beyond his powers of endurance, smashed his glass on the bar. This was in accordance with a prearranged plan, for the Salt Pointers were on mischief bent. A war of words ensued with the woman who was dispensing the drinks. The woman, against whom some insulting remark had been made, called for assistance. Her husband, Mr. Seigle, thereupon promptly shot, but did not kill Blake. Then the fight became terrific, for in those days the boys, especially the Salt Pointers, were fighters. Several of the participants were shot. It was fortunate that

Captain Timothy H. Teall's cadets, whose quarters were in the Granger Block, directly opposite, had just returned from their drill. Lieutenant William B. Olmsted called together the departing members of the Syracuse Cadets, and, surrounding the house, captured Seigle and several others and marched their prisoners to the old jail. When the cadets had departed the mob ransacked the house and made a bonfire of all the furniture. The cadets returned in time to save the building from being burned. The prisoners were tried the next day before Major William A. Cook, Justice of the Peace, and they were acquitted. Several of those who attacked the house were put under bonds to keep the peace. The German landlord, besides having his furniture totally demolished, mourned the loss of $300, which had been stolen from him. And after that he had no peace. He retired early every night, locked himself securely in, and stationed a guard at his door. He was glad to sell out his business the following April to Eliphalet Welch; and then he departed for Milwaukee.

Mr. Welch had formerly been associated with George Babcock, his nephew, in conducting a temperance restaurant, called the Syracuse Lunch, in the basement of the wooden building which was located where the Onondaga County Savings Bank building is now. Mr. Babcock had purchased that lunching place from Elisha Ford, June 20, 1839; and

considerable money had been made there, the trade
coming mostly from the Erie canal packet boats which
landed near by. It was thought at that time that
Mr. Welch had made a great mistake in moving to
the corner of Warren and Railroad streets, as that
location was considered too far removed from the
centre of trade. But Mr. Welch enlarged and improved the building and made it a very desirable resort for ladies and gentlemen. Welch's Coffee House,
as the place was called, soon acquired an excellent
reputation, and it was as well known throughout the
country as an eating house as was the old Syracuse
House, which had a national reputation. In those
days the depot stood in the centre of the street between Salina and Warren streets.

Mr. Welch was given a key to a door on the eastern
side of the depot, in consideration of his allowing an
extra track, which passed from a switch at Salina
street around the south side of the depot, to be placed
in front of his coffee house, there joining the main
track. In this way he was enabled to secure some of
the passengers for his eating house.

Much of the success of Welch's coffee house was
due to Mrs. Welch, who was an excellent pastry cook,
and to George Babcock, who was an excellent mana-
ger. But, on account of his wife's failing health,
Mr. Welch sold out his business, April 1, 1851, to
John L. Cook and Emilus Gay, and retired to his

farm of thirteen acres, located about where Cortland
avenue enters South Salina street. He died September 10, 1874, at the age of 78, and is remembered for
his gentlemanly manners and his kindhearted, gen-
erous disposition. His surviving children are Mrs.
Laurence W. Myers and Mrs. George H. Hosmer.
Elisha Ford, aged 85 years, and George Babcock,
aged 80 years, are still living. Cook & Gay continued the place for one year, and then Mr. Babcock
bought out Mr. Gay's interest, the firm continuing as
Cook & Babcock for three years. During that time
the business was so prosperous that the firm made a
yearly net profit of $7,000 above living expenses. Mr.
Babcock then sold out his interest to Mr. Cook, who
took into partnership his sons, John L., jr., and
Austin D., the place being then known as Cook &
Sons' Coffee House.

There is not a resident of this city, who lived here
a quarter of a century ago, who does not entertain
pleasant recollections of Cook's Coffee House. It was,
indeed, a famous eating house. So popular had the
place become, that the little two-story wooden building became altogether too small for the many customers, and an additional building was added on Railroad street, which was reserved exclusively for ladies,
and an extension was made on Warren street for the
kitchen. There was also a large open shed built on
Warren street to accommodate the horses of the farm-

JOHN L. COOK.

ers. The main entrance was on Railroad street with a side entrance on Warren street. The front part of the room was reserved as a meeting place; and here could be found, during some parts of the day, every professional and business man in the city. Then came the bar, which extended across the room, parallel with Railroad street. Beyond that was the dining room. A large table, extending east and west, was surrounded by small tables, with two small private rooms on the Warren street side. At noon time the table was spread with an excellent twenty-five cent dinner, each plate being ready for the customer, and provided with a capital repast, kept warm by me .ns of heaters, placed upon the table. It was not an unusual occurrence for a customer to wait for a seat to become vacant.

In those happy days, when a man could obtain a glass of Hersey's whiskey, which was made in Cazenovia and which was celebrated throughout the country, for three cents, and a pure Havana cigar for three cents, it was customary for each customer, upon paying for his dinner, to receive a cigar. And in those good old times the stores did not close till nine or ten o'clock. It was customary during the evenings for the merchants and their clerks, the lawyers and other professional men, to meet at Cook's Coffee House for a light repast, a social glass and a fragrant cigar. Mrs. Cook, who is still living, was celebrated

for her pastry, especially her lemon pie, which sold
for three cents. The fashionable ladies of the city
frequently took their meals in the room reserved for
them. Mr. Cook, an English gentleman of the old
school, greeted his guests with a happy remark or a
pleasant exchange of witticism, and did much by his
courteous manners to make his eating house popular,
though his success depended largely upon the excellent management of his wife. Among the regular
customers was "Counselor" Orcutt, an attorney who
enjoyed the reputation of being an eccentric character.
Promptly at nine o'clock every evening, just as the
clock was striking the hour, the door would open and
the Counselor would enter the room. He was always dressed in an old-fashioned blue coat with brass
buttons, a ruffled shirt, a blue pair of pantaloons,
gaitors about his shoes and a silk hat. The bartender
would place a glass of beer upon the counter; and
"Counselor" Orcutt, with his crooked iron cane
hanging from his left arm, the glass of beer in one
hand and a stub of a cigar in the other, would walk
up and down the room, always ready for an argument, which he sustained with some ability as he was
well read, and never leaving the place till all the other
customers had departed.

In 1867 the old building was removed to its present
location, the northwestern corner of Montgomery
and Jackson streets. It was purchased by Isaac

Manheimer and used as a grocery; and it is now occupied by his son-in-law, Moses Lichtenberg, as a grocery. It was succeeded by a larger building, which completely covered the former site. Mr. Cook named his hotel The Vanderbilt in honor of Commodore Vanderbilt, in order to give it the advantage of a world-renowned name and thus add popularity to his hotel. The Commodore was so well pleased with this honor that he sent Mr. Cook a fine engraving of himself, and the picture still hangs in the office of the hotel. The Vanderbilt House was opened March 18, 1868, Cook & Sons being the proprietors. It was the first hotel in the city to be furnished with parlor mantles and grate fires. Charles Dickens was the first guest. When he came to Syracuse March 9, 1868, to give his readings of "The Christmas Carol" and the Bardell-Pickwick trial, at the Wieting Hall, he was allowed to take the corner room directly over the parlor in order that he might have a grate fire in his room, even though the hotel was not ready for its guests. When Cornelius Vanderbilt, or Commodore as he was generally called, was married Saturday morning, August 21, 1869, at London, Canada—Miss Frank Crawford being the favored lady—he stayed at the hotel which had been named after him. The Commodore was then 73 years old, and that was his second marriage. The bridal party reached Syracuse Saturday evening, the special car stopping in front of the hotel.

The Commodore and his wife hastened to their apartments, where they remained during their stay, their
meals being there served to them. But the waiters
had cause to remember the short stay, which ended
Sunday morning, as the venerable railroad king left
fifty dollars to be scattered among them.

Mr. Cook sold his hotel in 1879 to Daniel Candee,
Horace Candee and Earll B. Alvord. The place has
since been run as the Vanderbilt, and it is now one
of the leading hotels in the city. Mr. Cook died November 4, 1890, at the age of 83. He was survived
by his sons John L., jr., Austin D. and Major Abel
G. and his daughter, Mrs. Lyman B. Dickinson. His
daughter Mary Jane, who married Marsh C. Pierce,
died some years previous. His son Austin died in
March, 1891. Mr. Cook was a prominent man in his
day. He was the Democratic Alderman from the
Sixth Ward in 1858 and one of the original committee
by whom Oakwood cemetery was bought and laid
out in 1859. He was also elected Assessor.

In the old Cook Coffee House there were several
fine paintings by Sanford Thayer, a local artist of
widely recognized ability, who painted many valuable
pictures. But there was one picture which used to
hang in that famous eating house, and which now
hangs in the bar room of the Vanderbilt, that can
recall many pleasant recollections to the theatre goers
of thirty and forty years ago. A card on the picture

reads thus: "Compliments of R. W. Jones. This picture hung on the wall in the old Welch Coffee House on this site, about forty years ago." The picture represents two women in their stage costume for "Asmodeus, or the Little Devil's Share." As there was some resemblance in the face and hands especially, and also in the form, of the shorter of the two figures to Susan Denin, the picture passed as a likeness of the Denin sisters, Susan and Kate. But the picture was not a likeness. These Denin sisters were the reigning actresses in those days, and they became famous in starring throughout the United States. They were great favorites in Syracuse, especially with the "Salt Pointers," as the residents of Salina were called; and they were always given an especially enthusiastic reception whenever they appeared in the National Theatre, which was formerly the First Baptist church, and which is now the site of the Universalist church. They will be remembered as appearing in their great play, Jack Sheppard, as well as Asmodeus, Romeo and Juliet, in which Susan appeared as Romeo and Kate as Juliet, and also in Grandmother's Pet.

The Denin sisters were fine actresses, singers and dancers, and they were blessed with elegant figures, which made their presence very attractive. Susan was an unusually beautiful woman in face and figure. She was the shorter of the two. She married Fletcher

Woodward, son of Arnold Woodward, a former prominent dry goods merchant in this city. The marriage was not a happy one, as Woodward was of a jealous disposition. Susan made large sums of money on the stage, but Fletcher was improvident. While returning from California by steamer, Fletcher is believed to have shot an actor of whom he was jealous. Susan nursed the actor, who died a few months afterwards in New York; but as no one was found who would swear against Fletcher, the murderer was never found. Susan was afterwards divorced from her husband. When she next appeared at the National Theatre, Fletcher and some of his friends attempted to hiss her from the stage. But there were a number of Salt Pointers in the theatre, and they notified him that if the hissing continued they would throw him and his friends out of the building. It is needless to add that the hissing ceased, for the Salt Pointers were famous for their fighting propensities. Susan thanked her admirers for their kind protection. She is remembered as having resided in this city in the Woodward homestead, on the southeasterly corner of Railroad and Clinton streets, and she was a welcomed guest in social circles. Susan afterwards married Captain Frank Barroll. Her daughter is now living in Portland, Oregon, a lovely woman and the mother of five children. Susan died in 1875 and is buried in Indianapolis, Ind. The picture was purchased by

Richard W. Jones from Mr. Cook; and it formerly hung on the walls of the Citizens' Club, of which Mr. Jones has been President for some years. About a year ago Mr. Jones gave the celebrated picture to the Vanderbilt House.

CHAPTER III

AN EARLY HOUSE OF GOD

The old, dilapidated wooden building on the north-westerly corner of Madison and Montgomery streets is the most historic ecclesiastical landmark now remaining in Syracuse. It was the first Episcopal as well as the first Catholic church in the village of Syracuse; and it was the third building in this place to be used exclusively for religious purposes. The first religious society organized in the village was of the Baptist denomination, the society being organized in the winter of 1819–20. The First Baptist Church edifice was erected in 1824. The First Presbyterian Church edifice was built in the summer of 1825 and dedicated in January, 1826, the society having been organized December 14, 1824. This old building was completed in 1827 for the St. Paul's Protestant Episcopal Church, though religious services were first held there in July, 1826. In February, 1842, the edifice, with all its fixtures and appointments, including the organ but excepting the

(42)

HARVEY BALDWIN.—From a recent photo. of an old-fashioned ambro-type.

THE OLD ST. PAUL'S CHURCH.—From an old painting

bell, was sold to the congregation of St. Mary's
Roman Catholic Church for about $600. The first
Roman Catholic Church of Syracuse was organized
December 25, 1842.

A meeting of those interested in organizing St.
Paul's Church was held May 22, 1826, in the old district school house which stood for many years in
Church street, in the rear of the former First Baptist
meeting-house. The Rev. John McCarty presided,
and John Durnford and Samuel Wright were elected
wardens; and Amos P. Granger, Archy Kasson,
James Mann, Matthew W. Davis, Mathew Williams,
Barent Filkins, Othniel H. Williston and Jabez
Hawley were elected vestrymen. The question of
erecting a church edifice of their own had been previously discussed, the preliminary steps having been
taken in 1824. In 1825 The Syracuse Company gave
to this congregation the triangular lot, bounded by
Warren, East Genesee and East Washington streets,
where the Granger Block now stands, under the express agreement that a church should be built thereon.
In September of that year the frame of an edifice, 41
by 52 feet, was raised and covered in, and in the following July the first regular service by a missionary
began, though the building was not completed till
1827. In those early days that triangular piece of
ground was a fine little green meadow. John Durnford advocated the selection of this meadow for the

proposed site for the church edifice, but Archy Kasson and John Rodgers, the other members of the Site
Committee, offered an objection to the lot, saying it
was too far from the village, whose central location
was where the old red mill stood, now the location of
the High School building in West Genesee street on
the east bank of the Onondaga creek. But the Site
Committee finally coincided with Mr. Durnford in his
choice and the report was adopted.

The church edifice was a plain, unpretending building, painted white, with green blinds, clapboarded,
buttressed angles and surmounted with a square
tower, with pinnacled corners. The windows were
lancet shaped, and there were three on either side, in
front two full length and one shorter over the entrance, and one in the west end over the pulpit, fitted
with seven by nine plain glass. The triangular lot
was greater in its area than it now appears. The
front faced the east and between it and the apex of
the triangle was a grass plot, set with shrubbery.
The rear or west wall was within a very few feet of
the east line of Warren street, and the whole plot was
entirely surrounded with a plain picket fence. In
front of the church, at the further end of the triangle,
was located a well of superb water, the common resort
of the residents of that neighborhood. The accompanying illustration is from a picture painted and
given to the church by Miss F. L. Dickinson; and the

painting may now be found in the vestry room of the present St. Paul's Cathedral.

The Rev. John McCarty, who was the first clergyman of St. Paul's church, resigned in the latter part of 1826 from his pastoral charge of the parish and also from the one at Onondaga Hill; and he was succeeded in the following December by the Rev. William Barlow, who became the first resident missionary of the church in the village of Syracuse. Mr. Barlow was an uncle of the members of the Barlow family, all at that time living here and occupying prominent positions in society. He continued his services until the autumn of 1828. From this period until 1830, a space of more than a year and a half, the parish was left without a rector. The Rev. Palmer Dyer of Hartford, Conn., entered upon the rectorship of this church May 1, 1830. One of his first acts was the establishing of a parish library, which was the first public library established in the village. Its volumes from some cause eventually became scattered and the remnant was absorbed either by purchase or gifts in the library of the Syracuse Academy. This parish library did much towards building up a church sentiment and in allaying a strong sectarian opposition. In those early days, when the common people were more unenlightened than they are to-day, there was a considerable feeling against the Episcopal church, which was looked upon as resembling the Catholic church, against which there was an intense, bitter feeling. It will be remembered by the older citizens that in the winter of 1847–48, Dennis McCarthy, who afterwards became distinguished as State Senator, and Dr. James Foran, a finely educated and leading physician, gave lectures twice a week on the doctrines of the Catholic church in the public hall, which was built on the triangular lot where the Granger Block now stands after St. Paul's church was removed. Those lectures were of the nature of debates, as they were participated in by representatives of the Protestant religion, especially of the Methodist denomination. But happily, through the influence of education, that sectarian prejudice is now greatly removed.

In 1833, Mr. Dyer resigned, and the parish from that time until May, 1835, except for a short period of about six months, when the Rev. Richard Salmon officiated, was without a resident rector. Mr. Dyer was succeeded by the Rev. John Gregg, who officiated for about six months. In October, 1835, the vestry resolved to recall the Rev. William Barlow, who, however, declined the call. The Rev. Francis Thomas Todrig became rector in December, 1835, and on the 28th of May following, was instituted according to the forms laid down in the prayer book. This is the first and only instance of the institution of a rector in this manner, in this parish, from its organization till the occasion of the Rev. Dr. Henry Gregory in

1840. These two clergymen, Messrs. Todrig and Gregory, were the only ones thus instituted as rectors in St. Paul's church in this city. Mr. Todrig had formerly been a member of the Roman Catholic church. He resigned in July, 1836, and from that date till December of the same year, the parish was again vacant. The Rev. Clement M. Butler accepted the charge December 4, 1836, and continued to officiate till May, 1838. He was succeeded, July 15, 1838, by the Rev. John B. Gallagher, who resigned November 1, 1840.

In March, 1840, the first definite action relative to a change of location of St. Paul's Church edifice was had. The Rev. Dr. Henry Gregory became rector December 1, 1840, and continued as such for nearly eight years, when he became rector of St. James Church in this city, in order that he might carry out his ideas on free pews in churches. The church lot was sold March 8, 1841, at auction, by order of the Court of Chancery, to Daniel Elliott, Joseph I. Bradley and Samuel Larned for $8,000; and the new lot, corner of Warren and Fayette streets, where the Government building now stands, was purchased for $3,500. The last sermon preached in the old edifice previous to its removal, was on April 10, 1842, by the Rev. Henry Gregory, D. D., an eloquent, able and highly esteemed gentleman. The church edifice now passed into the hands of the Roman Catholic

Church, from which time it was called St. Mary's
church. The corner stone of the new St. Paul's
church, which was a marvel of beauty in its day, was
laid July 12, 1841, and the building was completed
early in the following year.

The Rev. Father Michael Haes was the first resident Catholic priest in the village of Syracuse. He
assumed charge of St. Mary's Church, the old building having been removed to the corner of Montgomery and Madison streets, then an open common, a spot
low and marshy and altogether undesirable for residences or for buildings of this character. The lot
was given by The Syracuse Company to the Catholic
Society, who transferred it to Bishop McCloskey of
Albany, who afterwards became Archbishop of New
York. The title now stands in the Board of Trustees
of St. Mary's Church. Previous to the year 1842,
there were only a few Catholic families in the village
of Syracuse. During the administration of Father
Haes the church grew rapidly, and in 1848, the year
when Syracuse became a city, the church edifice was
considerably enlarged and improved. The general
external appearance of the building, however, does
not vary much from its former aspect, except that a
spacious basement was finished off and the building
was lengthened and an addition of two windows made
on either side, and a section was added to the tower,
on which there was placed a cross. In 1852 the

THE OLD ST. MARY'S CHURCH. From a recent photograph.

congregation of St. Mary's Church became so numerous that there was organized the Church of St. John the Evangelist, the edifice for which was erected under the charge of Father Haes in 1854. This church is now St. John's Cathedral, an outgrowth of St. Mary's Church.

The Rev. Father Haes died in 1859, and he was succeeded by the Rev. Father James A. O'Hara, a man of unusual ability and an eloquent and comprehensive speaker. Father O'Hara was the first American student who graduated from the University of Sapienza, a famous seat of learning, and honored with the degree of Doctor of Divinity. Through his ardent and strenuous efforts the site of the present St. Mary's Church edifice, at the intersection of Montgomery, Jefferson and East Onondaga streets, was purchased from Peter Burns for $30,000. The laying of the corner stone of the new St. Mary's Church, the most costly and beautiful church in the city, was held November 8, 1874. And it is worthy of note, as showing the kindly feeling which then existed among the different churches, a very marked contrast to former times, that considerable financial aid was given by people of other religious denominations. The new St. Mary's Church edifice was dedicated December 6, 1885. The Rev. Father John Grimes became assistant to Dr. O'Hara, November 10, 1882, succeeding the Rev. Father James J. O'Brien, who was removed to Fonda.

Dr. O'Hara died December 26, 1889, and he was succeeded by the Rev. Father Grimes, February 6, 1890. Under the administration of Father Grimes the congregation has steadily increased, and the church is in an excellent and prosperous condition.

The old building has been suffered to remain unused since it was abandoned in 1885. One Sunday in 1832 as Richard A. Yoe, one of the few early settlers now living, was coming out of the old St. Paul's church, he was asked by a man if Captain Hiram Putnam, then President of the village, was inside the church. The man said that a passenger on one of the line canal boats, which carried freight as well as passengers, had been abandoned by the boat's crew because he was sick, and that the passenger lay in the marsh grass between the two locks, Nos. 48 and 49. When Captain Putnam came out, he and Mr. Yoe and the man went to the canal, found the sick passenger and took him in a wagon to the old pest house, which was then on the hill just north of Rose Hill cemetery. The passenger died that same afternoon, and it was found that he had the Asiatic cholera. His was the first case of cholera in Syracuse. Many deaths followed during that year. It might be also noted that the first case of Asiatic cholera appeared in the United States during 1832. The old bell which hung in the tower of the old St. Paul's church, the only part not sold to the Catholic Church, was sent

to Troy and recast for the new St. Paul's church in
Warren and Fayette streets.   When that church was
torn down in 1885 for the beautiful St. Paul's Cathedral, corner of Montgomery and Fayette streets, the
bell broke in being taken down and it was again recast in Troy.   It now swings in the present cathedral,
of which the Rev. Henry R. Lockwood, S. T. D., is
the able and esteemed rector.

CHAPTER IV

MONEY OF EARLY DAYS

Prior to 1830, the date when the first bank was established in Syracuse, the banking business of this county was carried on mostly by the Bank of Auburn, of which Daniel Kellogg of Skaneateles was President, a. d by the Cayuga County Bank of Auburn. In those early days there were very few men in the present limits of Syracuse who were worth $10,000. If a man was worth $5,000, he was considered wealthy. There was not a great deal of money in circulation; and of the money then used most of it was Mexican and Spanish silver. There was not much English money, comparatively, and very little American or Federal currency. When the Safety Fund banks were authorized by this State in 1829, the banks, incorporated under that act, issued bank notes which were readily received as money by the merchants throughout the entire country. The cities where this money was redeemed were Albany and New York. The banks in the Western States, and even in

(52)

SHINPLASTER OF THOMAS S. TRUAIR.—From a lithograph.

Pennsylvania, were not considered very sound, and the paper money they issued was called "wild cat" money, subject to a discount by the banks in New York city. The bank notes issued in this State and the New England States, under the Safety Fund protection, were the only ones that were redeemable in New York city at par, the exchange being one-half of one per centum on a dollar.

The barter trade, which had prevailed quite extensively in the very early days, had passed away when banks were established. The salt, which was the main product in those days, was then paid for either by note or cash, and it was sold on four and six months' time. The merchants were rather slow in payments; but they were very reliable, as they obtained enormous profits on small sales. They would visit New York city twice a year for the purpose of purchasing goods, and they would give their notes on sixty or ninety days' time. Under the Safety Fund law they were required to have two endorsers, as the people in those early days were not worth much money, and there was a consequent lack of confidence. The notes issued by the banks, and which passed into circulation as money, were found to be so very convenient that the merchants themselves, in order to obtain change in sums less than one dollar, issued shinplasters, redeemable in sums of one or more dollars. This method of making small change was introduced in

1840. But there was no great amount of security in the shinplasters, as they were issued simply on the credit of the merchant; and the people took them at their own risk. A large amount of worthless paper money, issued both by banks and individuals, was then in circulation; and counterfeit money was very common. Thompson's Bank Note Detector was issued every week, and when a very clever counterfeit appeared, an "extra" was issued. Each bank had some peculiar mark of its own by which it could tell whether its bank notes were genuine or counterfeit.

This was the condition of the money market in Syracuse up to 1861, when the civil war broke out, bringing hard times and a great stringency in money. Gold and silver money became very scarce, as it was hoarded by the people, and it was very difficult to obtain small change in sums less than one dollar. In the following year it would frequently occur that one would go months at a time without seeing any silver currency. The great difficulty in making change in 1862 is shown in the manner in which the taxes were collected for that year. Thomas S. Truair was City Treasurer at that time. He was enabled to make change for the city taxes which were due in October, as he had thoughtfully provided himself with small change for that occasion. But he foresaw that he would be unable to procure sufficient small change for such part of the county tax as would come into his hands for collection in December. Mr. Truair, as City Treasurer, applied to the Common Council for authority to issue a form of bank note called a corporation order, similar to those which were then issued by other cities. One of these corporation orders reads as follows : "Treasurer of the corporation of the village of Rondout, pay to the bearer twenty-five cents at the Bank of Rondout when like orders are presented in amounts of one or more dollars. By order of the Board of Trustees." This was signed by the President and Clerk of the village, and dated October 1, 1862.

But the Common Council of Syracuse, after looking into the matter, decided that it had no authority to issue corporation orders. After consulting with Frank Hiscock, who was then District Attorney, and who afterwards became United States Senator, Mr. Truair decided to issue some shinplasters on his individual account. The plan which he originated was worked out by George J. Gardner, who was then Cashier of the Onondaga Bank. This plan resulted in the issuing of shinplasters which read as follows : "Bank of Salina, pay to the bearer in current funds fifty cents when presented in sums of one or more dollars. Secured by special deposit." These shinplasters were signed by Thomas S. Truair, and they were numbered and dated Syracuse, N. Y., November 1, 1862. They were issued in amounts of five, ten, twenty-five and fifty cents. The method of issuing them was very simple. The shinplasters were lithographed by Hatch & Company of New York, and they were all sent direct to the Bank of Salina. Mr. Truair borrowed $1,000, which he deposited in the Onondaga County Savings Bank. He was given a certificate of deposit for that amount and turned it over to the Bank of Salina, where he received shinplasters to the amount of $1,000. These shinplasters, thus secured by this certificate of deposit, were gladly received by the other city banks, the railroads, the Internal Revenue, the postoffice and city departments in sums of $100. After thus receiving $1,000 for the shinplasters, Mr. Truair returned his borrowed money.

The plan succeeded so well that the shinplasters drove out of circulation the individual notes of the merchants. Very few of the more responsible men in Syracuse did not issue similar notes, because it was almost impos ible to obtain small change. The people would even buy postage stamps and use them for change, but the postage stamps would stick together and thus became very inconvenient. The shinplasters issued by Mr. Truair, amounting in all to about $5,000 and issued for about six months, enabled the City Treasurer to make small change which was universally accepted for money. They were greatly preferred to the shinplasters of the merchants, which were generally prepared in a cheap manner, being simply printed on a card and signed by the merchant. There were a great many counterfeits of the merchants' shinplasters. Thomas Rice, a grocer of Syracuse, James Frazee & Company, millers of Baldwinsville, and Thomas S. Truair, were almost the only ones in this county who used lithographing in making their shinplasters.

It took some little time for the postage currency, which the Government first issued in 1862, to find its way into general circulation; but when it did come it superseded all other forms of obtaining fractional currency. The Government shinplasters continued in circulation until the resumption of specie payment in 1879. It is now a rarity to see the shinplasters issued by the Government. In the early times it was quite frequent to see advertisements prepared by merchants to resemble shinplasters and bank notes. A great many of such advertisements were fraudulently passed upon foreigners as money. At length a law was passed which prevented the issuing of bank notes, excepting by national banks, and also all forms of fractional currency. When the Government called in its shinplasters by resuming specie payments, the people showed their appreciation by gladly accepting the silver money in place of the paper money. In redeeming the shinplasters, it is said that there has been about $7,000,000 of the shinplasters either lost or destroyed; so that the Government is just so much ahead.

CHAPTER V

THE THREE EARLIEST BANKS

The recent stringency in the money market recalls the fact that during the great periods of financial stringency, leading up to panics that have swept over the country, leaving business ruins in their track, Syracuse has been able to continue her wonted industries and mercantile operations with very little of individual disaster to mark the time as one of peril. The banking institutions of this city have been managed with an exceptionally high degree of financial ability. In the early days of business transactions in this city, especially in the village of Salina, where the salt industry was centred, there was very little money in circulation. Salt was the staple article used in bartering for produce, clothing, household utensils and everything that was needed. It did not require much capital for its operation, while the returns were sure and continuous. The State required a certain quantity of salt to be constantly kept in the storehouse, provided by the Superintendent of the

(58)

ONONDAGA COUNTY BANK NOTE.—From an old counterfeit bill.

Onondaga Salt Springs, in order to meet the demands
. of the citizens of the State who depended on obtaining their supply from the salt reservation. It was
sometimes customary for the Salt Superintendent to
give certificates for deposits of salt in the public storehouse, and these certificates passed from one to
another as cash, so that the public storehouse in substance became a bank.

The first bank to be organized in this county was
the Onondaga County Bank, which was chartered in
1830, with a capital of $150,000. When organized, it
was located at the east end of the east wing of the
Syracuse House in East Genesee street. It was afterwards located in the second floor, northwestern corner, of the old bank building, corner of South Salina
and Washington streets, where the White Memorial
Building now stands. Its first President was Oliver
R. Strong of Onondaga Hill, father of Col. John M.
Strong, Canal Collector for the port of Syracuse; and
its first Cashier was Moses S. Marsh of Pompey,
father-in-law of Edward S. Dawson, President of the
Onondaga County Savings Bank. In 1839 Mr. Marsh
became President, and Hamilton White was made
Cashier. Mr. Marsh was succeeded by Oliver Teall,
father of Col. William W. Teall, who is the father of
Oliver Sumner Teall, famous in New York city as an
eccentric individual. Mr. White continued as Cashier.
George J. Gardner, Oliver Teall's son-in-law, who

entered this bank in 1843, as a Bookkeeper, became
Teller, and Charles Tucker was made Bookkeeper.
These officers remained in the bank until the expira-
tion of its charter in 1854, when the banking business
was continued by Mr. White as a private banker.
Some of the directors in this bank, aside from the
officers already mentioned, were Horace White, John
Wilkinson, Moses D. Burnet, Johnson Hall, Thomas
D. Davis, Hiram Putnam, Harvey Rhoades, David
S. Colvin and James R. Lawrence.

The Bank of Salina was chartered in 1832, with a
capital of $150,000. Its first President was Nathan
Munro of Camillus, and its first Cashier was Ashbel
Kellogg, the father of ex-Lieut-Gov. Thomas G.
Alvord's first wife. The directors at an early date
were Dean Richmond, William Clark, David Munro
of Camillus and Daniel Kellogg of Skaneateles. At
the death of Nathan Munro, Ashbel Kellogg became
President and Miles W. Bennett, formerly of Camillus, became Cashier. Mr. Kellogg continued as
President till 1845, when he removed to Michigan,
where he died in 1848. He was succeeded by David
Munro of Camillus. The largest stockholder in this
bank was Daniel Kellogg of Skaneateles, who was
also President of the Bank of Auburn. In 1851-52,
the date of the first city directory, the officers were:
David Munro, President; Miles W. Bennett, Cashier;
Timothy Brown, Teller; Walter C. Hopkins, Book-

BANK OF SALINA NOTE.—From an old genuine bill.

keeper and Discount Clerk. The city directory of 1854–55 gives these officers: David Munro, President; James Lynch, Vice-President; Timothy Brown, Cashier; T. J. Leach, Teller, and John H. Slaven, Bookkeeper. Mr. Brown removed to Madison, Wis., the following year, and he was succeeded by Cornelius L. Alvord. The city directory for 1856–57 gives the following officers: President, vacant; Cashier, James Munro; Teller, T. J. Leach; Directors, Robert Townsend, John Rice, Lewis H. Redfield, John B. Burnet, James Noxon, Allen Munro, Joseph Battel, James Munro, James M. Munro and Isaac Hill. Thomas G. Alvord became a director the following year. In 1859, James Monroe became President and George B. Leonard became Cashier.

The Bank of Salina was originally located at the corner of North Salina and Wolf streets. It was afterwards moved into what was known in the old city directories as 15 South Salina street, about where A. W. Palmer now has his clothing store, between Genesee and Washington streets. The charter expired in 1864, when the business was succeeded by the Third National Bank. Of all the names mentioned above as being connected with these two early banks, the only ones now engaged in banking business, and almost the only ones now living, are George B. Leonard, Cashier of the First National Bank, and Thomas J. Leach, Cashier of the Salt Springs

National Bank, though Thomas G. Alvord was the first President of the Salt Springs National Bank. The Third National Bank, successor to the Bank of Salina, was organized with James Munroe, President, and Francis H. Williams, Cashier.

Another of the early banks, and one closely allied with the other two, was the Bank of Syracuse, chartered in 1839 with a capital of $200,000. It was located in the second floor, southwestern corner of the old bank building, corner of South Salina and Washington streets, where the White Memorial Building now stands. Its first officers were John Wilkinson, President, and Horace White, Cashier. Mr. White was the father of Andrew D. White, ex-President of Cornell University. Upon the death of Mr. Wilkinson, September 19, 1862, Hamilton White became President; and he was succeeded for a short time by John H. Cheddell, and he by Andrew D. White. In 1856, Horace White was succeeded as Cashier by Orrin Ballard. The bank continued business until 1865, when it was reorganized as the Syracuse National Bank and continued as such until 1877, when it closed its affairs and retired from business.

The Onondaga County Bank and the Bank of Salina were chartered under the Safety Fund system, which was first authorized in 1829. Every bank belonging to that system received a special act of

BANK OF SYRACUSE NOTE.—From an old counterfeit bill.

incorporation from the Legislature. These charters were for a limited period, generally having about twenty years to run. That system was regulated by a general law, which was incorporated into every charter, by which each bank was required to have all its capital paid in before it commenced business; and it was also required annually to contribute one-half of one per centum upon its capital to a common fund, deposited with the State Treasurer, until such fund should amount to three per centum upon the capital of each bank. This fund was denominated the Bank Fund, and was to be applied to the payment of the debts of any insolvent bank contributing to the same; and, in case the fund was at any time diminished by payments from it, the banks were again required to make their annual contributions, till each had in deposit the three per centum on its capital stock. This fund, in common parlance, was called the Safety Fund, which finally gave name to the system.

There was so much political influence mixed up with the Safety Fund Bank, preventing the establishment of any bank that was not in accord with the leading politicians, that the Free Bank system, as it was styled, was established in 1838. The Bank of Syracuse was chartered under the new system. By this system every individual and association was authorized to engage in the business of banking, and on depositing with the Comptroller the stocks of

the United States or of any State which should be or be
made equal to a five per centum stock, or such stocks,
and bonds and mortgages to the same amount or less,
on improved, productive and unincumbered real estate,
worth double the amount secured by the mortgage,
over and above all buildings thereon, and bearing an
interest of at least six per centum per annum, the
Comptroller was required to deliver to such individual
or association an equal amount of bank notes for
circulation. Associations under this law were a
species of corporation. But there was nothing in the
act that required individual bankers to deposit any
particular amount of securities before they commenced business. The country was then flooded with
stock from almost every State, and the consequence
was that numerous banks sprung into existence under
this law. Repudiation soon followed. Many States,
that did not repudiate, failed to meet their obligations, confidence was impaired, credit was shaken,
and stocks generally depreciated in the market. The
consequence was that many banks failed.

The time when these pioneer banks were chartered
was a period in which banking capital could be employed very profitably and to the great advantage of
the public. The bank stock books were open to the
public, and anyone could subscribe for as much stock
as he wanted. It frequently happened that the subscriptions exceeded the capital stock. The State

Comptroller then allotted a pro rata share of the stock to each subscriber. Of course a man of sufficient means could buy up the stock of other men, and thus obtain control of the bank. The three early banks of this city were ably managed, and they were successful.

CHAPTER VI

THE SYRACUSE ACADEMY

The Syracuse Academy, knowledge of which is fast passing into a tradition, was once a celebrated school of learning, and it rivaled the celebrated academies at Pompey, Onondaga Valley, Elbridge and other towns in this county. It was located in East Fayette street, commonly called Academy street, directly in the rear of the present Onondaga County Orphan Asylum, which faces East Genesee street. After the Academy building had passed into the hands of the Orphan Asylum in 1846, and the new asylum building was completed in 1885, the old academy building was torn down and the brick taken to Geddes. The brick was used in building the Butler Manufacturing Company's building, erected in West Fayette street, between the old Thomson's Infirmary and the Onondaga Pottery Company. The building, as it now stands in Geddes, closely resembles in its construction the old academy building. When first built for an academy it was a three-story building,

(66)

the design being to add wings, but afterwards a fourth story was added. The academy building was long and narrow, though strongly built, and it had a cupola in which there was a bell. The grounds were large and laid out in a beautiful manner, the walks sloping from Lodi hill, or Academy hill as it was called, to the streets on either side.

The Syracuse Academy was incorporated by act of Legislature, dated April 28, 1835, the incorporators being Oliver Teall, Harvey Baldwin, Aaron Burt, William I. Dodge, Thomas Spencer, Lewis H. Redfield, Elihu L. Phillips, Thomas Rose and S. W. Cadwell. The President of the Board of Trustees was Harvey Baldwin, the Clerk, or Secretary, was Lewis H. Redfield, and the Treasurer was Thomas Rose. The land was purchased by the institution May 25, 1835, from Aaron Burt and Harvey Baldwin for $1,000, and it is described as being in the village of Lodi, now Syracuse, commencing on the south line of Third South street (now East Fayette street) eight rods east of Chestnut street (now Crouse avenue) and running easterly sixteen rods on the south line of Third South street, and thence southerly twelve rods. In the deed it was provided that the land should be used for the sole and only purpose of having enclosed thereon an academy or other buildings for the instruction of youth and the diffusion and promotion of literature and science, and when not so used or

otherwise appropriated the land, with the appurtenances, should revert to Messrs. Burt and Baldwin,
unless the institution should pay $1,500.

The academy grounds were part of a purchase of
sixty acres made by Harvey Baldwin shortly after he
came to Syracuse from Onondaga Valley in 1826.
The land was formerly a farm owned by Rufus Stanton, who had before 1810 cultivated thrifty fields of
wheat near the Salina street bridge over the Oswego
canal, and who kept a tavern in 1811 just south of
the site of the bridge on the east side of the street.
Mr. Baldwin sold one-third of the land to Mr. Burt,
and another third to Oliver Teall, and the land was
known as the Baldwin, Burt and Teall tract. In
those early days all that portion of the city lying
between Mulberry street and Lodi on the south side
of the canal was an unclaimed cedar swamp. The
present Fayette Park was then a favorite resort for
foxes, rabbits and wild fowl, forming a capital sport-
ing ground. The Genesee turnpike passed through
this unhealthy swamp, and it consisted of an ill laid
corduroy road that tested the strength of the horses
and wagons, and the skill and moral training of all
teamsters and passengers having occasion to pass that
way. It was the purpose of the purchasers of this
tract to build on the highlands of Lodi a city which
should rival Syracuse.

The year 1835, in which the academy was started,

was chiefly notable in the village of Syracuse, whose population in 1830 was 6,929, for the introduction of paved streets, the result of the vote of the citizens being to pave Salina street between Fayette and Church (now Willow) streets. In that year also the bounds of the original village were considerably enlarged. But there was a great need of educational advantages for the youth. The children of such parents as could afford it were sent to the academies at Onondaga Valley or Pompey or Utica, or to some of the colleges. Syracuse was in need of an academy of her own. Through the exertions of Messrs. Baldwin, Teall and Burt and some others friendly to the cause of education, the charter for the Syracuse Academy was obtained. Under many discouraging embarrassments the building was completed in the fall of 1835, and the academy was opened in January of the following year. It was supplied with competent teachers and supported by the benefactions of the citizens, besides drawing its share of the educational funds of the State. The academy was well supplied with educational facilities, and it had a fine library, many of the books coming from the parish library of the old St. Paul's Church. Richard A. Yoe, agent of the Austin Myers estate, is probably the only one of the original stockholders now living.

The first principal of the academy was a Mr. Kellogg, who came from New York. The next

principal, and the one that gave most distinction to
the academy, as he was an excellent instructor, was
Oren Root, the father of Elihu Root, the distinguished
lawyer of New York, and of the Rev. Oren Root,
Professor of Mathematics in Hamilton College. Principal Root taught mathematics and the classics. His
assistant during the first part of his principalship was
Albert G. Salisbury, who afterwards taught in the
district school built in 1839 on the ground occupied
by the old Putnam school and who became the first
clerk of the Board of Education. Mr. Salisbury was
succeeded as teacher by Joseph A. Allen, an excellent
disciplinarian, who taught English branches. When
Mr. Root went to Hamilton College about 1844, where
he became Professor of Mathematics, Mr. Allen was
made Principal. His assistant was Oliver T. Burt,
son of Aaron Burt, and he taught mathematics and
the classics. J. B. Clark was at one time one of the
teachers. Miss Frisbee was at one time principal of
the female department, and she was a highly cultured
woman. She was succeeded by Miss Buttrick, a sister
of Mrs. Oren Root. During the time that Mr. Allen
was principal, the academy was discontinued, and
Mr. Allen and Mr. Burt opened a private school in
the brick building on the west side of Mulberry street,
corner of East Washington street, just south of the
blacksmith shop.

The instructors of the Syracuse Academy were men

and women of more than ordinary ability. Almost all the men afterwards became distinguished. Mr. Root was a fine mathematician, and he is remembered by the graduates of the academy, as well as of Hamilton College, as one of the best of instructors. Mr. Allen, who married Lucy Burt, daughter of Aaron Burt, afterwards kept a music store in Syracuse, under the firm name of Allen & Phelps. He returned to Massachusetts, where he became distinguished as a teacher, meeting with great success. He is now living at Westborough, Mass. But the Syracuse Academy was not a success financially. It was built on the college dormitory plan, but the pupils came almost entirely from Syracuse. After a few years the enterprise of the people began to be aroused, jealousies in reference to the academy being a speculation for building up the village of Lodi were awakened, and district school houses sprang up and were patronized. In those days every one, who sought the gratification of political ambition or to enact a part on the stage of life with a view to the applause of his fellow men, hastened to mount the common school hobby, as it was called, for education had become a hobby. The result was that the common schools and the free schools profited by the popular agitation, and the Syracuse Academy went into a decline.

The Trustees of the Syracuse Academy executed

a mortgage, June 22, 1836, to The Syracuse Company, the owners of the greater part of the village of Syracuse, for $3,000. The conditions expressed in the deed or the reversionary interest retained by Messrs. Burt and Baldwin were removed in favor of The Syracuse Company for one dollar, the mortgage being acknowledged July 2, 1842, and recorded five days thereafter. This mortgage was foreclosed May 22, 1845, the principal and interest then amounting to $4,398.83. John Townsend of Albany, one of the members of The Syracuse Company, bid in the property for $2,000, and he sold it to the Onondaga County Orphan Asylum, March 18, 1846, for $3,000. Bradley Cary and Herman H. Phelps, who did the carpenter work on the academy, were judgment creditors subsequent to the mortgage, as appeared at the time of the foreclosure. The stockholders of the Syracuse Academy waived all their rights in favor of the Orphan Asylum. Although the Academy was not a financial success, it was an excellent school, and it educated many of the children of the early settlers, who have become prominent citizens of this and other cities.

THE RECRUITING STATION.—From a recent photograph.

CHAPTER VII

THE RECRUITING STATION

On the south side of West Water street, between Clinton and Franklin streets, there recently stood a two-story stone building, the first stone building erected in the village of Syracuse; and it remained till recently in almost the same appearance as when first erected by Judge James Webb. This building was one of the most historic landmarks of what was once the village of Syracuse, though the present location seems strangely out of place, as it is now in the centre of the wholesale trade. The building was owned and occupied as a dying and scouring works by Mrs. Eliza Smith, widow of Alexander Smith who died in 1890. It was built of Onondaga blue lime stone. The walls were almost two feet in thickness, the owner evidently intending that his home should indeed be his castle, capable of withstanding the bloody onslaught of the Indian or the bombardment of the more civilized soldier.

Timothy C. Cheney in his "Reminiscences of Syracuse," published in pamphlet form in 1857, says: "Judge Webb built the stone house lately used as a United States recruiting office on Water street in 1824, and occupied it as a dwelling house." The records in the County Clerk's office show that the lot whereon this building stood, 42 feet frontage, was purchased September 3, 1829, for $127.28, by James Webb from Moses D. Burnet, who was the trustee of The Syracuse Company, and who received his deed of trust June 18, 1825. The Syracuse Company was formed in May 1824, having purchased the Walton Tract, and being composed of William James of Albany, who owned five-eighths; Isaiah Townsend and John Townsend of Albany, who owned two-eighths; and James McBride of New York, who owned one-eighth. In 1819, when the ultimate success of the Erie canal was assured, Judge Joshua Forman, the founder of Syracuse, removed from Onondaga Valley to Syracuse and built a residence about on the site of the present wholesale grocery store of G. N. Crouse & Company, being on the northeast corner of the block in which the Smith dye house is located. In 1821 there was but one store in Syracuse, excepting two or three small groceries, and it was kept by General Amos P. Granger, who came from Onondaga Hill.

Among the list of business men who settled in

Syracuse up to 1825, as mentioned in "Clark's Onondaga," the name of James Webb does not appear. But it does appear that Mr. Webb, at the first meeting for the election of officers of the village of Syracuse, held May 3, 1825, was elected one of the three Assessors. The population of Syracuse in 1825 was 600. James Webb was engaged in the storage and forwarding business, his store being located on the west end of what is now the Onondaga County Savings Bank building, directly opposite the Syracuse House. He sold the residence June 11, 1832, to John F. Wyman, the consideration being $1,650.

One of Judge Webb's daughters married Horace Wheaton, who was elected to the Assembly in 1834 and who was appointed Mayor of Syracuse by the Common Council in 1851, Moses D. Burnet having declined to qualify. Another daughter married Col. George T. M. Davis, a lawyer by profession, who was for some years under Dr. William Kirkpatrick, the Superintendent of the Salt Springs at Salina. Colonel Davis afterwards removed to Louisville, Ky., where he became a prominent newspaper man, being the editor of the Louisville *Commercial* and the rival of George D. Prentiss. He became Colonel in the Mexican war, and afterwards located in New York city, where he became an authority on financial questions. His daughter married George Francis Train, whose remarkable and eccentric history is well known

throughout the entire country.   Judge Webb moved
from Syracuse, about the time he sold his residence,
to Alton, Ills., in the wilds of the wilderness; and
there he died.

John F. Wyman, the second owner of this old stone
building, established the Syracuse *Advertiser* in 1825,
in company with Thomas B. Barnum, who, however,
soon withdrew and was succeeded by Norman Rawson.
The *Advertiser* was continued by Rawson & Wyman
until the autumn of 1826, when the firm dissolved,
Mr. Wyman continuing alone until the spring of
1829.   The Onondaga *Journal*, published at Onondaga
Hill by Vivus W. Smith, was then united with the
Advertiser under the name of the Onondaga *Standard*,
the publishers being Wyman & Smith.   Silas F.
Smith, brother of Vivus W. Smith, says that he lived
with his brother, Vivus, who was older than himself,
in the old stone building, erected by Judge Webb.
Mr. Wyman sold a half interest in the property,
December 5, 1833, to Henry Ogden Irving, who lived
in Orange, Essex county, New Jersey, for $1,150.
The other half was sold to Mr. Irving December 5,
1834, at the same price.   Mr. Irving sold the property
February 17, 1853, to George Everson and Giles
Everson, the consideration being $2,500.   The Everson
brothers, both residents of Syracuse, dealt quite extensively in real estate in those days.   They sold the
property May 10, 1854, for $2,700 to Anstis Slattery,

a woman who made " her mark " on the deed recording the sale of the property. The next owner of this historic residence was Jefferson Phillips, a blacksmith, who purchased it April 7, 1856, for $2,700. He sold it to Huldah Bradley, wife of Christopher C. Bradley, April 5, 1857, for the consideration of $2,800.

Mr. Bradley settled in Syracuse about 1822, and for many years he was the head of a thriving foundry business. He held the office of Village Trustee, County Treasurer and other responsible positions. His sons, Christopher C. and Waterman C., founded the business of Bradley & Company, manufacturers of power hammers and carriages. The Bradley family in those early days lived on the lot directly west of the stone building erected by James Webb, the place till recently being occupied by the wholesale hardware store of Robert McCarthy & Son. At that time the south side of West Water street was occupied by residences and was considered a desirable location. The stone building was sold July 1, 1862, to Wheeler Armstrong, a large iron manufacturer of Rome, the price of the property being $2,000. Mr. Bradley was the agent for the property till September 13, 1865, when the next and the present owner became Eliza Smith, wife of Alexander Smith. The property was sold for $2,500.

For many years prior to 1851–52 this old stone building was used as a recruiting station. The massive strength of its walls, unusually strong for a residence, made it especially well adapted for this soldier-like occupation. The building was a two-story one with a strongly built cellar, which could on occasion be used as a guard room for refractory soldiers; and the walls, nearly two feet thick, offered an excellent defence should it so happen that they were to be put to that use. It is remembered by the old residents of this city that this building was used by the government as a recruiting station as far back as the Mexican war and even prior thereto, probably as early as 1835, after Mr. Wyman had sold the property to Mr. Irving. Among those graduates of West Point who were placed in command of this recruiting station were Captain John C. Robinson of the Eighth U. S. Infantry, who became a Brigadier General in the army, commanding the third brigade of the first division of the first corps, and who eventually became Lieutenant Governor of this State. Lieutenant Christopher C. Auger was another officer in charge; and he became distinguished in the army, rising to the rank of a Major General. Lieutenant "Bonny" Phillips was another officer in charge. He was removed to Texas and died in New Orleans. Lieutenant Russell, afterwards a General in the army, was another officer remembered as one of those who had charge of this recruiting station. Lieutenant Kirby Smith, afterwards a Colonel in the Mexican war, was another officer in charge of this station.

George Murray, now deceased, rented this building in 1851-52, and he used it as a dye house, to which use it was ever afterwards put. In the spring of 1861, Mr. Murray sold out his business to Alexander Smith, who rented the building until September 13, 1865, when his wife purchased the property. Mrs. Smith says that one day Mr. Bradley, the agent for Mr. Armstrong of Rome, told her husband that he would give him just one hour in which to decide whether to purchase the property or not. By purchasing the property Mrs. Smith became possessed of the first stone building erected in the village of Syracuse, an old and historic landmark, and a valuable piece of property.

Col. John M. Strong, Canal Collector, says that he well remembers James Webb as a fine-looking, well-built man, six feet in height and a man of means and prominence in the early history of Syracuse. Judge Webb owned a farm in Onondaga Hill. His brother, Jabez Webb, who was a Supervisor, owned an adjoining farm; and he was killed at the raising of a mill on his farm. Jabez Webb had two sons, John and Ezra, the former locating in Cicero, where his descendants are now living, and the latter locating in the western part of the State. James Webb's two daughters, mention of whom has already been made, were attractive, beautiful young ladies, the belles of Onondaga Hill. Mr. Webb became clerk of the

Board of Supervisors when he came to Syracuse, an important position which he held for some years thereafter. He removed to Alton, Ill., with his son-in-law, George T. M. Davis, who became member of Congress from that district. Mr. Webb sold his farm to Rodger Billings, who gave Billings Park to the city; and Mr. Billings sold the farm to Judge Oliver R. Strong. In 1842, after the old Webb farm had been owned by Judge Strong two years, Judge Webb returned to Syracuse for a visit, and then went back to Alton, Ill., where he died.

This old landmark was destroyed on the night of December 8, 1893. A fire had started in one of the adjoining buildings, causing a large brick wall to fall upon it. Little was saved from the ruins excepting the eastern wall. Another building, similar in design, was erected in the course of a few months.

THE ALVORD BUILDING.—From a recent photograph.

CHAPTER VIII

THE OLD ALVORD BUILDING

As a reminder of the important part which the village of Salina once took in the prosperity of New York State, greater comparatively than the part now taken by the city of Syracuse, the student of that early history finds a lasting monument in the old Alvord building, now standing on the northeasterly corner of North Salina and Exchange streets. When this building was erected in 1808 by Elisha Alvord and his brother Dioclesian, it stood on the corner of Free street, through which the Oswego canal now passes, and Canal street, which is now called North Salina street. It is the first brick building erected within the present limits of Syracuse and one of the oldest landmarks in this part of the State. Ex-Lieut-Gov. Thomas G. Alvord, son of Elisha Alvord who settled at Salt Point in 1794, says that this old building to-day is the strongest and most durable building in Syracuse, as its walls are two feet thick up to the first story and eighteen inches thick from there to the

(81)

roof, while the joist and other parts of the woodwork
are still in an excellent condition. The building, built
upon honor, cost a small sum as compared with the
prices now paid for similar structures, because of the
low price then paid for labor and material, about
fifty per centum less than at the present day. The
brick were made by David Marshall on the banks of
the Yellow Brook, near where it crossed South Salina
street, between Jefferson and Onondaga streets; and
the stone in the cellar were quarried in the line of
what is now Center street, in the First ward.

The Alvord brothers kept a hotel in this building
till 1813, when they dissolved partnership, the building
coming into the possession of Elisha Alvord. The next
occupant was Major Ryder, commonly called Bull
Ryder, who kept a hotel there till the building was
sold to William Clark in the early 20's. Mr. Clark
not only bought this building, but also considerable
land in front of it, including what is now Exchange
street and the lot directly opposite, where the State salt
building was afterwards erected, the purchase price
being $12,000. When Exchange street was opened in
1828 the appraisers valued "the interest of William
Clark in said street at $279," and further appraised
"the value of the land in front of William Clark at
$418.50."

Mr. Clark was one of the most prominent merchants
at that early day, keeping a store of general merchan-

dise and dealing largely in salt. In 1828 he built an addition to the building, extending it to the canal. He afterwards rented part of the building on Exchange street as a drug store to Dr. Proctor C. Sampson and Dr. Lyman Clary, two celebrated physicians. Dr. Clary's son, O. Ware Clary, recently kept a rubber store in South Salina street, between Washington and Fayette streets. This drug store was conducted from 1832 till nearly 1840, when the store was absorbed in Mr. Clark's general store. Mr. Clark at one time took into partnership, under the firm name of William Clark & Company, his brother-in-law, James Beardsley, who afterwards returned to New Orleans, where he became the editor of the New Orleans *Bee*. Ex-Lieut-Gov. Alvord, oftentimes called "Old Salt," for the great service he rendered Syracuse in protecting the salt industry, occupied an office in this old building, over the drug store, from 1833 to 1846, excepting three years, during which he occupied an office in the State building, directly opposite, in partnership with Gen. Enos D. Hopping, brother-in-law of Dean Richmond.

William Clark sold out his business in 1841 to Myles W. Bennett and Noadiah M. Childs, who carried on the business for five years under the firm name of Bennett & Childs. Mr. Childs was the active business partner, while Mr. Bennett continued as cashier of the Bank of Salina, which stood at the corner of North Salina and Wolf streets. Mr. Bennett was succeeded by Thomas Earll, son of Judge Nehemiah H. Earll, who was member of Congress for two terms from Onondaga Hill. Their firm, Childs & Earll, remained in business from 1846 till 1849, when Mr. Childs continued alone in the old Alvord building till 1856. Mr. Childs bought the building from William Clark in 1853, the purchase price being $4,500.

After the fire of 1856, which destroyed some six or seven acres of buildings and residences, mostly located in the block inclosed by Exchange, North Salina, Wolf and Park streets, though there were some buildings destroyed on Wolf and North Salina streets, notably the Bank of Salina and the Eagle Hotel, the latter being located where E. J. Eddy's store is now located, N. M. Childs removed to the Crippen block, corner of Park and Wolf streets, which is now occupied by H. A. Moyer, the wagon manufacturer. Mr. Childs continued in business till 1881. He is now the agent for the Dillaye estate, residing at 406 Townsend street, hale and hearty at the age of 87 years. He and ex-Lieut-Gov. Thomas G. Alvord, still in vigorous health at the age of 84 years, a salt manufacturer, residing at 514 Turtle street, are the only survivors of the old inhabitants mentioned above.

The upper floor of the old Alvord building, consisting of three stories, was used as a public ball room, where much dancing was enjoyed in those early days, but it was not so used when Mr. Clark occupied the building. When N. M. Childs was President of the Board of Education in 1858, this upper floor was used for a winter school, during the close of canal navigation. The young fellows who worked in the salt yards and along the canal in those early days—the "Salt Pointers," as they were called—enjoyed the well-earned reputation of being rather tough, and it was a difficult matter to find a school teacher who was capable of preserving order. Mr. Childs' says that Henry A. Barnum, who was afterwards distinguished as a General in the civil war, then 25 years old, was the teacher in that winter school for one or two winters, and that young Barnum proved that he had plenty of pluck, and succeeded in governing the school, notorious for its being decidedly tough.

After Mr. Childs moved into the Crippen block in 1856, the old Alvord building was rented for various purposes, though it was mostly vacant. In 1873, the building was sold to Albert Freeman and his son, Hoyt H. Freeman, then doing business as A. & H. H. Freeman, the purchase price being $3,500. That firm carried on a pork packing business and dealt in flour and feed for dairy purposes, besides owning five canal boats. In 1878, the firm dissolved. Hoyt H. Freeman carried on business alone at the corner of Wolf and North Salina streets, where the Bank of Salina was formerly located and where the Freeman block now stands. Albert Freeman took into partnership his other son, Horace P. Freeman, under the firm name of A. & H. P. Freeman, who conducted a salt and feed mill and broom manufactury till 1886, when Albert Freeman died. The business was continued a year or two afterwards by Horace P. Freeman. Hoyt H. Freeman purchased the building, after his father's death, and he now uses it as a store house, he being of the firm of Freeman & Loomis (H. H. Loomis,) manufacturers of willow clothes baskets. In 1880 or 1881, Albert Freeman rented a portion of the building for an oil stone manufactory to Allan H. Gillett, father of William A. Gillett, and who is now agent for an oil stone firm in New York city. The building was also occupied by a man named Billings, a peddler, who kept a rag and tin store, and who sold out his business to a man named Ayres.

The history of this old Alvord building, now known as the Freeman building, reveals the history of Salina, well known throughout the State as Salt Point. Prior to the opening of the Oswego canal, Free street was the great business thoroughfare of the village. The farmers would come from different parts of the State—from Oswego and Ogdensburg, two important towns on the north, and from Buffalo, another equally important town in the west—mostly in the winter time; and they would barter their provisions for salt. The old people, who lived in those

early days, and who are now living, can remember
the time when Free street, from Park to Canal (now
North Salina) street, was filled with the farmers'
sleighs. At that early day, the society of Salt Point
was of a refined, intellectual and literary character.
After the Oswego canal was opened in 1825, the
business thoroughfare was moved to Exchange street,
and most of the business was carried on by canal
navigation. The early merchants of Salina rented
the large island at Oswego, covering several acres of
land, and would use it for storing their salt to be
shipped westward on the lakes. As the surrounding
country became more thickly settled, the business
thoroughfare, after the destructive fire of 1856, was
moved to Wolf street, because of the building of the
plank road to Central Square.

As an example of the fluctuation in the price of
real estate in Salina, from those early days till now,
it might be noted that William B. Kirk, the father
of ex-Mayor William B. Kirk, sought at one time to
purchase the property where the Kearney brewery
now stands, at the corner of North Salina and Wolf
street; but he did not have sufficient money. And so
he purchased property at the corner of South Salina
and Fayette streets, then known as a popular tavern,
afterwards called the Kirk House, and now known
as one of the finest business blocks in the city,
called the Kirk block.

CHAPTER IX

A FOREMOST JOURNALIST

The large, old-fashioned brick house at the southwestern corner of West Onondaga street and South avenue, which was occupied for many years by Vivus W. Smith, who, as editor of the Syracuse *Journal*, exerted a very great influence upon the early political history of this State, is soon to be torn down by Oscar F. Soule and to be replaced by a double dwelling house for Mr. Soule and his son, Frank C. Soule. This house is one of the earliest houses erected in this city, and it is the place where political consultations were held between Horace Greeley, editor of the New York *Tribune*, Thurlow Weed, editor of the Albany *Journal*, and Vivus W. Smith, editor of the Syracuse *Journal*.

The house was erected in a very substantial manner in 1830, when the village of Syracuse had a population of 2,500, by Zophar H. Adams, a builder, who had a brick yard between his house and Onondaga creek. Mr. Adams did much of the early village

THE HOME OF VIVUS W. SMITH.—From a recent photograph.

jobbing, having teams, wagons and ploughs; and he
made roads, carted off rubbish and cleaned the streets.
He is remembered as the man who made Warren
street from Jefferson street to Billings Park.   His
was the only house at that time west of the creek.   It
stood on the old Cinder road, built in 1827–28 on low
land running through a wooded territory, consisting
principally of oak and hickory, interspersed with
some hemlock.

The house was purchased in 1847 by Mr. Smith,
who lived there until he died in 1881.   Its capacity
was very much enlarged, making it a very roomy and
pleasant dwelling house.   It seemed at the time as
though Mr. Smith was going into the country, as all
the territory west of the creek was farm land up to
1860.   Philo N. Rust, the original landlord of the old
Syracuse House, who had a national reputation as the
most celebrated hotel keeper in central New York, had
a fine garden of fifty acres near by; and John Wilkinson's farm of 120 acres adjoined it on the west.   The
house on the opposite side of the street was occupied
by the Rev. George H. Hulin, editor of the *Religious
Recorder*, afterwards occupied by General Henry W.
Slocum and now occupied by N. M. White.

Mr. Smith had moved from the house built by
Elias W. Leavenworth in East Fayette street, about
opposite where the Grand Opera House now stands.
He had formerly lived in Onondaga Hill, where he

removed in 1827 from Westfield, Mass. When the
Court House was removed from Onondaga Hill to
Syracuse in 1829, Mr. Smith moved to Syracuse and
lived in the house between the one built by Joshua
Forman, the founder of Syracuse, and the one built
by James Webb, afterwards known as the recruiting
station; and here it was, in West Water street, between South Clinton and Franklin streets, that Carroll
E. Smith, the present editor of the Syracuse *Journal*,
was born.

This old landmark, about to give way to modern
improvements, was a meeting place in the early days
for all the leading politicians, influential in the Whig
party in this State. In those early days, it was the
custom of the political leaders to make tours at least
once a year throughout the State and visit each
county seat, calling together their trusted leaders for
the purpose of discussing campaign issues. William
L. Marcy, Edward Crosswell, Martin Van Buren
and other men of national reputation made these
yearly tours. But it was with William H. Seward,
Horace Greeley and Thurlow Weed, the great newspaper men, that Mr. Smith was most closely intimate.
They would sometimes come together, though more
frequently alone, just as one friend would visit
another.

The most marked man of them all, and certainly
the most eccentric, was Greeley, whose white hat and

white coat, with pantaloons of one leg tucked inside
his boot leg, made him a noted character. Whether
he affected this peculiarity in his personal appearance
from design, or whether he was simply careless and
absent-minded, are matters of conjecture. Another
peculiarity of this noted man, and one which must
have caused his host considerable vexation, was his
insisting upon having a tub of cold water for a bath
every night, and then literally emptying the water
upon the carpet during his vigorous efforts to keep
himself spotlessly clean.

Thurlow Weed, for more than a quarter of a century, came to Syracuse at least once a year; and he
would quietly drive over the old Cinder road and
renew his acquaintances at Onondaga Valley, where
he lived when a boy. His father, Joel Weed, was a
laboring man at Nicholas Mickles' furnace, which
was located in what is now Elmwood Park; and
he was a very remarkable man, noted for his
strong sense and great fund of general information,
obtained mainly from his devouring the newspaper
exchanges in the office of Lewis H. Redfield, publisher
of the Onondaga *Register* at Onondaga Valley.

It was in that newspaper office that young Thurlow first imbibed his liking for newspaper work.
When the son was twelve years old, he also worked
in Mickles' furnace. He afterwards became one of
the greatest men the country ever produced, being

called the Maker of Presidents, as Warwick of England was called the Maker of Kings. His first silver dollar was earned by selling to Joshua Forman a fine salmon, which he caught in Onondaga creek, formerly a fine stream of water and abounding in salmon and trout.

Those four newspaper men, who were very close friends, were possessed of broad information and great knowledge of the world. Mr. Smith was naturally a very reticent man and apparently cold, but when among his friends he would be companionable, humorous and an entertaining conversationalist. He was a great student of various branches of knowledge, and much given to scientific investigation. Greeley and Weed had great confidence in him; so much so that when they were absent on their European trips they would entrust the editing of their papers to him; and Mr. Smith would edit the New York *Tribune* or the Albany *Journal*, as the case might be. After the break between Seward and Greeley in 1860, Smith went with Seward and Weed. The characteristic of Smith in his newspaper work was his clear, forcible editorial expressions. He was a journalist for fifty years, and he was recognized as one of the strongest writers in the State.

In those days an editor would write from one to three editorials a week, which would fill about as many columns of his newspaper. The papers were all mod-

VIVUS W. SMITH.

eled after the papers of Europe. There was very little of local news in them, as a reference to the old files will clearly show. The first paper to establish the local column was the Syracuse *Journal*, the plan originating with Edward Cooper in 1846, when that paper was published by Barnes, Smith & Cooper, consisting of Henry Barnes, Augustus S. Smith (brother of Vivus W. Smith) and Edward Cooper. Mr. Weed of the Albany *Journal* originated the short paragraph in journalism, which is now the most effective weapon. Greeley of the New York *Tribune* effected the long and elaborate editorial, which was very convincing in its argument. He originated the "em" dash at the commencement of each paragraph. And it may be added that while he was very careless in his dress, he was exceedingly careful of his manuscript, though his handwriting, to one unaccustomed to it, was very difficult to read. There were many italicised words used in those days, but the modern type-setting machines have no italics. Seward was connected with Weed in the Albany *Journal*, and he became distinguished through his State papers while he was Secretary of State under President Lincoln.

It has been noticed that this old house, which was really a mansion, so large and roomy was it, was never painted. Some of the bricks were of the natural color, some were painted, some were mixed brick and some were those which had been in the original part built by Mr. Adams. Mr. Smith was frequently joked about the outside appearance of his house; but as he had no pride for outward show, he refused to paint it, saying it was good enough for him, though he sometimes threatened to paint it a sky blue, that it might be different from other houses. His widow, Theodora M. Smith, died in 1893. His newspaper, through which he gained his great reputation as a politician and journalist of the highest rank, is now edited and managed by his son, Carroll E. Smith.

Vivus W. Smith, the most distinguished newspaper writer of Syracuse, was born in Lanesborough, Mass., January 27, 1804. After a short experience in a newspaper office at Westfield, Mass., he came to Onondaga Hill in 1827, and bought out the Onondaga *Journal*, which he published till 1829, when he removed to Syracuse. In company with John F. Wyman, who had established the Syracuse *Advertiser* in 1825, he established the Onondaga *Standard*, the two papers having been united, and the firm name being Wyman & Smith. In 1837 he dissolved his connection with the Democratic party and established in 1838 a Whig paper, entitled the *Western State Journal*. In 1841, he went to Columbus, Ohio, and spent three years there editing the *State Journal*, a Whig paper. He returned to Syracuse and resumed the editorship of his former paper, which is now called the Syracuse *Journal*. In the fall of 1846, he was elected County Clerk, and served for three years. He was appointed by Governor Clark in 1855, Superintendent of the Onondaga Salt Springs, which office he held for ten years. In 1873, he was appointed Canal Appraiser by Governor John A. Dix. Mr. Smith married, in 1832, Caroline Earll, the daughter of Jonas Earll, jr., of Onondaga Hill, by whom he had one son, Carroll E. Smith. His wife died in April, 1835. In 1839, he married Theodora Morey, daughter of David Morey of Syracuse, by whom he had three children: Fillmore M., Seward V. and Florence A. Mr. Smith died in 1881.

CHAPTER X

THE CITY BOARDING HOUSE

The three-story brick building on the northwestern corner of West Genesee and North Clinton streets, part of which has now been torn down so as to widen North Clinton street, was considered a very handsome building in the early days. It was known as the Dana House, having been built by Deacon Daniel Dana, but its correct title was the City Boarding House. The residence part at the west of the building was connected with the eastern part, under which were the stores, and the whole was used for a fashionable boarding house. Indeed, it was the most fashionable boarding and lodging house in the city. In the angle at the extreme eastern part of the building, which was cut away when North Clinton street was widened in 1858, there was a small building used for a blacksmith shop and various offices. An account of this landmark will recall the names of several men who were once prominent in the history of Syracuse.

(96)

THE CITY BOARDING HOUSE.—From a recent photograph.

The land whereon the building stands was originally part of the Walton Tract, which was purchased in 1814 for $9,000 by Forman, Wilson & Company, composed of Joshua Forman, Ebenezer Wilson, jr., and John B. Creed. Forman & Wilson kept a country store in Onondaga Valley. Mr. Creed married Mr. Forman's daughter Mary, who, after her husband's death, became the wife of Moses D. Burnet. About the time of this purchase, Forman, Wilson & Company built and started a large slaughter house and packing establishment in a grove north of Church street (now West Willow street), where a large business was done till 1817. During the latter part of the war of 1812 they filled contracts for the army. It was their ambition to found a city on the present site of Syracuse. But misfortune overtook them; for the Walton Tract was sold by the Sheriff, Jonas Earll, jr., October 26, 1818, to Daniel Kellogg and William H. Sabin, for $10,915, to satisfy a claim of $10,000, (reduced from $15,000,) against Joshua Forman by the Bank of America of New York, and a claim of $452.62 against the firm by the Ontario Bank of Canandaigua. Messrs. Kellogg and Sabin sold the two western lots, April 1, 1824, for $350 to William Mead, a tailor, and Zina Denison, a wagon maker, both of Onondaga. They sold the property to Seth K. Akin, of the town of Salina, June 17, 1824, for $850. On November 26, 1830, Mr. Akin, then of New

Bedford, Mass., sold the property to Daniel Dana
for $1,300.

Mr. Dana came to the village of Syracuse about
1824 from Albany, originally from New England, and
was for a year or two employed as paymaster by the
Syracuse Salt Company.   He then opened a small
grocery and grain store in the block standing where
the Clinton block now stands, on the southwestern
corner of West Genesee and North Clinton streets.
There he continued in business for several years, till
his brother, Major Dana, came here and joined him,
under the firm name of D. & M. Dana.   That firm
built the block of three stores on the northwestern
corner of Warren and East Water streets, where for
several years they successfully carried on one of the
largest grain and country stores in this section of the
State.   Their principal competitor was Joseph Slocum, who was one of the three Assessors for the
village during the years 1828-'29-'44 and '45, and who
was the father of Mrs. Russell Sage of New York
city.

Mr. Dana, or, as he was generally called, Deacon
Dana, built his residence on the property he purchased from Mr. Akin in 1830.   This location was
then considered the best in the village.   Several of
the prominent citizens resided in the neighborhood.
This brick dwelling house was very grand and stylish
in its day, especially as it was ornamented with an

iron railing around the front stone steps. This iron
work was made by Joseph I. Bradléy, an uncle to
Christopher C. and Waterman C. Bradley, and it was
the first work of that kind used in the village. And
it was considered surprising as well as extravagant in
Deacon Dana that he should build such a fine house,
as he was very simple in his habits and not given to
expensive outlay of money. But though the Deacon
was a close business man, good at driving a bargain
and careful in expenditures, he was a pompous little
man, always well dressed in the black swallow-tail
commonly worn by the gentlemen of those days; and
he carried a gold-handled cane with much dignity of
manner. He was a nervous man, always ready for
an argument, a close student of the Bible, possessed
of a large acquaintance throughout the State, and he
was a prominent member of the First Presbyterian
Church. He was an enterprising, capable business
man, though during the last few years of his life he
became rather eccentric. Mr. Dana does not appear
to have held any public office, excepting that he was
an elector for James K. Polk in 1844. He was a
Democrat of the old school and a strong party man.
He was an applicant for the postmastership of the
village at that time, but the office was given to Col.
William W. Teall, who served from 1845 to 1849.

On July 8, 1824, Messrs. Kellogg and Sabin sold
the two eastern lots for $250 to Daniel Hawks, jr., of

Hannibal, Oswego county. On March 18, 1829, Mr. Hawks, then of the town of Clay, sold the property for $1,025 to Dr. David S. Colvin, a prominent Democrat, who sold it to John B. Ives, December 5, 1835, for $3,400. Mr. Ives was a very successful contractor, building railroads and canals, and he resided at Jamesville. His widow, Mrs. Ann Eliza Ives, daughter of B. Davis Noxon, is now living at the Empire House. The property was sold by Peter Outwater, jr., one of the Masters in Chancery, whose daughter married Andrew D. White, ex-President of Cornell University, on the claim of John V. L. Pruyn, a prominent citizen of Albany, to Daniel Dana, September 25, 1845, for $2,250.

Deacon Dana then erected the brick building, unusually large and handsome for those days, and, connecting it with his dwelling house, rented it to David B. Blakely, who kept the City Boarding House. Mr. Blakely and all his family were very musical, and he frequently gave concerts. He was succeeded by James A. Durnford, who for several years kept the boarding house. Some of the older and prominent residents of this city boarded at that fashionable place.

Deacon Dana, after dissolving partnership with his brother, Major, occupied the two stores for his grain and grocery business. But because of his failing health, his business was not as thriving as formerly. His eccentricities took a religious turn, and he would

appeal to his friends to make repentance of their sins
and prepare for the hereafter. His kindly and courteous, though pompous, manners remained with him
to the last. He died at his residence December 21,
1858, aged sixty-seven years, and he was buried at
Rose Hill cemetery. Owing to the infirmities of his
afflicted widow the funeral was held at the First Baptist Church, which was near by, the services being conducted by the Rev. Dr. Sherman B. Canfield, pastor
of the First Presbyterian Church. Major Dana lived
several years thereafter. He is remembered as a careful, methodical business man, though, in his later
years, much given to buying large quantities of mis-
cellaneous goods sold at public auction.

The entire property was sold November 6, 1858, to
John Ritchie for $11,500. Mr Ritchie was a partner
with David Leslie, as Ritchie & Leslie, and they kept
a very fine grocery in Robbers' Row, being succeeded
by D. & J. Leslie. Mr. Ritchie then retired from
active business, though he kept the open sheds for
farmers, on nearly the opposite side of the street,
which business is now carried on by his son, John
Ritchie. His daughter is the wife of Wilbur S. Peck.
The property has since changed hands, part of it being
sold to the city in widening North Clinton street.

Deacon Dana had no children. His brother, Major
Dana, who survived him several years, is survived by
a daughter, Mrs. Mary Dana Hicks, widow of Charles

Hicks, who was a promising young attorney. Mrs. Hicks was a teacher of drawing in the public schools; and it was her work in this department that brought her to the attention of L. Prang & Company, fine art publishers of Boston, Mass. She is an artist of considerable ability, and she has charge of an art department in Prang's art works in Boston, living in Cambridge, Mass.

THE WEIGH-LOCK HOUSE.—From a recent photograph.

CHAPTER XI

THE WEIGH-LOCK HOUSE

One of the old landmarks of this city, and one of which little has been written, is the weigh-lock house at the foot of Market street on East Water street and on the heel-path side of the Erie canal. The house, a low, long, dingy-looking brick building, was erected by the State for the enlargement of the Erie Canal. The contract was awarded to William D. Champlain, James Thorn and Edward Fuller, and it was dated September 28, 1849. Champlain and Thorn did the mason work and Fuller was the carpenter. The contract price was $7,950 with $333.37 as items of extra work, making the final estimate $8,283.37. These accounts were settled November 19, 1850, so that the building was doubtless completed by that time.

The house stands to-day practically in the same condition as when erected, excepting that improvements were made in the winter of 1892 to the interior of the second floor, where the Superintendent of the Middle Division, the Superintendent of Section No.

(103)

6, the Division Engineer, and the Resident Engineer have their offices. The first floor with the weigh-lock on the north side facing the canal presents a romantic, picturesque appearance; and it is here that the Canal Collector and his assistant have their offices. The Inspector of Boats also has his office on this floor.

The year of 1893 was one of the most prosperous seasons known in several years by the boatmen, especially on the Erie canal. By far the greater part of the merchandise transported by the canal consists of grain, stone, clay, lumber, coal and iron and other ores. The best year on all the canals was in 1868, when the total movement of articles amounted to $305,301,920, representing 6,442,225 tons of freight. The amount of produce cleared from Syracuse during the season of 1824, four years after the middle section of the canal was first opened for navigation, was 12,065 barrels of flour, 2,862 barrels of provisions, 2,565 barrels of ashes, 76,631 barrels of salt and 64,240 bushels of wheat; and the amount of toll received at the Syracuse office during that season was $18,491.58. It will be seen that the village of Syracuse as early as 1824 was not only a shipping point for salt, the most important product, but also for wheat and flour. This was a prosperous wheat-producing county in the early days, and there was some thriving flour mills in the vicinity of Syracuse. Since

1883, tolls have been abolished on the canals, by amendment to the State Constitution at the preceding fall election. During the year of 1893, ending September 30, the appropriations from the State for constructing and improvements in the middle division of the Erie canal were $209,300, showing that continued and large expenditures are being made on this great and important regulator of railroad freight rates.

The former Canal Collector's office stood between the bridges spanning the junction of the Erie and Oswego canals. A foundation of hewn timber was laid upon "Goose Island" on the north side of the towing-path, and upon this was erected a small frame house, which was designated as the Canal Collector's office. Dr. David S. Colvin was the Collector in 1824, and he employed Benjamin C. Lathrop and B. F. Colvin as clerks in his office. The old weigh-lock was completed that year. It was built upon an entirely different plan from the one now followed; the weight of the boat being determined by measuring the quantity of water it displaced. Deacon Thomas Spencer then owned and occupied the old boat yard near the Oswego canal. This boat yard, afterwards owned by John Durston and now the site of the Durston block, corner of James and Warren streets, was then considered out of town, the easiest approach being by the tow-path. But it was convenient to both the Erie and Oswego canals, the principal part of the business consisting in building and repairing the canal boats.

In 1824, soon after the completion of the Erie canal through Syracuse, it was thought necessary to have a basin where boats could run in and be out of the way of navigation. It was decided to locate the basin in what is now the western part of the present weigh-lock and extending south half-way to Washington street, taking in the former site of the old Market Hall, now the northern portion of the City Hall. As there was no current in the water that was in the basin, the place became a miserable, nasty hole; and it was the dread of all the inhabitants, because it tainted and infected the whole atmosphere with disease.

A little low frame building stood on the bank of the basin partly hid by the bushes that grew in great profusion in that region. Joseph Thompson kept a small grocery in the building, and derived most of his custom from the canal boatmen by furnishing them with supplies. A small barn stood on the south side of the basin, with a path on one side leading into it, which was used as a watering place for cattle and horses. In those days there was a large number of scow-boats used to transport wood for the salt blocks. They were not in use more than half of the time, and this basin, or frog pond, as it was called, became filled with these unsightly craft. Many of them were neglected and sunk to the bottom, and they were afterwards found by the workmen in excavating near the present City Hall.

It was not until 1845 that the final abolition of this old canal basin, long regarded as a necessary evil, was accomplished, and the erection of a public market building on its site carried out. It was a project which had been discussed three years. The plan was to erect a building with market stalls on the ground floor, which were to be leased for the sale of provisions, as had been and is the practice in New York and other cities; and a commodious hall was to be provided on the second floor. The location of this new market was the subject of numerous and warm discussions, but the place finally selected was between Montgomery and Market streets, where the canal basin had long existed as a nuisance, the cost of the land being $5,000.

After the completion of the building, and to overcome the seeming reluctance on the part of some of the market-men to give up their former place of business for the market stalls, a paper was drawn up which the leading dealers signed, agreeing to try the new plan. This was in March, 1846. The stalls were accordingly taken and lavishly provided with meats, and the square in front of the building was the daily resort of farmers' teams for the sale of various kinds of produce. It all looked well, quite metropolitan,

but it did not pay. Customers did not like it and
neither did the rival dealers, and the project was soon
abandoned. But the public hall was a great convenience, and in it was transacted for many years all the
public business; and it was often occupied for other
purposes. It will be remembered that the market
place was convenient for public out-of-door gatherings
when distinguished visitors were in town. General
Scott in 1852 reviewed the military companies of the
city in front of the City Hall and there made an
address. In the same year an elaborate stand was
erected on this square for the reception of Louis
Kossuth.

It is perhaps a singular coincidence that the first
movement in the Halls of Legislation, relative to the
Erie canal, was made by a member from Onondaga,
Joshua Forman; that the first exploration was made
by an engineer of Onondaga, James Geddes; that the
first contract was given to, and the first ground broken
by a contractor, John Richardson, who had been several years a resident of Onondaga; and all of whom
had been judges of Onondaga's county courts and
members of the Legislature from Onondaga county.
Mr. Forman introduced the great project in the Legislature in 1808; Mr. Geddes submitted to the Surveyor
General his report of three different routes for constructing the Erie canal in 1809.

The first contract, given to John Richardson of

Cayuga, was dated June 27, 1817, and the remaining
part of the whole middle section was under contract
very soon thereafter; and on the 4th of July following, the excavation was commenced at Rome with
appropriate ceremonies. In 1819 the middle section,
from Utica to Seneca river including a lateral canal
to Salina, about ninety-four miles, was reported by
Governor Clinton in his annual message of 1820, as
completed. By the opening of this portion of the
canal the resources of Onondaga were more fully
ascertained and developed. And finally, November
1, 1825, a period of only eight years and four months,
it was proclaimed to the world that the waters of Lake
Erie were connected with those of the Hudson river
without one foot of portage, through one of the longest
canals in the world; and the cost, according to the
books of the Comptroller, including the Champlain
canal, was $8,273,122.66. After the canal was com-
pleted, all things were ready and the water was let in.
For a long time it would not flow further west on the
Syracuse level than the stone bridge, now called the
swing bridge, at the junction of Salina and Genesee
streets, as the water all disappeared in a bed of loose
ground. Many despaired of ever making the canal
tight; but after a deal of perplexity this place was
stopped and the water run on to the Raynor block,
northwestern corner of West Water and Franklin
streets, and there performed the same freak, and it
was several weeks before this level could be filled.

If the canal benefitted the people of Onondaga, the men of Onondaga were principal promoters of the undertaking in all its incipient steps. Two men of Onondaga labored faithfully and effectually throughout; Judge Geddes as an able engineer, Judge Forman as an unwavering promoter of the canal's utility. These two men furnished more solid information relative to the canal than all others put together. Till they took hold of it, the whole matter was considered by most men but an idle dream, a delusion, a false, unfeasible project. Oliver Teall was appointed the first Superintendent on the Erie canal, and Joshua Forman, the first Collector; office at Syracuse.

The weigh-lock at Syracuse and the one at Troy are the only ones along the Erie canal that are now in good condition and capable of weighing the canal boats. Since the canals are now free there is no necessity of weighing the cargoes for the purpose of collecting the tolls; but this weigh-lock is very useful in finding the weight of cargoes for the benefit of the canal captain, the shipper and the purchaser.

The weight of each canal boat is registered in the Collector's office. When the weight of the cargo is desired, the boat is run into the slip, directly in the rear of the weigh-lock house. The gates are then closed and the water in the slip is taken out through a tunnel which runs under the canal and into Onondaga creek, near the High School building. The boat then rests upon a cradle, suspended by strong beams from above, and it rests high and dry, just as ships do when placed in a dry dock. The weight of the cargo is then easily ascertained by means of fine scales used for that purpose. This weigh-lock is also used when repairs are necessary to be done on a disabled boat; and if it were not for this weigh-lock, there would be no place along the canal where such repairs could be done. And if it were not for this weigh-lock, acting as a dry dock, the disabled boats would, of necessity, sink into the canal, thus obstructing further travel along this great water way.

In the early days travel in the packet boats and in the line boats, which also carried freight, was quite popular and common. But it was slow traveling and far from pleasant if the journey was a long one, since the continued scraping of the towing line, the bumping of the boat against the sides of the canal, and the noise of the horses which were also quartered in the boat, interfered with the passenger's slumbering and prevented him from enjoying pleasant dreams. The canals met a serious competition in transporting both passengers and freight when the railroads came into use. The Syracuse and Utica railroad went into operation July 3, 1839; the Auburn and Syracuse Railroad in 1841; and the Oswego and Syracuse, October, 1848. But the speed of these early railroads was very slow as compared with the rapid transit of to-day. The

maximum speed was about fifteen miles an hour, with
an average of from seven to ten.

The stage coach driver was slow in relinquishing
his profitable trade to either the packet boat or the
railway car. It is remembered that Jason C. Woodruff, who afterwards filled the office of Mayor of Syracuse, and who excelled all other stage drivers on the
road, would wheel up his coach-and-four, "as he cut
a clean 6 and swept a bold 8," in front of the Syracuse
House, and offer a wager that he could reach the end
of the journey quicker than either the railroad car or
the packet boat. But so great was his skill and so
excellent his horses that he had no takers. The stage
coach is now almost forgotten and the canals are
maintained mainly to regulate railroad freight rates;
but there is no question but that the village of Syracuse is the offspring of the Erie canal, and that the
villages of Onondaga Valley and Salina, by declining
to render material assistance to Judge Forman in his
canal undertaking, lost their golden opportunity.

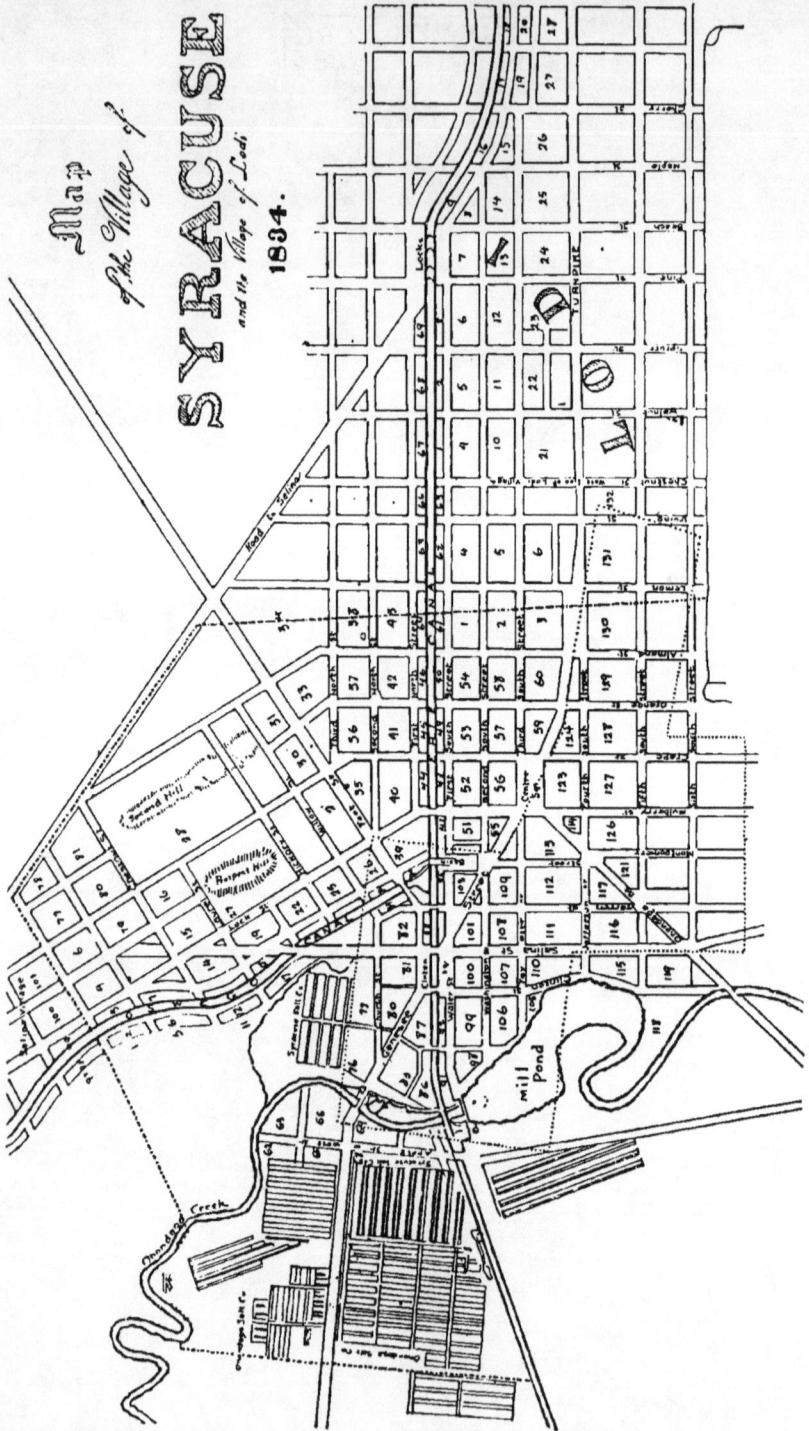

Map
of the Village of
SYRACUSE
and the Village of Lodi
1834.

CHAPTER XII

CHENEY'S REMINISCENCES

The following are the "Reminiscences of Syracuse," from the personal recollections of Timothy C. Cheney, compiled by Parish B. Johnson. These reminiscences give a description of Syracuse in 1824, and they were published in pamphlet form in 1857. They are invaluable, since they contain almost the only authentic records of Syracuse at that early date. Very few of the pamphlets are now in existence. Mr. Cheney was one of the earliest settlers in the village of Syracuse, and he was intimately connected with the business and history of the place, both as a village and a city. His reminiscences give an account of the most important local events that have transpired, and brief sketches and anecdotes of several of the early inhabitants :—

My father, with his family, came to this county in the winter of 1811 and '12. This county then formed part of the "Military Tract," and was the residence of large numbers of Revolutionary soldiers,

(113)

who had obtained the land for their services in our
war for freedom. They were generally athletic, hardy
and energetic, and well fitted to settle a new country.

We lived on Onondaga East Hill about two years.
My brothers and myself went to school in an old log
school-house to our worthy citizen, D. B. Bickford.

A tavern was kept there by John C. Brown,
brother-in-law to Harvey Baldwin.

Onondaga East Hill was then a place well
adapted and frequently used as a rendezvous for regiments of soldiers passing from the Eastern States to
the Niagara frontier.

Fragments of regiments and companies of British
prisoners generally camped there for the night by the
side of a small stream, while on their way to and
from the different places of detention or exchange.

I well remember going one fall in a wagon with
my father, to Salina, after a load of salt. We went
through Onondaga Hollow by the way of Mickles'
Furnace, to what was then called the "Corners,"
now Syracuse. At that time there was no road
where the present Tully Plank Road now runs; that
part of the country was still in its natural state.

We stopped at a tavern on the present site of the
Empire block, kept by Mr. Bogardus, an old
Revolutionary soldier. The house was a small one,
and was, I should judge, about twenty by thirty feet
square, and a story and a half high. I do not recollect

of seeing any other houses, though there may have
been two or three small ones.

I well recollect that it was a cedar swamp from
the Corners to Lodi, and a corduroy road where the
Genesee turnpike now runs. The road was covered
with an arch of cedars, and it looked very much like
an arched railroad tunnel a mile in length. The Corners, at that time, comprised the whole of Syracuse.

At that time nearly all of the first settlers of this
county were alive, and as a boy I knew them.

I was well acquainted with General Asa Danforth, and used to visit him frequently to listen to his
stories about the Revolution and partake of the
delicious musk melons with which he bountifully
supplied me.

I was at that time but six years old, and he must
have been over seventy-five. I well remember the
feelings of sorrow and regret I experienced as I saw
him borne to his grave. He was buried on the knoll,
next north of the old stone arsenal, and was removed
from that place to the family burial ground of Thaddeus M. Wood, and a few years ago his remains were
again removed and placed in the cemetery at Onondaga Hollow.

Arthur Patterson and Dr. Needham of Onondaga
Hollow are the only persons now living who acted as
pall bearers on that mournful occasion.

General Danforth came to this county in the year

1788, and settled in Onondaga Hollow, with the permission of the Indians.

At that time there were full five hundred Indians belonging to the Onondaga tribe. Many of their old men were engaged in the Revolution. They fought for his majesty, George III, against the American forces.

They had also fought against General Sullivan soon after the Revolution, in three small battles in this valley. Two of those battles were fought within the corporate limits of this city.

General Sullivan came up the Susquehanna with a large force, landed near Elmira and crossed over the country west of this place, until he reached Onondaga Lake. He passed round the lake until he reached the ground now occupied by the Salt Springs Pump House, which used to be Henry Young's sand bed. At this point he fought a severe battle with the Onondagas and defeated them. The Indians retreated to the foot of the hill, where the Water Works reservoir is now located, and encamped. In the morning General Sullivan sent out his scouts, who discovered and captured a couple of Indian spies in a large tree. From these two Indians they obtained information in regard to the camping place of the Onondagas.

The General formed his army in the form of a crescent and advanced over the hill, completely taking the Indians by surprise, while busily engaged in cooking breakfast, and shutting off every avenue of escape. At that time the flats near the foot of the hill were covered with water at all seasons of the year.

The Indians, discovering their situation, fought like savages while any hope was left, and then wildly plunged into the creek and escaped by swimming. Large numbers of them were killed in the water. General Sullivan rapidly followed up his advantage, and completely destroyed the castle and the largest portion of the village.

In the village they found a negro lock-smith engaged in repairing the locks of the Indians' guns. He was immediately seized by the infuriated army and hung and quartered in less than fifteen minutes.

The young chief, Anteauga, was engaged in both of these battles, and distinguished himself by his great bravery. He was presented by General Washington with an oblong silver medal, which he always wore afterwards, as a token of friendship and fidelity to this Government. The medal is probably still in the possession of his relatives on this Reservation.

The Onondagas were nearly destroyed by this incursion of General Sullivan into their country. They shortly afterwards came to terms, and were thenceforth allies of the American Government.

This city was known from 1806 to 1809 as

"Bogardus' Corners;" from 1809 to 1812 as "Milan;" from 1812 to 1814 as "South Salina;" from 1814 to 1817 as "Cossit's Corners;" from 1817 to 1820 as "Corinth;" and from that time it has ever been known as Syracuse, the name given it by John Wilkinson, he being the first postmaster.

Mr. Cheney came here to reside in March, 1824. He boarded on Church street, and used to cross "the green" where the old Baptist church (now the National theatre) stands, on his way to work.

One morning in the spring as he was going to his work, the thought came across his mind that he might live to see the time when the "Corners" would become a large and flourishing place, and that when that time did arrive it would be pleasant to look back to the year 1824 and be able to tell how many houses were then erected.

From where he stood every house in the village could be distinctly seen. He counted them and found there were but twenty-three finished houses and six or seven under way.

How few there are, if placed in the same circumstances with Mr. Cheney, would have conceived and carried out such an idea? And yet that wild dream of the future has come to pass. "The Corners" have grown until now they fill the vast boundaries of Syracuse—the "City of Salt" and "Isms."

At that time it was thought the "Old Red Mill"

would be the business centre of the future city. What citizen of Syracuse during the past ten years does not remember the old Red Mill? We, the compiler, well remember its old walls. In our more youthful days it was one of our favorite places of resort. We remember the feelings of awe and wonder we were wont to experience as we watched the great wooden water-wheel turn, turn, with a uniform motion, as if striving to get rid of the great weight of water let fall upon its time-worn frame from the moss-covered flume. We remember curiously watching the tin boxes of the elevator as they wound rapidly upward, bearing their burdens of grain or flour; of listening to the ceaseless bur-r-r-r of its different run of stone, and the clatter of the hopper as it supplied their greedy mouths. We remember the great bolter and the wooden spout from which issued a great dusty stream of bran or shorts; the huge box, into which was emptied the farmers' bags of grain to be weighed and then let down into a bin below, through a square hole in the bottom. And we do not forget the dark frown that would overshadow that fat, jovial face of the miller as we, boy-fashion, dipped our unresisting hand into the wheat bin and commenced that great delight of boys, making gum.

We remember still later, when the old mill had been abandoned, and the great wheel had ceased to turn the complicated machinery, of crawling burglar-like into one of its back windows and playing "hide and seek" within its deserted walls; of trembling and turning pale as we were startled by the noise made by some ancient rat as it clattered across the floor; of starting noiselessly down the stairs as the declining sun threw a dim and dismal light through its mildewed windows, looking right and left, expecting every instant to behold some ghost or other frightful apparition; until we reached the street, when, drawing a deep sigh of relief and casting a sidelong glance at the old mill, we would start on the homeward track; and we remember the old wooden bridge across the creek and race, from which we first witnessed the ordinance of baptism.

Excuse us, kind reader, for indulging in these sweet, sad memories of the past. At times we delight to revel in the shades of other days, and the old Red Mill and rickety wooden bridge, with many pleasant associations, hold a prominent place in our memories.

The old Red Mill was built in 1805, and set in operation the following year by Mr. Walton of the famous "Walton Tract." It was situated on the east bank of the Onondaga Creek, near the present substantial bridge spanning the creek on West Genesee street. In 1850 the old mill with its ancient companion, the wooden bridge, was removed to make room for the present artistic super-structure. The motive power was furnished by a mill race, leading from the old mill pond, now Jefferson Park. The mill dam stood where the present Water street bridge has been erected, and the pond extended as far south as Cinder road bridge. The waste water from the mill ran directly into Onondaga Creek.

The old mill contained two run of stone, and Henry Young was miller in 1824.

When it became necessary to remove the old mill dam, the Syracuse Company employed Mr. Young to make a pond west of the salt office, to be filled by the waste water from the canal, and to dig a race from the pond to the mill.

While he was engaged in digging the race he removed an old pine stump standing in front of the dwelling of E. F. Wallace, measuring four feet in diameter. At the foot of this stump among the roots he found the bones of a large Indian, a tomahawk, beads, knives and a rude earthen pot containing black and red paint. The paint was as fresh and perfect as though mixed the day before. Mr. Young claimed that the bones of this Indian, with the tomahawk, knives and pot of paint, had lain there for two hundred years. He had known the spot of ground for forty years, and the tree had been cut before he saw the place. The tomahawk found with the Indian is now in the possession of Mr. Cheney. It is a small iron hatchet with a pipe bowl for a head. The handle of this instrument was too much decayed to be preserved. This hatchet must have been brought here with the French Jesuits in 1656, and was obtained from them by this Indian, who, to judge from the quantity of trinkets and ornaments buried with him, must have been a very rich man.

A little southwest of the old Red Mill, on the race leading from the dam, Captain Rufus Parsons built a mill for the purpose of making linseed oil. In 1824 it was in full operation.

Southeast of the old mill, on the same side of the race, there stood a saw mill. It was built in 1805. In 1824 it was run by Frederick Horner.

That year pine lumber sold at the mill for four dollars per thousand, and hemlock for two dollars and fifty cents. Even at these prices, "store pay" had to be taken.

Mr. Hickox built a tannery that year on the present site of Walters' sheep-skin factory. Part of the old building is now standing. Mr. Hickox also built the house on the corner of Mill and Mechanic streets.

In 1824 that portion of our city now occupied by the Syracuse Pump House, was covered with a dense growth of small trees and bushes. Among these trees, near the present sand bed, stood a grave stone which had been erected a great many years before to the memory of a poor Indian trader who was murdered on that spot by the Onondagas. The inscription on the grave stone recorded the name of "Benjamin Newkirk, 1783." With Newkirk came Ephraim Webster. By reason of some act on their part displeasing to the natives, a council was held, at which it was agreed to kill them. Newkirk they immediately dispatched with a tomahawk. Webster's time had to all appearances come; he was escorted by two Indians to the place of execution. Arrived at the spot, he told his conductors that he wanted to drink once more before he died. The request was granted; whereupon he took his cup and drank the health of the Chiefs in a flattering speech. The speech captivated an old man so greatly that he exclaimed: "No kill'm." After some parley he was released and adopted into the tribe.

Soon afterwards he was married to a squaw. She did not live long. He married another, with the understanding that she was to remain his wife as long as she kept sober. He lived with her near twenty years, although he contrived many plots to get her intoxicated, that he might get rid of her and marry a white woman, as the whites became numerous. At the end of this period, with the aid of milk punch, he succeeded in his cruel attempts. The morning following her disgrace, she arose and without speaking a word, proceeded to gather together her personal effects, and left for her friends, no more the wife of Webster. Of a sensitive mind, and possessing a large share of self-respect, grief so preyed upon her that she died in a short time after the separation. One of her sons is now the principal Chief of the Onondagas, and is a man of unblemished character. After his second wife left him, Webster married Catharine Danks, a daughter of one of the early settlers of this county.

Webster was very serviceable in the war of 1812 in commanding the Indians, and acting in the capacity of a spy for General Brown. He was a perfect Indian in manners; could speak all the dialects of the American and Canadian tribes, and was a very shrewd and sagacious man. He used to make journeys into Canada, and, pretending to be intoxicated, lie around the fort at Kingston, for the purpose of obtaining information to communicate to the General at Sacket's Harbor. In order to get over the St. Lawrence, he would steal a boat, which upon landing on the other side he would set adrift; and on returning he would repeat the theft. The General and he were in close communion, and the nature of their interviews was known only to themselves. When on these Canadian expeditions, he would disguise himself with a coloring substance, that gave him the exact appearance of an Indian, and that could not be washed off from the skin by any ordinary process. He always pretended that his errand among the red coats was to obtain food or whiskey, and among the officers of

recent importation he met with uniform kindness;
but the old ones, who knew him well, usually sent
him away with a kick or a curse.

A little east of Newkirk's grave, myself and other
boys used to dig up the remains of Indians for the
purpose of getting possession of the beads, kettles,
knives and other implements of warfare, or an orna-
mental dress that had been buried with them—this
being the spot where the slain on both sides in the
first battle General Sullivan had with the Onondagas
were consigned to their final resting place.

Across the creek west of the old Red Mill there
were but few houses standing in 1824, and only two
or three more were built that year.

The house Hon. George F. Comstock now owns
and occupies, was occupied that year by John Wall.
He boarded the hands employed by Cyprian Hebbard,
step-father of George Stevens, of this city. Mr. Hebbard now resides in Onondaga Valley, and is a man
seventy-one years of age.

In 1824, Mr. Hebbard was engaged in building the
salt works on both sides of Genesee street, west of
the Onondaga creek.

A small yellow house then stood on the present
site of Allen Munroe's new house, and in 1824 was
occupied by Sterling Cossit, formerly landlord of the
old Mansion House.

The house now standing on the corner of West

and Genesee streets, lately occupied by D. O. Salmon, was built that year by Henry Young, the miller. His brother, Andrew Young, built the second house south of the corner on West street.

Old Mrs. Marble then lived on West street. Christopher Hyde lived nearly opposite of her residence. A carpenter named Patterson lived a little north of Mr. Hyde.

The house Joseph Savage has occupied so many years, was built in 1823 and finished in 1824. It was occupied that year by Calvin Mitchell, a contractor. He obtained the contract for building the railroad between Schenectady and Albany, one of the first railroads ever built in this State.

These were the only houses then standing on the west side of Onondaga creek and north of the canal.

The old house standing on the southeast corner of Genesee and Mill streets, was built several years before by Captain Rufus Parsons. The house now standing near the northeast corner of Genesee and Mill streets, was occupied by Frederick Horner.

Mr. Horner is now nearly eighty years of age, and is the only man now living in this city that ever saw George Washington.

About the time of the first invention of the grain elevator, inventors experienced great difficulty and expense in obtaining patent rights. Mr. Horner was then engaged in tending mill in New Jersey, and one

of the newly invented elevators had been placed in
his mill, and as yet had not been patented; though
the inventor was using every means in his power to
secure the desired protection of his skill. Washington, who was then President, was induced by the
invention to diverge from the direct route to the seat
of government at New York, and witness the performance of the elevator. Thus was Mr. Horner
afforded the pleasure of exhibiting to the Father of
his Country one of the first grain elevators. This was
the only time Mr. Horner ever saw the great Washington, and he remembers him distinctly as he
appeared on that occasion.

A little north of Mr. Horner's residence, Andrew
Young lived in a small wooden house which is now
standing.

The house that David Stafford lives in on West
Genesee street, was built by his father in 1824. He
was a carpenter by trade, and assisted in building the
old Baptist church and several other edifices.

A Mr. Cook built the house next west of A. Mc-
Kinstry's present residence on Church street.

Mr. D. Canfield built the house next east of
Public School House No. 4, and that year it was
occupied by the Rev. Mr. Barlow, the Episcopalian
minister.

Samuel Booth was the principal master mason at
that time, and owned and lived in a wooden house a

little east of Public School House No. 4. He did the mason work on the old Saleratus Factory, and was a prominent, influential mechanic.

An old yellow painted house then stood on the point formed by the junction of Genesee and Church streets, and was occupied by Deacon Fellows. The first house next west of the Baptist church was then standing.

Elijah Bicknall built the old Baptist church that year. Elder Gilbert was Pastor of the Church that year, and when the carpenters got ready to raise the building he mounted the timbers and made a long prayer for the blessing and prosperity of their work. Mr. Bicknall also built the small yellow house east of the old church, fronting on Church street.

L. A. Cheney purchased the lot fronting on the corner of Franklin and Mechanic streets that year, for two hundred and fifty dollars. It was then considered one of the most desirable lots in the village, on account of its being so near the centre of business. He had his choice, and selected that in preference to all others in the village, at the same price. Few persons, if any, then thought that the south side of the canal would ever be anything.

The old wooden house east of the foot bridge on Franklin street was built that year by Matthew L. Davis, and was kept the same year as a tavern by William Hicks. Mr. Davis also built the present residence of William L. Palmer on Genesee street. While Mr. Palmer's family were engaged in cleaning house last spring, they explored a large hole in one of the numerous cupboards, and discovered the remains of a linen pillow case marked "Matthew L. Davis." This pillow case must have lain in that hole upwards of thirty years. It was probably stolen by some mischievous rat and deposited in that place.

A little east of Mr. Hicks' tavern, Mr. P. Clarke occupied a small frame house.

The salt fields back of Church street were in full operation that year.

The house Mr. Driscoll lived in between Church street and the salt works, was built that year by Mr. Ryder. He also built two small houses on Mill street.

Where Public School House No. 4 now stands, there was standing, in 1824, an unpainted frame house, twenty-five feet square, a story and a half high, with a roof sloping four ways. This building contained one room, very high between joints, which was warmed by a large box stove. The room was furnished with old-fashioned, inconvenient school-house furniture, and in this room William K. Blair, for five days and a half in each week, taught the young ideas of Syracuse how to shoot.

The Universalists held regular meetings every Sabbath in this room.

The celebrated Orestes A. Brownson occasionally preached Universalism in this school-house to the inhabitants of Syracuse.

The house now occupied by Henry Fellows on West Genesee street was occupied by Widow Creed (now Mrs. M. D. Burnet) as a boarding house.

The house on the corner of Franklin and Genesee streets, the present residence of George B. Walters, was built that year by Henry Gifford. Mr. Gifford cut some of the sleepers for his house from the ground now occupied by the residence of John Crouse, on the corner of Fayette and Mulberry streets.

D. Canfield lived in a small house next east of Booth's on Church street.

B. Filkins lived next to him on the same side of the street.

John Wall built a small house east of Filkins' for the Syracuse Company.

Miles Seymour built the house on the southwest corner of Genesee and Franklin streets. He also built and kept a blacksmith shop on the corner of Clinton alley and Genesee street, the present site of the Dana block.

The Rev. Dr. Adams lived in a small wooden house on Franklin street, between the canal and Genesee street. The house was built in 1824 and occupied by Dr. Adams in 1825.

Hiram Hyde built the house near the centre of the block, between Clinton and Franklin streets.

Henry Newton lived in a small yellow house next west of John Ritchie's new store.

The old Eagle Tavern, kept by Frederick Rhyne, then stood on the present site of John Ritchie's store, and did a large business.

Joel Cody owned and lived in a small wooden house where the new Baptist church now stands. Attached to the house he had a large, well-kept garden, stocked with fruit trees and grapes, running back to Church street. Mr. Cody was at that time captain of a packet boat running between Utica and Rochester, and was noted for his eccentricities and love of fun.

East of Mr. Cody's house two brothers by the name of Woodward built a large frame house, which was kept by them for a hotel for about a year. Afterwards, Mr. Gates, son-in-law of Sterling Cossit, kept the house until it was accidentally burned.

The present residence of P. S. Stoddard was occupied in 1824 by Squire Bacon. He kept his justice office in the basement.

The present residence of Daniel Dana stood between Woodward's tavern and a small house standing next to Captain Cody's, occupied by a weak-minded man named Cohen.

Deacon Dana came here in 1825, and worked in the salt works, packing salt.

Monday, July 5, 1824, marks the date of the first celebration of our National Independence ever held in this city.   The Syracuse *Gazette* of July 7, 1824, published by Mr. Durnford, gives the following account of the celebration:

"At the morn's early dawn, the day was ushered in by the thunder of cannon bursting upon the stillness of the hour; and at sunrise a national salute was fired from Prospect Hill, on the north side of the village.   As the spiring columns of the cannon's smoke disappeared, the star spangled banner of our country was then seen floating majestically in the air from the top of a towering staff erected on the summit of this hill for the occasion.   At about twelve o'clock, a procession was formed in front of Mr. Williston's hotel, under the direction of Colonel A. P. Granger, marshal of the day.   An escort, consisting of Captain Rossiter's company of Light Horse, an artillery company under the command of Lieutenant J. D. Rose, and Captain H. W. Durnford's company of riflemen, with their music swelling and banners flying, preceded the procession which moved to the new meeting house (the old Baptist church).   Here the usual exercises took place, and an oration was pronounced by J. R. Sutermeister, which was received by the large assembly with a universal burst of approbation.   The procession then formed again and moved through the village to the summit of Prospect Hill, where, under a bower, a numerous company partook of a cold collation prepared by Mr. Williston, landlord of the Mansion House.

"It was a truly interesting sight to see among our fellow citizens who participated in the festivities of this day, about thirty of the remnant of that gallant band of patriots who fought in the Revolution. These spared monuments of our country's boast honored the company with their presence throughout the day, giving a zest to the festivities rarely to be found in common celebrations of this national anniversary."

The principal object of attraction on that day was the Rifle Company, composed of the young men of the county, and commanded by Captain H. W. Durnford, Lieutenant James H. Luther and Orderly Zophar H. Adams. They were dressed in red Scotch plaid frocks and pants, trimmed on the bottoms and sides with a bright red fringe. They wore leather caps with long red feathers, and carried the long Indian rifle, with powder horns and bullet pouches. As they marched through the streets, they presented a gay and imposing appearance.

Prospect Hill was then fully forty feet higher than at present. The trees and bushes were removed from its summit for the purpose of the celebration.

The aged veterans fast disappeared, and at the next celebration only about half the members were present. The second year following, they were still fewer in number; and finally all sank into honored graves, amid the regrets of many true patriots. In 1824, the thirty veterans who were present walked in the procession, but in the succeeding years time had made so great inroads on their ranks and constitutions that carriages were provided for their accommodation.

A little Irishman named John Dunn had a blacksmithing and horse shoeing shop next east of Captain Parsons' house, on the corner of Genesee and Mill streets. He was a jolly, whiskey-loving fellow, and afforded a great deal of amusement to his customers.

East of David Stafford's house, there stood a large yellow painted carriage factory, carried on by a Mr. Martin. Between the factory and Stafford's house, there was standing in 1824 a large pine tree.

The old yellow stores, now Taylor & Company's saleratus factory, were erected in 1824. Samuel Booth had the contract for and performed the mason work of the building. Daniel Elliott, of Auburn, performed the carpenter work.

Matthew L. Davis occupied the store on the corner of Genesee and Clinton streets, as a dry goods store.

Heman and Chester Walbridge occupied the store next to him, as a dry goods and general assortment store.

A man from New York kept a bookstore in the same block, in the store next to the canal. The store on Genesee street was occupied by Samuel Hicks as a hat store.

A one and a half story wooden store, between the

Eagle tavern and Hicks' hat shop, was occupied by Matthew L. Davis, previous to his going into the corner of the then new block.

Before the new stores were completed, the Walbridges occupied the old store formerly standing on the corner of Clinton alley.

B. B. Batchelder occupied a store next to him, and kept a general assortment of all descriptions of goods.

A. Root occupied the third store from the corner, as a boot and shoe store.

These old buildings were all removed last summer to make room for the new Court House.

Clinton Square, the famous resort for our wood dealers from the country, was then a large green, upon which many a game of base ball was played by the young men of the village. The packet boats used to land their passengers on the towpath, and they would cross the green to the old Mansion House.

The Mansion House stood on the ground now occupied by the stately Empire block. It was built in 1805 by Henry Bogardus, and kept by him as a tavern for several years. Back of the house, Mr. Bogardus erected his barns and out-houses. He also set out a large orchard of apples and other fruit. Some of the old apple trees are still standing and bear a very excellent variety of fruit. Mr. Bogardus had no regular bar in his tavern, and was accustomed to set his liquors and glasses out upon a large table.

The proprietorship of the Mansion House changed hands several times during its existence. In the spring of 1824, Sterling Cossit was the landlord. That spring the house was enlarged and renovated, and O. H. Williston assumed the proprietorship.

The Mansion House was a shabby, patched up old concern, requiring additions and alterations every year, until it looked like a relic of other days. It was the scene of many a hard "Salt Point spree," and had its old walls been gifted with the power of speech, they could have told many a strange tale of hard fought, strongly contested battles between the sturdy residents of Salina and Syracuse. The greatest rivalry existed between the two places in 1824, which manifested itself in "free fights" every time the residents of either town crossed the boundary line. That year the Salt Pointers strained every nerve as far as building and business were concerned, to outstrip the rapid growth of Syracuse; but every exertion proved unavailing. Syracuse shot ahead like a race horse, and has ever since maintained the ascendancy.

In 1845, the old Mansion House and attending buildings were removed to make room for the Empire block. The Empire block was commenced in 1845 by John H. Tomlinson and Stephen W. Cadwell of Syracuse and John Thomas of Albany. The building was finished in 1847, when John H. Tomlinson became sole owner. Mr. Tomlinson was killed by a railroad accident at Little Falls in the summer of 1848. He was an active, energetic, enterprising man, and carried on more business than ten ordinary men could well accomplish. He was a native of this county, and died deeply regretted by a very extensive acquaintance throughout the State.

In the fall of 1848, the Empire was sold under the hammer to John Taylor of Newark, New Jersey. It was afterwards purchased by James L. Voorhees and John D. Norton. In 1850, Colonel Voorhees became sole owner, and during the summer of 1856 he made large and important additions and improvements on the original building, until it is now one of the largest, best built and arranged blocks in the city.

Colonel Voorhees came to this county in the winter of 1812-13. He settled in Lysander, about 20 miles from this city. The Colonel was then eighteen years of age. He started in life with an axe, and has hewn himself into a position of great wealth and influence. In his early days, the Colonel passed under the familiar nickname of the "Dutchman" and "the tall pine of Lysander." He has been engaged since his boyhood in the lumber business in all its departments, from the office of "chopper" to the position of the extensive landed proprietor. In the years 1844-45 and '46, he was engaged in the construction of the extensive Atlantic docks, in the port of New York. He is now sixty-two years of age, and appears as hale and hearty as a man of forty, and even now transacts an amount of business that would require the time and energies of three or four common men to accomplish.

In 1824, the people used a peculiar kind of hay scales. A load of hay was drawn under a roof, four chains were lowered and attached to the hubs of the wagon, and by means of pulleys and a windlass the load of hay was hoisted into the air, and the weight determined by a huge pair of steelyards in the loft of the building. Such an inconvenient contrivance for weighing hay stood a little north of the Mansion House.

The house now standing in the northeast corner of Clinton alley and Clinton street, now occupied by George B. Parker, was built in 1824 by Asa Marvin. The house next east of it was built by John Wall for the Syracuse Company.

The present residence of J. D. Dana, on the corner of Church street and Clinton alley, was built that year by a Mr. Denslow. The old canal stables on Clinton alley were in full blast in 1824. They were owned by John A. Green, father of our well known grocery merchant of that name, and are now a part of the new Court House lot.

In 1824, General A. P. Granger was the proprietor of a store containing a general assortment of all descriptions of wares and merchandise, on the present site of the Star buildings. Hiram Deming was his clerk. His store was a long, two story building, fronting on Salina street. The building stood back from the street a few feet, and had a green fence of posts and cross bars between the street and house, to which his customers fastened their teams when they came to trade. The south end was occupied by the store, and the north end of the house and the second story the General occupied as a dwelling house. Between the fence and the house a considerable quantity of shrubbery had been set out, forming a miniature flower garden. The General was one of the principal men of the village, and on the occasion of LaFayette's passage through Syracuse (June 8, 1825), during his last visit to this country, he was made the orator of the day.

The General performed the duties of the office to the entire satisfaction of every person present on that occasion by making an excellent and appropriate speech to the assembled citizens, from the deck of a canal boat, in honor of the distinguished visitor.

At the time of LaFayette's visit to this place, there lived at Onondaga Hollow a large, athletic man named Moore, familiarly known under the appellation of "Donakeedee." This man was engaged in the Revolution, and served as a private in LaFayette's regiment. While in the army he had been nick-named, on account of his extremely large head,

"Cabbage Head." LaFayette came from the west by the way of Marcellus, Onondaga Hill and Onondaga Hollow. While passing through the Hollow, Moore was brought before him, and he was asked who it was. LaFayette regarded the man a moment, and then exclaimed: "Why, it's Cabbage Head." This story will serve to show the remarkable memory of the great LaFayette. He had not seen "Cabbage Head" for forty-two years, and yet his memory of the man was perfect.

A few moments after LaFayette had made his final bow to the assembled citizens, and retired to the cabin of the boat in which he was then traveling, a large scow boat loaded down with men, women and children, arrived from Geddes to see the great and illustrious companion of Washington. LaFayette being informed of their arrival, again ascended to the deck, amid the prolonged cheers of the multitude, said a few words to his Geddes visitants, and, bowing, proceeded on his way to Utica.

LaFayette was a man of medium height, well proportioned, and stood very erect for a man of his age. He had a large head, full features, a rough, swarthy skin and beard cut smooth. He wore a very curly, light brown wig, rather inclined to red, and was dressed in a straight bodied black coat, black silk vest, Nankeen pants and calf skin shoes. He was very polite and pleasing in his address, in fact a most perfect and polished gentleman in every respect.

LaFayette's son, George Washington LaFayette, accompanied him on his last visit to this country. He was a larger man than his father. The top of his head was bald, what little hair he possessed being brown. He was a very good looking man, free and easy in his manners, and dressed in black.

In 1824, Salina street bridge consisted of one single stone arch, barely high enough to admit of the passage of the small boats used in those days. A stone wall was raised about three feet above the level of the roadway on each side of the bridge, and was covered with flag coping full three feet broad. This wall formed a favorite lounging place for the lazy people of Syracuse. They could lie on the coping and watch the boats as they passed up and down the canal, and at the same time witness all that transpired in the village. Occasionally one of the numerous loafers would go to sleep and roll off into the canal, thus furnishing food for the gossiping tongues of the villagers for many a day and week.

In 1824, Stephen W. Cadwell and Paschal Thurber bought out a man by the name of Cummings, who kept a lot of pet bears, wolves, monkeys and other wild animals on the ground now occupied by Cadwell and the Doran brothers on James street. This Cummings was a miserable old fellow, and everybody was glad to get rid of him.

Between Cadwell's and Granger's corner there were

three or four old rookeries standing, occupied by different persons, who derived the principal part of their trade from the canal boatmen.

East of Cadwell's, a man named Brockway occupied a little shop as a meat market. Next to the meat market, there stood a large frame building painted red, a miserable old shell at best. East of this red house, on the corner now occupied as a grocery by B. C. Lathrop, a store house was kept by E. L. Clark in a large wooden building, since burned.

In 1824, that portion of James street styled "Robbers' Row" had been surveyed and laid out as a street, but had not been worked. The trees and brush had been cleared off and the passage of teams had made considerable of a trail. Stores and houses on the south side of the street had their front entrances opening on the towing path. The gable ends and back yards of the houses were on James street.

James street proper was at that time only an Indian trail, leading over the hills to what was then Foot Settlement, now the first gate. The eye of the lonely wayfarer on that trail was not gladdened by the sight of the lordly and palatial residences of the upper ten that now give a grand and aristocratic appearance to this beautiful street.

The only object on this trail which then served as a resting place to eyes (if there ever were such, wearied with continuous watching of swaying trees and

falling leaves in the dense forest where God speaks to
man through the rustling leaves, the sighing wind
and the joyous appearance of all nature, as with a
human voice) was the dwelling house of Major Burnet, erected that year by Rodney Sargents, of
Auburn. This house stood on a slight eminence now
occupied by the new residence of Major Burnet.
The house fronted the south, and had a path, or
rather, an impromptu road leading directly to the
towing path on the Erie canal. The house then stood
far out of town, and the only avenue of approach for
teams was by the tow path and the private road.
Persons on foot could reach the house by taking the
trail and beating through the underbrush.

The old collector's office stood between the bridges
spanning the junction of the Erie and Oswego canals.
A foundation of hewn timber was laid upon "Goose
Island," on the north side of the towing path, and
upon this was erected a small frame house which was
designated as the canal collector's office. Dr. Colvin
was the collector in 1824, and employed Benjamin C.
Lathrop and B. F. Colvin as clerks in his office. The
Doctor resided in a small frame house on Salina street,
a little north of Waggoner's corner.

The amount of produce cleared during the season
of 1824 from this office was 12,065 barrels of flour,
2,862 barrels provisions, 2,565 barrels ashes, 76,631
barrels salt, and 64,240 bushels of wheat. The amount

of toll received at the office during the season of 1824 was $18,491.58.

The old weigh lock was completed that year. It was built upon an entirely different plan from the one now followed; the weight of the boat being determined by measuring the quantity of water it displaced.

Deacon Spencer then owned and occupied the old boat yard (now John Durston's) near the Oswego canal. The boat yard was then considered out of town, the easiest avenues of approach being by the tow path.

Deacon Spencer lived in a small frame house adjoining, and west of the present "Greyhound Inn," on the corner of James and Warren streets.

Between Deacon Spencer's residence and Waggoner's corner there were two small edifices. The first one was occupied and used as a blacksmith shop. The other was the residence of Widow Cushing, who obtained a scanty subsistence by retailing milk to those needing this product of her only cow.

A little mercurial Frenchman, named Lewis, a brother-in-law of Sterling Cossit, resided in the first house north of Dr. Colvin's on Salina street.

James Sackett commenced building in 1824, a little north of Dr. Colvin and the Frenchman. He was a very eccentric man, and at times was feared and disliked by all his neighbors, because he would persist in indulging in the most eccentric habits.

Dr. Colvin's, the Frenchman's and Mr. Sackett's were the only houses on the block opposite of the Empire in 1824.

A small frame house stood on the ground now occupied by the Noxon block. It was then occupied as a dwelling by Isaac Stanton.

Amos Stanton, the father of Isaac and Rufus Stanton, came here to reside in 1805. He engaged in the manufacture, during the winter, of salt. That article then sold for three dollars per barrel. In 1816 the price had been reduced to two dollars per barrel, and in 1824 it was sold for $1.50 per barrel.

Mr. Stanton then, in 1805, owned one square acre of ground, including the land now occupied by the old "Ogle Tavern," near the Oswego canal bridge on Salina street. Mr. Stanton had this acre of land cleared and converted into a wheat field. He also hired a few acres southeast of his lot, and worked the whole as a farm in the summer time.

When the Oswego canal was built, they cut diagonally through Mr. Stanton's acre.

The Ogle Tavern was occupied as a private dwelling house in 1824.

Mr. Bogardus, of the Mansion House, built a small frame house near the present site of Corinthian Hall, which he occupied while building the Mansion House. Paschal Thurber lived in it in 1824. The house stood on the bank of a small natural creek, since arched

and formed into a sluice way for the passage of the
surplus water of the new weigh lock.

On the north side of the Oswego canal, the house
lately known as "Church's Grocery," then belonged
to the widow of Peter Wales, and was occupied by
her as a dwelling house.

The land north and east of Widow Wales' house
was covered by a young growth of trees and underbrush, the only clearing being the patch of ground
near the old Centre House, upon which Harry Blake
had built himself a dwelling and commenced to farm
it.

There were no other dwellings between Syracuse
and Salina. It was then two miles between the two
places, and Salina street was a mere wagon track cut
through the timber and known as Cooper street. The
name was derived from the circumstance that several
coopers put up shanties and used all of the available
timber for the purpose of making salt barrels, about
the year 1806.

A little cluster of five or six cheaply built, white-
washed houses, known as White Hall, stood on the
first block north of the new Catholic church.

I think there were three or four salt blocks standing near the canal. They were built in the old fash-
ioned style, with the side towards the canal, a chimney in the middle and a fire built at both ends of the
block. I think there were two or three little houses
near the blocks, occupied by the salt boilers.

With the exception of these few buildings and a
little patch of cleared land, formerly part of Stanton's
farm, all that portion of the city lying north of the
Erie and east of the Oswego canals, was covered with
a heavy growth of timber and underbrush, with numerous paths leading to the various spots where wood
had been cut for the purpose of making salt.

The first lock formerly stood but a few yards east
of Mulberry street bridge.

"Vinegar Hill" then, as now, consisted of several
shanties and old rookeries, erected there to catch the
trade of the passing boatmen.

In 1840, Captain Joel Cody finished his contract
for building the present first lock. The old one was
torn down and "Vinegar Hill" removed to its present
quarters.

In 1824, a small boat, half the size of the common
boats of the present day, made regular trips every two
hours between Syracuse and Salina.

Augustus Spencer was the first captain of this boat.
He was succeeded by Captain William Stewart, the
present famous landlord of the Syracuse House. Captain Stewart commanded his boat with great dignity,
and treated his passengers with the utmost politeness
and attention. The gallant captain exhibited as much
pride while pacing the quarter deck of his small craft
as do the commanders of the ocean steamers of the
present day.

The first circus that ever performed in Syracuse occupied the vacant lot on the corner of Church and Salina streets, at present occupied by the Onondaga Temperance House.

The first horse show was attended by nearly all the citizens, and a full delegation of Onondaga Indians; and Syracuse immediately acquired a reputation as a " good show town," which it has preserved even to the present day.

The success of this circus led to the building of a circus house in 1825 by Andrew N. Van Patten and John Rodgers, on the ground now occupied by the stables of the Onondaga Temperance House. This circus house was subsequently turned into a livery stable with a cooper's shop in the rear, and a long two story building, owned and occupied by Mr. Goings as a carpenter and joiner's shop, was erected on the towing path in the rear of the circus building with an alley of about twenty-five feet between the buildings.

On the evening of Friday, August 20, 1841, a fire broke out in the carpenter's shop, which was occupied by Charles Goings. The building was soon surrounded by a crowd of firemen and citizens, using their utmost efforts to extinguish the flames, when suddenly a terrible explosion took place, filling the air with flying cinders, and scattering death and destruction around. This catastrophe was one of the most distressing events that ever occurred in the

history of this or any other city, and we have therefore given a very full description of the calamity,
copied from the files of papers of that year.

[A condensed report from the newspaper files referred to is as follows: The alarm of fire was given
at half past nine o'clock.   The wooden building
situated on the tow path of the Oswego canal, nearly
in the rear of the County Clerk's office and occupied
as a joiner's shop by Charles Goings, was on fire.
The fire appeared to have commenced in the top of
the building.   The cry of "Powder! Powder! There
is powder in the building!" was heard.   The immense crowd rushed back, but the move was only
momentary.   Most of those nearest the fire maintained
their position, and very few appeared to place any
credit in the report.   Suddenly, a tremendous explosion took place, completely extinguishing the fire and
demolishing the building.   The explosion lasted some
three or four seconds, and its effects were felt for over
twenty miles around.   The noise of the explosion
having ceased, all was still for a moment, and then
the most heart-rending groans were distinctly heard.
Everything was in total darkness.   All was confusion.
Although the sight of the dead and the dying was
horrible, it was scarcely less than that of the living
inquiring for their relatives—parents for their children, and wives, almost frantic with despair, for their
husbands.

[On Saturday the village was shrouded in mourning. The stores were all closed. Business was out of the question. Hundreds of people from the country towns came hurrying in, on learning the awful intelligence, to see the spot so fruitful with distress, and to know the particulars of the sad affair. Sunday was a busy day in entombing the dead. Early in the day the funeral procession commenced from different directions, and from the several churches; and there was one continual succession of corpses passing to the lonely sepulchre. The several churches were crowded. The clergymen were most solemn and impassioned in their addresses. A deeper sadness never pervaded so large congregations.

[Parley Bassett, the Coroner, summoned the following persons to form a jury of inquest: Johnson Hall, as foreman; Pliny Dickinson, Lewis H. Redfield, D. S. Colvin, William A. Cook, Thomas T. Davis, Samuel Larned, Rial Wright, Philo D. Mickles, Harmon W. Van Buren, Daniel Elliott, Ashbel Kellogg, Thomas G. Alvord, Elijah W. Curtis, Jared H. Parker, Amos P. Granger. The Coroner's jury closed its business on Monday evening, August 23. The report showed that Hugh T. Gibson, Ezra H. Hough, Thomas Betts, Elijah Jones, Zebina Dwight, William Conklin, Benjamin F. Johnson, Elisha Ladd, George W. Burdick, Isaac Stanton, William B. Close, George Gorman, Horace

T. Goings, Charles A. Moffit, Loren L. Cheney, Horatio N. Cheney, John Durnford, jr., Hanson Maynard, Noah Hoyt, Joel Kohlhamer, Matthew Smelt, James M. Barker, Charles Miller, Benjamin T. Barker, Charles Austin—twenty-five in number—came to their deaths by the explosion of 27 or 28 kegs of gunpowder in a carpenter and joiner's shop, then on fire. In the belief of the jury, the shop was set on fire by some person or persons unknown to the jurors. The powder was the property of William Malcolm and Albert A. Hudson, and was secretly stored in the shop by Mr. Hudson and Charles Goings, with the knowledge and consent of Mr. Malcolm, contrary to the published and known ordinances of the village, and without the cognizance or consent of the village Trustees.

[A public meeting was held Monday evening, presided over by Hiram Putnam, President of the village. D. D. Hillis was made Secretary. A committee was appointed to obtain subscriptions and to afford relief to those families who needed aid in their sudden bereavement. The committee from Syracuse was composed of Daniel Dana, M. D. Burnet, A. P. Granger, Charles L. Lynds, and Wing Russell; from Salina, Ashbel Kellogg and Colonel E. D. Hopping. At the meeting, about $1,800 was subscribed, of which amount the firm of Malcolm & Hudson subscribed $500, and William Malcolm $500.]

On the south side of the Erie canal and on the corner now occupied by Stone & Ball, jewelers, and Sabey & Weaver, hatters, there stood in 1824, a two-story frame building, known as the "Coffin Block." The name was given to the block on account of it's fancied resemblance to that receptacle for the dead. The first and second stories on the extreme corner were then occupied by John Durnford as a book store, lottery ticket and printing office.

From this corner the first number of the Onondaga *Gazette*, the first paper ever issued in this city, was printed by John Durnford, our present worthy Justice of the Peace. The first number was issued Wednesday morning, April 2, 1823. In his "address" to the public, the publisher lays down the following views and principles:

"Notwithstanding it may be said the State already abounds with newspapers, yet the rapid growth of the country, and the happy location of this village, in connection with its other advantages, are sufficient to warrant the belief that ere long Syracuse and its vicinity will afford an adequate support to this establishment, and raise up a monumental trophy of the wisdom and enterprise of the canal projectors."

The price of the paper was $2 per year, payable half yearly, when received from the office or sent to mail subscribers; but when sent to village subscribers it was $2.50. The *Gazette* was a weekly paper,

published on a 12 by 17 sheet, four pages, with five
columns to the page. On the 31st of March, 1824,
the paper appeared under the name of the Syracuse
Gazette.

The Syracuse *Gazette* was published by Mr. Durnford until 1829, when Lewis H. Redfield of the
Onondaga *Register*, then published at Onondaga
Hollow, came to Syracuse, bought out Mr. Durnford
and united the two papers under the name of *The
Syracuse Gazette and Onondaga Register*. He continued to publish this paper until 1831, when it was
transferred to other hands.

In 1824, Henry W. Durnford occupied the first
store east of the Syracuse *Gazette* office, as a drug
store. He also kept an assortment of groceries,
crockery and liquors, and transacted a large and
profitable business.

That year it was deemed necessary, for the convenience of the public, to remove the post-office, then
under the charge of John Wilkinson, to some more
convenient location than General Granger's store.
Mr. Wilkinson made selection of Mr. Durnford's
store as the location for the new post-office, and consulted with him in regard to the matter. Mr. Durnford raised the objection of a lack of room for all the
purposes of the post-office. Mr. Wilkinson thought
different, and to convince the incredulous storekeeper,
crossed the canal and returned, bearing the whole

post-office, boxes, mail bags, mail matter, and all the
appurtenances on his shoulders.   This feat convinced
Mr. Durnford that he had plenty of room, in which
to accommodate the post-office.

The first store east of the drug store was occupied
by John Rodgers & Company, as a dry goods store.
Mr. Rodgers was an energetic, enterprising man, and
is now one of the millionaires of Chicago, and visits
the scene of his early prosperity yearly.

Between the store of Mr. Rodgers and the drug
store. there was a wide hall-like entrance leading to
the printing office in the second story, and the rooms
occupied as a dwelling by Mr. Van Velzer.

General Jonas Mann began in 1824 to build a store
on the corner now occupied by the bookstore of Peck
& Rudd.   He also commenced to build as a dwelling
house the present famous "Cook's Coffee House."
He moved his family here the next season, and
during the summer finished both buildings.

Henry Newton occupied the first store east of Mr.
Mann's building as a grocery and general assortment
store.   Mr. Newton afterwards formed a partnership
with A. Root, in the boot and shoe business, on the
north side of the canal.

Joseph Slocum carried on the dry goods business,
and also kept a general assortment of wares and
merchandise, next east of Mr. Newton's grocery.

A. N. Van Patten carried on the dry goods,

grocery and provision business in the first store east
of Mr. Slocum's grocery.

Over the store a man by the name of Thompson
kept a billiard table during the fall and winter.

Deacon Phelps kept a stove store and grocery on
the first floor, and a tin shop in the second story of
the first building east of Mr. Van Patten's store.
Between the tin shop and Warren street. there were a
series of vacant lots. These lots were subsequently
occupied by fine blocks of stores. In 1834, they were
all reduced to a heap of smouldering ruins. The
burning of these two blocks, comprising ten buildings
of different dimensions, with eleven buildings on the
north side of the canal, was the first great calamity
that ever befell the embryo city. This fire occurred
Friday night, March 15, 1834. The fire broke out in
the store of B. F. Rodgers, nearly opposite the
Syracuse House. The Syracuse House was saved by
the greatest exertions. The east wing, containing the
Onondaga County Bank, was several times on fire.
The loss caused by the fire was about $75,000, of
which one-half was insured.

On the corner now occupied by Murphy, McCarthy
& Company, hardware dealers, John Rodgers carried
on in 1824, the storage, forwarding and commission
business, in connection with his dry goods store.
The building was burned down afterwards.

White & Clark occupied the first store east, and

dealt in all descriptions of merchandise and produce. They were also engaged in the storage and commission business in the building then standing next east of their store.

Joseph Slocum occupied the first building east of White & Clark's storehouse, and carried on a general storage and commission business. There was but one other building then standing between Mr. Slocum's storehouse and the old canal basin. It was a little, low frame building, standing on the bank of the basin, partly hid by the bushes that grew in great profusion in that region. Joseph Thompson kept a small grocery in the building and derived most of his custom from the canal boatmen by furnishing them with "supplies." In 1824, the present site of the weigh-lock, market hall, hay market and public square, as far south as the railroad, there formed what was known as the canal basin. It was a miserable, nasty hole and was the dread of all the inhabitants, because it tainted and infected the whole atmosphere with disease. A small barn stood on the south side of this basin, with a path on one side leading into it, which was used as a watering place for cattle and horses.

In 1824, Parley Howlett and Barent Filkins built a slaughter house on the ground, and the same house is at present occupied by Joe Tasker's well known cottage.

Water street, east of the basin, had been laid off
as a street, but had not been worked to any extent.
A few trees and a quantity of underbrush had been
cut and a few rails laid in the worst miring places,
so that by dint of hard work and hard swearing a
team could be got through to old Mr. Russell's pottery. This pottery stood on the ground now occupied
by James L. Greenman, storage and commission
house. It was carried on by an old man named Russell, who manufactured jars, jugs, mugs, milk pans
and all other articles commonly made at such estab-
lishments. He resided in a small frame house a little
south of his pottery.

Mulberry street was almost impassible for teams
in 1824, the ground being very low and marshy in
that section.

The State owned a small frame house on the heel-
path side of the old first lock, which was known and
used as a lock house. The building is now standing
and forms part of Hatch, Rust & Randall's lumber
and coal office.

In 1824 all that portion of our city lying between
Mulberry street and Lodi on the south side of the
canal was an unreclaimed cedar swamp. The present
Fayette Park with the splendid residences of our
merchants and business men was then a favorite
resort for foxes, rabbits and wild fowl, forming a
capital shooting ground. North and east of the park

the sonorous croakings of the bull frog served to enliven the otherwise dismal scenery.

This swamp was full of rotten logs and stumps from which issued a deadly miasma containing the whole list of fevers, from the fever and ague to the typhoid and brain fever. The Genesee turnpike passed through this swamp and consisted of an ill laid corduroy road that tested the strength of horses and wagons and the skill and moral training of all teamsters having occasion to pass it.

Captain Oliver Teall owned and run two small saw mills on the north side of the Erie canal, near the Lodi locks. He obtained the water which moved his mills by tapping the canal. He was then Canal Superintendent under Henry Seymour, Canal Commissioner, and obtained the right to use the water for running his mills from the State.

It was this successful tapping of the great "Clinton Ditch" that gave the well known captain such a decided partiality to cold water over all other fluids. It was this very tapping of the Erie which led him to conceive and carry out the grand idea of tapping mother earth, filling a huge reservoir with the crystal nectar, and forcing it through great iron arteries and veins to the very heart and extremities of our flourishing city.

The captain lived in a small house built by the State for a lock house. There were about a dozen little houses scattered about the locks, and occupied by the employes on the locks and the canal.

John H. Lathrop kept a tavern in a medium-sized house, standing on the block lying southeast of the orphan asylum on the Genesee turnpike. He had a fine well on his premises affording the best water in the country. People coming from the east to trade or barter in Syracuse would stop with Mr. Lathrop, and from his house they would go to the village and trade during the day, returning as the shades of evening fell on the gloomy swamp to his house for food and lodging. They did this in preference to putting up at one of the village taverns and running the risk of the ague.

At that time Syracuse was considered as the most unhealthy spot in the valley, and people were inclined to believe that the city would be built on the Lodi hills in preference to the middle of a cedar swamp. But the projectors and proprietors of the embryo city did not waver even for an instant in their choice of a location for the village. The present large, flourishing, healthy, wealthy city is the reward of their judgment and faith.

The "Holden House" stood nearly opposite of Mr. Lathrop's tavern, and was then used as a dwelling.

At the foot of the hill, near the swamp, on the Genesee turnpike, Lemuel J. Benton commenced in 1825 to manufacture brick.

Henry Shattuck, the present policeman, and Abner Chapman, Supervisor from Onondaga, worked as moulders in this brick yard.

Coming west from the brick yard the mind's eye found nothing to remember, nothing to describe, but a low sickly cedar swamp and corduroy road, until you reached what now forms a large part of the heart of our city.

This swamp was the fear of all the inhabitants and the dread of all in search of a location for a future residence.   But the art of man has reclaimed the "Dismal Swamp," and it now forms one of the most beautiful and healthy sections of the city.

Samuel Phelps kept a blacksmith shop on the lot now occupied by the Home Association.   The shop was in a two-story building, with the front towards Genesee street.   The second story Mr. Phelps occupied as a dwelling.   The family reached their rooms by means of an outside pair of stairs.   The ground upon which the shop stood was so low and marshy that the fall rains made a large pond all around the building.   In the winter this pond formed a famous skating ground for the boys of the village.

In 1824, the remains of a small log house, formerly standing on the southwest corner of Genesee and Montgomery streets, were visible.   In this house Albion Jackson was born about the year 1802.   Mr. Jackson was the first white child born within the limits of this

SITE FOR OLD ST. PAUL'S CHURCH   161

city. Shortly after his birth, Mr. Jackson's father moved to Canada and was gone for some eighteen years before he returned.

The ground upon which the Granger block now stands was, in 1824, a fine little green meadow. That year John Durnford, Archy Kasson and John Rodgers were appointed a committee by the Episcopal Society, authorized and empowered to select a site for a church edifice.

Mr. Durnford advocated the selection of this meadow as the proposed site. The other members of the committee offered an objection to the lot "that it was too far from the village," but finally coincided with Mr. Durnford in his choice, and the committee reported accordingly. The report was adopted, and immediate measures taken to erect the necessary building.

Deacon Wright obtained the contract for performing the carpenter work, and assumed the general superintendence of putting up the building. The building was completed in the year 1825. It was used a number of years by the Episcopalians, and then sold to the Roman Catholics, who removed it to the corner of Montgomery and Madison streets, where it is still standing.

The millinery store of Mrs. Gillmore was erected in 1824 by John Rodgers, then one of the most enterprising men in the village. The mason work was performed by a man from Manlius, named Dwinnelle.

On the ground now occupied by the Bastable block, there stood, in 1824, a little frame house occupied by a Mr. Walker. These were the only buildings then standing on the block opposite the Granger block.

A small, yellow building, was then standing next east of "Cook's Coffee House," which has since been moved back and a brick front built to it.

Henry Van Husen owned and occupied a black-smith shop on the corner of Genesee and Warren streets, where the Tremont House now stands. His shop was a hard-looking concern, and was not much of an ornament to the village, even in those primitive days. The building stood about a foot and a half below the level of the mud sidewalk. His customers used to complain of the distance to be traveled and the great depth of mud to be waded through before his shop could be reached from the village. In rainy weather it was almost impossible to reach his shop on account of the mud.

The street and square was then some four feet lower than at the present day, and formed one of the worst roads for the passage of teams that can be imagined. I have frequently seen teams with an ordinary load get set in the deep mud, and remain for some time before they could be extricated.

Henry Durnford resided in a small white house on the ground now occupied by Gay's Hotel. The house fronted the south. He had a white fence around his lot, and a beautiful flower garden in front of his house. It was a very pretty, cozy, little dwelling.

About the year 1820, Buel & Safford purchased the ground now occupied by the Syracuse House, and commenced the erection of the Syracuse Hotel. During the progress of the building, Mr. Safford fell from the scaffolding and was killed. This accident caused a temporary suspension of the work, until the property went into the possession of Mr. Eckford, who completed the building in 1822.

The building was of brick, three stories in height, fifty feet square, with a roof pitching north and south, with brick battlements on the east and west ends, and chimneys on the ends of the upper brake. The front entrance was through the present shoe store of T. Ryan.

The stables stood well back from Genesee street, extending nearly to the present railroad depot. There was a large yard attached to the house and stables, in which stood a number of old dilapidated out-buildings. The entrance to the yard was through a large gateway, then standing on the present site of Butler, Townsend & Company's dry goods store.

After the premises fell into the hands of the Syracuse Company they were rebuilt and named the

Syracuse House.   The original building has since been enlarged and improved, and is now one of the best hotels in this region.

James Mann was the landlord of the Syracuse Hotel, which was then the headquarters of the different lines of stages.   In 1824 Jason C. Woodruff drove stage between Elbridge and this place.   He performed the duties of his office with great dignity, and was wont to wheel his favorite coach up to the door of the Syracuse Hotel with an exhibition of great skill and training.   From the post of driver, Mr. Woodruff, by his own unaided exertions, raised himself into the position of proprietor of a line of stages, and has since filled several offices of trust and honor in the county, with credit to himself and satisfaction to his fellow citizens.

Colonel Elijah Phillips had his stage office in an east room of the Syracuse Hotel.   The Colonel was very prompt and exact in his business operations, and for years a stage never drew up to his office without finding him ready to give or receive the way bill.   It was a common expression in those days that "Time and Colonel Phillips wait for no man."

Next east of the gate leading to the stables of the Syracuse House, a man named Waterbury owned a small frame building.   On the first floor he kept a little grocery.   His stock in trade consisted of a small quantity of poor whiskey, a few plugs of tobacco, a handful of pipes, and about eighty-eight cents worth of comic valentines. His family lived in the second story and reached their place of residence by means of a flight of stairs built on the outside of the building. That year Joel Owens bought out Waterbury's establishment, and still remains in possession of the property.

Next east of Waterbury's, there was standing a two-story building, considerable larger than its western neighbor. The first floor was occupied as a dwelling house. The second story was occupied by Jabez Hawley, as a chair factory. These old buildings were rather unprepossessing in their appearance, being of a dirty wood color, from having never made the improving acquaintance of a paint pot and brush.

A small house stood next east of Mr. Hawley's shop, which was occupied by a person whose name is forgotten, as a grocery and drinking house. It was originally painted white, but the color had worn off, and in 1824 the house had a forlorn and dingy appearance. Between this house and the blacksmith shop on the corner of Warren and Genesee streets, the ground was vacant.

Archy Kasson built a dwelling house in 1824, on the ground now occupied by the Central Railroad company's ticket office.

The square upon which now stands the Onondaga County Bank, Bank of Syracuse, Dillaye block,

Episcopal church and St. Charles Hotel, was in 1824 a vacant lot, covered with a few scattered trees.

In 1825, " The First Presbyterian Society of Syracuse" built a church on the ground now occupied by the new and beautiful Dillaye block. The church was finished in the fall and dedicated in January, 1826. The original church was enlarged and improved several years ago, but in 1849 the increasing demands of the society rendered it necessary to build a new edifice. It was accordingly sold, and the present ornament to the city erected in 1850.

The Rev. Dr. John W. Adams was ordained and installed pastor of the new church in June, 1826. Dr. Adams continued to act in that capacity until death claimed him as her own in 1850. Dr. Adams was a very exemplary man. He centered and united the affections of his whole flock about his great heart, and died after a long life of usefulness and devotion to his God, deeply mourned by all who ever had the pleasure and profit of his acquaintance.

This entire square, with the exception of the church lot, was afterwards offered to the county free of charge, if the Supervisors would agree to build the court house and jail upon it. After some deliberation on the matter, the offer was refused by the Board.

A small unpainted house, with an L, stood nearly on the opposite site of the Washington block. The main part of this house was occupied by Widow

Stewart, and the L by a Mr. Wheeler. Mrs. Stewart is the mother-in-law of John Hurst, our worthy Justice of the Peace. She is now over eighty years of age, straight and active as a girl of eighteen. She was one of the early settlers of this county, and formerly resided at Liverpool.

A farm house belonging to the Syracuse Company, and occupied by Jacob Hausenfrats, stood on the present site of Captain Thomas Wheeler's residence, on what was then a little knoll. The barn stood on the ground now occupied by the residence of William B. Kirk, and a corn house stood a little east of the dwelling.

Mr. Hausenfrats worked the farm on shares for the company, and had a large wheat field, extending from the First Methodist church west, nearly on the line of Jefferson street, to his house. Between the house and village, a small brook, called Yellow Brook, ran from the swamp and emptied into the old mill pond. The passage of water through this brook had cut a ravine over fifteen feet deep where it crossed Salina street. Previous to 1824, there was a bridge across this brook, on Salina street, but by means of a sluice, the ravine had been partly filled up, and the bridge removed.

All south of the wheat field was a young unclaimed forest, thickly overgrown with underbrush.

Zophar H. Adams manufactured brick in 1824,

on the west side of Salina street, a little south of the
farm house.   I think Dr. Westcott's residence stands
on the ground then used as a brick-yard.

South Salina street was then full six feet higher
than at the present day, and very irregular, passing
over a series of mounds or hillocks, the whole
distance, making a bad road to travel with a loaded
team.

That portion of our city now known as Onondaga
street, or Cinder road, was in 1824 a cedar swamp,
with any quantity of old logs, stumps and trunks of
fallen trees, slowly going to decay, and filling the air
with noxious vapors.   Wherever the land was
sufficiently firm and dry to afford a suitable soil, there
a very luxuriant growth of blackberry bushes had
sprung up, yielding innumerable quarts of that
delicious fruit.

This swamp was also a great resort for game, and
has been the scene of many hunting and blackberry-
ing adventures to the children of a larger growth, as
well as to the youth of Syracuse and vicinity.   The
swamp extended from the pond as far as Colonel
Johnson's present residence.

That year, the proprietor of Mickles' Furnace gen-
erously appropriated the cinders formed by his furnace,
to the filling up of the road through the swamp.   A
cart with two horses, driven tandem, and a man to
load, drive and deposit the cinders, was furnished by

the Syracuse Company, and the drawing of cinders
was continued until a coat of them had been placed
on the road a foot and a half thick. This gave it the
name of Cinder road, which it has ever since retained.

A man named Finch lived in a small log house
near the reservoir on the Cinder road. This man was
very dissipated, and finally died in that house.

Thurlow Weed's father lived, previous to 1824, on
the Cinder road near Colonel Johnson's, in a small
log house.

The canal basin, between Salina and Clinton streets,
was not as large in 1824 as at the present time. It
was so narrow as scarcely to afford turning room for
even the small boats used in those days. When an
extra amount of water was let into the canal the banks
of this basin were frequently overflowed, and the cel-
lars in the vicinity filled with water.

A small foot bridge, with stairs on each end, spanned
the canal several yards east of the present Clinton
street bridge. At the foot of this bridge on the southeast side, Deacon Chamberlain, father-in-law of ex-
Mayor Stevens, kept a meat market in a small frame
building painted yellow.

Hiram Hyde kept two store houses adjoining each
other on the ground now occupied by the old Raynor
block, a little west of Clinton street bridge. Mr. Hyde
was a son-in-law of Joshua Forman, and a man of
enterprise and integrity. He died in 1825 of consumption.

There were no other buildings on the north side of Water street, between Salina street and Onondaga creek.

LeGrand and William Crowfoot carried on the manufacture of brick on the ground at present occupied by Greenway's Malt House on West Water street.

In the spring of 1824, Kasson & Heermans carried on the hardware business in a small wooden building standing on the corner of Salina and Water streets. During the summer they tore down the wooden building and erected a three-story brick block seventy feet deep. The building was afterwards occupied by Horace and Charles A. Wheaton as a hardware store, and in 1849 it was destroyed by fire, together with a long row of small wooden buildings, extending nearly to the Townsend block.

Wieting block and hall was erected and finished during the years 1849–50. On the 5th of January, 1856, one of the coldest days during the winter, this beautiful block was burned to the ground. Dr. Wieting at once took measures for the erection of a new block if possible larger, better and more beautiful than the former one.

Cheney & Wilcox obtained the contract for performing the mason work on the building. Under their combined efforts and the superintending eyes of Dr. Wieting and H. N. White, the architect, the building rose like a phœnix from the ashes, larger,

better and more substantial and beautiful than the
former splendid block. The hall is one of the best in
the State, and is not excelled out of New York in
point of convenience and beauty. The Doctor deserves
great credit for his unremitted exertions and lavish
expenditure of money. The new hall was dedicated
on the 9th of December, 1856, eleven months from the
date of the destruction of the former building.

During the summer of 1824, William Malcolm put
up a frame building on the ground now forming the
centre of the Wieting block on Water street. He
occupied this building the following spring as a hardware store. Mr. Malcolm also built a dwelling house
on the present site of the Malcolm block. The Syracuse Company put up three or four small wooden
buildings west of Malcolm's, which they let to different
persons as stores and groceries.

Moses D. Burnet occupied a small frame building
standing a little west of the Syracuse Company's store,
as an office. A large hickory tree stood in front of his
office, affording a fine shade. Major Burnet was an
energetic, enterprising man, and in the spring of 1824
was appointed the agent of the Syracuse Company.
He has since occupied several offices of profit and trust
with ability and success. He was once elected Mayor
of the city, but refused to serve. The Major is a
whole-souled man, and is now quietly enjoying the
rewards of his early labors.

Ambrose Kasson lived in a small frame house standing a little west of Major Burnet's office. John Durnford occupied a dwelling next west of Mr. Kasson's. These two houses had very pretty yards in front, filled with flower beds and shrubbery.

Dr. M. Williams came to this place in 1824, and established himself in the practice of medicine. The Doctor for some months kept his office in the front room over General Granger's store, and boarded with him. He then moved to the south side of the canal, and occupied a part of Judge Forman's office, and boarded in his family. He subsequently became the son-in-law of Judge Forman.

The Doctor was a hard-working, go-ahead man, and by his influence contributed greatly to the prosperity of the embryo city. The village was known throughout the country as a most unhealthy locality. The Doctor combatted the idea with all his powers, claiming that the day was not far distant when the village would be a "city of refuge" for consumption patients. The prediction, to our knowledge, has proven true in a large number of cases, and we can safely claim that Syracuse is one of the most healthy localities in the State. Dr. Williams of to-day is the Dr. Williams of 1824, in dress and personal appearance. He does not appear to change or grow old in the least.

Clinton street was not passable for teams in 1824.

Judge Joshua Forman moved to this place in the fall
of 1819, and occupied as a dwelling the house now
standing next west of the " Climax House " on Water
street. In 1824 he was still living in the same house,
and had a large garden extending from Clinton street
down Water street to Franklin street, and back to
Fayette street. The garden was well stocked with
fruit, and was tended by a Protestant Irishman, named
Montgomery, a very intelligent, faithful man. The
Judge was the father of the canal and of Syracuse.

Colonel Stone, formerly editor of the New York
Commercial Advertiser, in giving an account of a
western journey, compares Syracuse in 1820 with
Syracuse in 1840 in the following language: " Mr.
Forman was in one sense the father of the canal.
That is, being a member of the Legislature in 1807,
he moved the first resolution of inquiry upon the subject of opening a channel of artificial navigation from
the Hudson river to the great lakes. And from that
day to the completion of the stupendous work, in 1825,
his exertions were unremitting and powerful in the
cause. Passing as the canal does, close by the head
of Onondaga lake, within a toss of a biscuit of some
of the salt springs, and within two miles of the principal and strongest fountain at Salina, Mr. Forman
saw the immense advantages which the site of this
place presented for a town; with the completion of
the middle section of the canal, Syracuse was begun.

At the period of my first visit, but a few scattered and
indifferent wooden houses had been erected amid the
stumps of the recently felled trees. I lodged for a
night at a miserable tavern, thronged by a company of
salt boilers from Salina, forming a group of about as
rough looking specimens of humanity as I had ever
seen. Their wild visages, beards thick and long,
matted hair, even now rise up in dark, distant and
picturesque perspective before me. I passed a restless
night, disturbed by strange fancies, as I yet well
remember. It was in October and a flurry of snow
during the night had rendered the morning aspect of
the country more dreary than the evening before.
The few houses I have already described, standing
upon low and almost marshy ground, and surrounded
by trees and entangled thickets, presented a very un-
inviting scene. 'Mr. Forman,' said I, 'do you call
this a village? It would make an owl weep to fly over
it.' 'Never mind,' said he in reply, ' you will live to
see it a city yet.'

"These words were prophetical. The contrast between the appearance of the town then and now is
wonderful. A city it now is in extent, and the magnitude and durability of its dwellings.

" As I glanced upward and around, upon splendid
hotels, rows of massive buildings in all directions, and
the lofty spires of churches glittering in the sun, and
traversed the extended and well built streets, thronged .

with people full of life and activity—the canal basins crowded with boats lading and unlading at the large and lofty stone warehouses upon the wharves—the change seemed like one of enchantment."

Judge Forman went to Washington to see Thomas Jefferson in regard to the canal, but did not meet with success, that great statesman remarking: "You are a hundred years too soon with your project." The Judge met and overcame all obstacles in his project of building a city at this point, and so long as Syracuse preserves a place in the list of cities, Joshua Forman will be known and honored by its inhabitants.

Judge Webb built the stone house lately used as a United States recruiting office, on Water street, in 1824, and occupied it as a dwelling house.

The first burying ground in Syracuse comprised a little knoll on Fayette street, near its junction with Clinton street. Fifteen or twenty persons were buried there, and their bodies have never been removed. Thousands are constantly passing over the ground, wholly unconscious that they are passing over the last resting place of those who once as proudly trod the soil of Syracuse.

The old burying ground on Water and Franklin streets was laid out in 1819 by John Wilkinson and Owen Forman, at the same time they laid out the "Walton Tract" into village lots. The first person buried there was the wife of Deacon Spencer, sister of

G. B. Fish, of this city. The second person buried there was a Mr. West, a circus rider, who was killed by a fall in the old circus house.

The old log dam across the creek on Water street was removed in 1824, and a large stone one erected in its place. The dam stood where Water street bridge now crosses the creek. The pond extended over a great extent of country, running up to the then new cemetery, up Fayette street to the old cemetery and up Clinton street to the Cinder road. In 1849, this pond was filled up by earth conveyed from Prospect Hill, and the great cause of sickness and death in our city was effectually removed. The ground thus made is now partly occupied by the freight depot and works of the Binghamton railroad, the coal yards of Messrs. Cobb and Hatch, Rush & Company, the residence of Jason C. Woodruff and a number of other buildings.

An old saw mill, pretty much used up, stood a little east of the stone mill, and was run by Maron Lee as sawyer.

The stone mill was built in 1825 by Samuel Booth for the Syracuse Company.

A man named Clapp, familiarly known as "Old Sandy," lived in the swamp on the ground at present covered by the round house of the Central Railroad Company. He was a very eccentric man.

The rest of the country west of the creek was a swamp full of rotten logs, stumps, brush, etc., the fear of all the inhabitants.

James Pease came here in 1824, from Lyons, by the canal, and brought a small frame house on a boat, which he put upon the ground now occupied by the Mechanics' Bank. In this house, Mr. Pease manufactured and sold boots and shoes for a great many years. He was a very exemplary man, and was liked and respected by the whole village.

In 1824, an alley was, by common consent, left open between Kasson & Company's hardware store, on the corner and Mr. Pease's shop, for the purpose of allowing teams to pass to the rear of the stores fronting on Water street. This alley was to remain open forever, but it is now covered by one of Dr. Wieting's splendid stores.

In 1824, Theodore Ashley bought out a man named Kneeland, who kept a chair factory next south of James Pease's shoe shop. Mr. Ashley entered into the manufacture of chairs and cabinet ware, and continued in the same branch of business until the time of his death in 1855. Mr. Ashley was a prompt business man, and fair in all his dealings. He was for several years City Sexton and died regretted by a large circle of friends and acquaintances.

There was standing in 1824, on the ground now covered by the Syracuse City Bank, an old frame building occupied for various purposes. In 1828, Grove Lawrence removed this old building and erected in its stead a fine brick block.

In 1819, John Wilkinson, in company with Owen
Forman, a brother of the Judge, came here from Onondaga Hollow, and under the direction of Judge Forman proceeded to lay out the Walton Tract into
village lots. This survey was not accomplished without the severest labor. The old lines and marks of
the tract were nearly obliterated, and it was with the
greatest difficulty that they found with any degree of
certainty the starting point of the original survey.
The survey was completed after several weeks of hard
labor. Part of the Walton Tract was laid out into
village lots, and the remainder into farm lots of from
five to ten acres. After the completion of the survey,
Mr. Wilkinson built an office on the corner now occupied by the Globe Hotel, and commenced the practice
of law. The office was a small one, being but twelve
by fourteen, and Mr. Wilkinson was heartily ridiculed
for putting his office out in the fields. That location
now forming the business centre of our flourishing
city was then out of town.

In February, 1820, a post-office was established in
Syracuse, and Mr. Wilkinson was appointed postmaster. In May, 1825, when the first election for village
officers was held, Mr. Wilkinson was elected clerk.

Mr. Wilkinson has since held several offices of
profit and trust, with honor and distinction. When
railroads were first successfully put in operation, Mr.
Wilkinson closely investigated their workings and

principles, and his gigantic mind comprehending on the instant their immense advantages and ultimate supersedence over the common post roads, he entered at once largely into railroad affairs, and is now emphatically a railroad king. He was for several years President of the Syracuse and Utica railroad, and by his influence succeeded in having the work shops of that road built at Syracuse, thus adding the hardy population of the Fifth ward to our city. He is now the President of the Michigan Southern road, and under his skillful management that road is now one of the best in the Union. Mr. Wilkinson is a great favorite with the traveling public, and is loved and respected by all railroad men, who would do anything for him.

In 1824, Mr. Wilkinson built a residence a little southwest of his office, where he resided a number of years. He now lives in one of the most beautiful palaces on James street. Mr. Heermans built a house a little south of Mr. Wilkinson's, which he occupied as a dwelling for a number of years.

The Syracuse Company built a frame house in 1824, on the ground at present covered by D. McCarthy & Company's mammoth stores.

Kirk's Tavern was built by John Garrison in 1824. The house is now standing, and is kept by E. G. Smith. At the time it was built, the mud on Salina street was hardly wadeable. Overshoes were of no account in those days, and boots were hardly a protection against the mud and water. Mechanics at work in the village refused to board there, giving as a reason that the house was so far out from the main village, and the street was so muddy they could not get to their meals. Mr. Kirk came here in 1826, and opened the house as a tavern. He was for a number of years the sole proprietor, and enjoyed the reputation of being a first-rate landlord. He was a favorite with the country people, and his house was always filled with them. He retired from active life several years ago, and is now quietly enjoying his well-earned riches. None know him but to love and respect him.

A man named White built a small frame house on the ground now occupied by the gothic house a little south of the Pike block. There were no other buildings on the south side of the canal in 1824.

Salina street, from the canal to Fayette street, was then from three to four feet lower than at the present day, and during the spring and fall was nearly impassable from the great depth of mud. There were no sidewalks, and pedestrians were compelled to pick their way along the street as best they could. Teams frequently would get set in the mud, and require great exertions to extricate them. This portion of the street has since been filled up, and the southern portion been cut down to its present level.

The land west of Salina street was then covered with scattered pine trees, oak underbrush, fallen logs and old stumps, down to the creek and pond, which have all long since bowed their heads to the dust and given place to the stately stores and residences of our merchants and business men.

Game of all kinds then abounded in great profusion in the valley, and the crack of the sportsman's rifle was heard where now are our most populous streets. What was in 1820 designated as a place which would cause "an owl to weep" when flying over its broad territory, has now become a large, prosperous, growing city, whose name is known throughout the length and breadth of the land. A Syracusan can now be found in every corner of the earth, and the exclamation: "I hail from Syracuse," is almost as common as "There goes a Yankee." "Syracuse salt" and "Syracuse isms" are spoken of in every place in the Union.

The family of John Savage was the first Irish family that located in Syracuse. Mr. Savage was the father of Richard Savage of this city. He was a jovial, whole-souled man, and a general favorite in the village.

The only colored family residing in Syracuse in 1824, was the family of Isaac Wales. "Uncle Ike" came to Manlius from Maryland, as a slave of the Fleming family, about the year 1810. He worked on

the canal while it was being dug, and soon accumulated enough money to purchase his freedom. Eighty
dollars was the stipend and price which he paid for
himself. He married soon after obtaining his
liberty, and settled in this place, which has ever since
been his home.

Andrew Fesenmeyer was the first German that
located in Syracuse.

Captain Jonathan Thayer came here in 1824. He
was a very useful and humane man, and in nursing
the sick of the village he was always ready and willing
to grant his services. In 1832, when the cholera
prevailed here to such an alarming extent, he over-
taxed his constitution in taking care of Elder Gilbert,
Pastor of the First Baptist church, and others. The
last person he laid out was Dr. Day. He performed
this melancholy duty at 12 o'clock noon, and before
midnight he had gone to his final resting place,
mourned by all who knew him.

On the 1st of March, 1809, an act passed the
Legislature, creating the town of Salina. On the
20th of March, 1809, the first town meeting under
this act was held at the house of Cornelius Schouten
in Salina village. Syracuse then formed part of the
town of Salina, and was not incorporated as a village
until the winter of 1824-25. Up to that time Syracuse
flourished under town laws, together with such rules
and regulations as were from time to time adopted by

mutual consent, and acknowledged as the established regulations of the embryo city.

At a meeting of the freeholders and inhabitants of the village of Syracuse, held pursuant to notice, at the school house in said village, on Tuesday, the 3rd day of May, 1825, the following officers were chosen and proceedings had: Trustees, Joshua Forman, Amos P. Granger, Moses D. Burnet, Heman Walbridge and John Rodgers; Clerk, John Wilkinson; Treasurer, John Durnford; Pound Master, Henry Young; Constables, Jesse D. Rose and Henry W. Durnford; Overseers of Highways, First District, Henry Young; Second District, John Garrison. This statement of the meeting is certified to by Daniel Gilbert, Justice of the Peace, Syracuse, May 3, 1825.

I stated in a former chapter of the "Reminiscences of Syracuse" that Frederick Horner was the only man now living in this city who had ever seen General Washington. In casting my eye over the city at that time, I did not think of the venerable Major S. S. Forman, although I had frequently conversed with him about Washington, his dress and personal appearance, and also about the evacuation of New York by the British army. Major Forman did not tell me his age, but he is a venerable man. His brothers were officers in the American army during the Revolution. They were stationed in New Jersey and were engaged in the battle of Monmouth and several other severe engagements fought in that State. Major Forman is a man of wealth, and has filled several public offices in this State with honesty and ability, and has always borne an unblemished character throughout a long and useful life. He is one of the last of that indomitable race of men who lived during the Revolution, and no history has yet recorded the names of their equals.

I have been kindly furnished by Mrs. John O'Blennis of Salina, with the following facts in regard to the early settlement of that portion of our city. Mrs. O'Blennis is now over seventy years of age, and her memory in regard to the early settlement of Salina is as perfect as though the occurrences which she relates had taken place within a year. She is the daughter of Isaac Van Vleck, one of the first settlers in Salina.

Mr. Van Vleck moved to Salina from New Galway, in Saratoga county, with a family of four children. He arrived in Salina on the 2nd day of March, 1792. Mr. Van Vleck's family was the sixth family that settled in Salina. A Mr. Whitcomb came to Salina with Mr. Van Vleck. They found at Salina a Mr. Hopkins, engaged in the manufacture of salt in what were then called "salt works."

These salt works consisted of an eight or ten-pail kettle hung to different poles, each end of the pole being placed in the crotch of a post set in the ground, and a fire built under the kettles between a few stones

which were laid up on each side to condense the heat,
and no improvement has been made on that mode
since that time. The salt manufactured at that time
was of a greyish color. This color was produced by
boiling the bitterns in and mixing them with the pure
salt. The art of separating the impurities of the salt
was discovered by a Mr. Dexter, a blacksmith, two or
three years after that date.

John Danforth, a brother of General Asa Danforth,
lived in Salina in 1792, and was engaged in the manu-
ufacture of salt. He was one of the few fortunate
enough to own a kettle large enough to make salt in.
He sold the salt for fifty cents per bushel at the works.

Pharis Gould, father of Pharis Gould of this
county, lived in Salina in 1792. He was also a salt
manufacturer.

A surveyor by the name of Josiah Olcott was a
resident of Salina at that time. He was engaged in
laying of and surveying the roads in and about the
country, and in laying out the streets of the village
then in embryo. When not engaged in surveying he
was employed as an adviser and middle-man about
the salt works.

There was also a man by the name of Sturge, with
his family, then living at Salina. Mr. Loomis was
also a resident there at that time. James Peat and
several others came that year.

These early settlers were all attracted there by,

and had something to do with, the manufacture of salt. They lived very highly on game and fish, of which there was a very great supply.

The Onondaga lake and creek were filled with as fine salmon and other varieties of fish as were ever eaten by any people. The inhabitants were supplied with fish and game by the Indians in great abundance.

There were no clearings in or around the village except here and there a place where nature had refused to do its work of rearing lofty trees, and had left a small prairie-like spot of green. These places the emigrants took to cultivate and settle upon. There was such an open space near the salt spring, a little south of the pump house. There were also several such open spots on each side of Onondaga creek that were occupied by the Onondaga Indians; they having built small brush and bark huts, which they used while fishing and hunting, but not as permanent residences. Their permanent place of abode was where the present Indian castle and village now stand.

There were a great many Indians belonging to this tribe living at that time. They were continually roving in all directions, seeking game and watching their enemies.

At that time there was not a very good feeling existing between our people and the inhabitants of Canada and the frontier.

The Indians had a perfect knowledge of all that

transpired on the frontier. This knowledge they communicated from tribe to tribe by means of runners. They had a perfect and systematic arrangement of this human telegraph, by means of which they communicated with each other from Albany to Buffalo with the greatest precision and despatch.

The head chief, Kiactdote, was one of the most cautious and observing men that ever ruled this tribe. He had perfect command of them, and exerted a great influence over them. To illustrate his power, I must relate an incident which took place in 1793.

At Green Point, on one of the small prairies, a Mr. Lamb had settled with his family. He had a daughter fourteen years old, who was left in his rude house alone while he attended to his agricultural pursuits. Mr. Lamb heard a noise in the house, and going there he saw a young Indian kissing his daughter and taking other improper liberties with her. He was so enraged that he picked up a junk bottle belonging to the Indian and struck the savage on the head, killing him on the spot. He then fled to the settlement at Salina for safety.

The Indians in the vicinity declared they must have the life of Mr. Lamb, according to their custom of "life for life." The people called the chiefs together and with Webster as interpreter, related the circumstances as they transpired. Upon receiving this information, a council of the tribe was called at Salina.

(It was the last council ever held there.) When the council had assembled, Kiactdote stepped into the ring formed by the Indians, threw off his blanket, gave three whoops, making a motion with both hands at the same time. The meaning of this performance was: "Pay attention to what I say." He then related the whole circumstances to the nation, and said that it was the first time an Indian had ever been known to insult a white squaw. Although they had many, many prisoners of white blood, no Indian had ever been found so low as to degrade himself and tribe by insulting a white squaw until this occurrence. He declared that killing was justifiable, and that Mr. Lamb must not be punished. His decision was acquiesced in and adopted by the tribe, with the proviso that Mr. Lamb should pay to the relatives of the Indian killed a three year old heifer, which was to cement peace and good will between the posterity of both parties forever. The Indian was buried on the spot where he was killed.

At that time the whites used to require the children to drive their cows one mile from the settlement and watch over them during the day, for fear of being surprised by the enemy from Canada.

In 1793, the ill will between the inhabitants of New York and Canada had risen to such a point that it was deemed necessary for the security and protection of the inhabitants in and around Salina, to erect a Block House. The State caused an immediate survey to be

made, and the location for the Block House determined upon. A spot of ground directly in front of
the Salina Pump House, near where the canal now
runs, was selected as the proposed site. The building
was finished before 1795. It was twenty feet in height,
with port holes arranged in each story to fire from, in
case of necessity. The Block House was used as a
defence against the occasional incursions of guerrilla
parties from Canada, which the inhabitants feared
more than the Indians.

Among the persons present when the Block House
site was selected were Baron Steuben, Moses DeWitt
of Pompey, Isaac Van Vleck, William Gilchrist, General Asa Danforth, Mr. Olcott of Pompey, and Aaron
Bellows.

Baron Steuben and Moses DeWitt took supper and
lodged at Mrs. O'Blennis' father's house. The Baron
was a large, corpulent man, pleasing in his address
and manners.

The Rev. Mr. Sickles, an itinerant minister, used
to stop at Mr. Van Vleck's on his way through the
country to and from the frontier.

Mr. VanVleck's house was a common stopping place
for most all travelers through the country. He did
not keep a tavern, but he afforded rest to the weary
and food to the hungry.

At that time the inhabitants of Salina did not have
any wells. The water they used for drinking and

cooking was brought from a fresh water spring under the hill near what was then the marsh.

The lake at that time was five or six feet higher than at the present day, and covered the flats at certain seasons of the year.

In 1792, Mr. Gould built what was called a mud house. It was similar to a stick chimney, narrow strips of boards being laid flat-ways about half an inch apart, and the open spaces filled with mud. The roof was made with split logs running lengthwise from the peak to the eaves.

The first frame house was built by General Danforth and Mr. Van Vleck in 1793. The lumber, or most of it, was brought from Little Falls and Tioga Point in batteaux. The nails came from Albany.

That year Thomas Orman, Simon Phares and William Gilchrist came to Salina. Mr. Orman brought the first cauldron kettle for the manufacture of salt. Aaron Bellows came that year and established a cooper shop for the manufacture of salt barrels. Mr. Van Vleck went to Albany that year and brought a large copper mill and placed it in Mr. Bellows' cooper shop, which all the families used to grind their corn with. This was an improvement upon the scalloped stump and sweep.

There were no grist or saw mills in this section of the country at that time. There was a small saw mill at Jamesville, but it was not accessible from Salina as there were no roads for the passage of teams. Benjamin Carpenter kept the first store at Salina. He kept a large variety store and traded in furs, salt, etc., with the Indians and settlers. He commenced business in 1795.

In 1794, Patrick Riley, Mr. Thompson and several others came to Salina to live. The village at that time had increased to thirty-three persons, and of this number thirty were sick; only three being able to attend to their sick neighbors, which they did with the assistance of the Indians.

In 1794, Elisha Alvord, then a young man, in company with several others came to Salina to reside. Mr. Alvord was elected the Supervisor of the town of Salina at its first town election. He was the father of Thomas and Cornelius Alvord, now residents of Salina.

In 1794, Judge Richard Sanger, Mr. Andrews of New Hartford, Thomas Hart of Clinton, Oneida county, Mr. Butler of Pompey, Mr. Keeler of Onondaga, Asa Danforth of Onondaga Hollow and Elisha Alvord of Salina, formed a company called the "Federal Company," for the purpose of manufacturing salt. They put up some of the first six kettle blocks. The company failed in 1801 by inexperience in the business. They had wood merely by cutting it, and sold salt readily at high prices.

Dioclesian Alvord came here in 1796, and hired

part of the "Federal Works" with four kettles. He
added two more, and with his six kettles he could
manufacture eighteen to twenty bushels of salt per
day, which he readily sold for fifty cents per bushel.
The pump house was then out in the water, and Mr.
Alvord had to take a skiff to reach it. The water was
pumped by hand and conveyed in troughs to the reservoir made of hollow logs.

The first law suit tried in Salina was the suit of
Dr. Barber against John Lamb. The suit was in regard to alleged overcharges on the part of the Doctor,
and was tried before 'Squire Kinne of Manlius, who
came there to accommodate the parties. Dr. Barber
was one of the first physicians in the village of Salina,
and son-in-law of John Danforth of that place.

In 1792, there were about six log and two mud
houses in Salina. Three of these houses stood on
Salina street, and two or three stood on the spot where
Widow Miller now lives. These were built together,
or adjoining each other, with separate entrances.

Village lots were not in market in 1792, and when
a person wanted to build he took such a location as
suited him, and put up his house. When the lots
came into market the person building got a pre-emp-
tion title for forty dollars.

In 1795, Judge Stevens, the first Salt Superintendent, William Gilchrist and Isaac Van Vleck of Salina,
conceived the idea of levying duties on salt. It was

thought that the "duties" were not so much for the
profit of the State as for the advancement of the personal interests of different parties in Salina. The
idea originated by these men has been a source of
very great profit to the State, the State having received, prior to 1843, in duties upon salt, over
$3,000,000. The first duties on salt were four pence
per bushel. Upon the opening of the canal, the duty
was raised to one shilling per bushel. The duty is
now one cent.

In 1801, Judge Stevens had collected a considerable
amount of moneys for duties, and was on the point of
proceeding to Albany to make a deposit, when he was
prevented by sickness and died.

In 1795, the State purchased of the Onondagas the
salt lake now called Onondaga lake, with a strip of
land one mile in width extending entirely round it,
with the exclusive right to all the salt springs for $500,
and the annual payment of one hundred bushels of
salt. The State has from time to time sold to different individuals all of the land thus purchased, with
the exception of 549 acres, for which, prior to 1843,
they had received in the aggregate $58,428.25.

The early inhabitants of Salina were a tough,
hardy race of men, and withal they were intelligent,
energetic and enterprising. They were governed solely
by the common law until 1809, when the first town
election was held in the town of Salina.

The village increased gradually, and the salt kettles kept pace with the increase of the inhabitants, until now "Salt Point" and "Salt Pointers" and "salt kettles" are known all over the habitable globe.

In 1824, the village of Salina was about one-third as large as at the present day, and its inhabitants were known as a most intelligent, enterprising set of men. It grew rapidly during that year.

The first tax levied upon the inhabitants after the incorporation of the village of Syracuse, was in the fall of 1825. It amounted to $250, a striking contrast to the sum now levied upon the city of Syracuse for municipal purposes. Henry W. Durnford was the collector, and John Durnford was his bondsman.

In the year 1802, Judge Oliver R. Strong came from Berkshire, Mass., to the county of Onondaga, and located at Onondaga Hill. He was among the first of the settlers who acted in an official capacity, having been appointed a Deputy Sheriff in 1803, by Elijah Rust. This office he held for several years. In 1808, he was appointed County Treasurer by the Board of Supervisors, and served in that capacity for the extraordinary term of twenty-two years. He has been one of the Judges of the county, and President of the Onondaga County Bank for a long period. In all the relations of life, he has borne a reputation for integrity second to no man in the community.

In 1803, Judge Strong, in connection with Cornelius

Longstreet, acted as clerk of the election. At that time the elections continued for three days, and the polls were held half a day in a place. The town of Onondaga at that time embraced a large extent of territory, and it was no light duty to act in the capacity of an inspector or clerk of the elections. The responsibility, too, was much greater than at the present time, as the ballot boxes had to be strictly guarded over nights.

In 1802, the village of Onondaga Hill consisted of four framed buildings—two of them erected that year—seven or eight log dwellings or huts and two log taverns. One of these taverns was kept by Daniel Earll, the grandfather of Jonas Earll, former Canal Commissioner. His house stood on the site of the office subsequently occupied by Nehemiah H. Earll, and which still remains on the original lot. The other public house stood about where the store of Mr. Eastman now stands, and was kept by William Lard. Mr. Lard was a man of energy and enterprise, and many of his descendants still reside in the county. One of the log huts was used as a blacksmith's shop. A store was kept by Walter Morgan, but did not have much business.

Medad Curtis was the only lawyer in the place. He was a man of ability, and was intelligent and trustworthy; and he enjoyed the unbounded confidence of his neighbors. His practice was lucrative.

Two physicians, Dr. Thayer and Dr. Colton, were in practice in 1802. They did a large and profitable business, as the inhabitants, like those of all newly-settled countries, were subject to diseases of a bilious character. Few persons were proof against these insidious diseases.

At the time referred to, this county was settling with great rapidity. Many of the settlers were Revolutionary soldiers, who received their land for services rendered their country in the stirring and eventful contest with Great Britain, and came here to enjoy the blessings of peace and independence which had been acquired by their courage and patriotism.

In 1794, Onondaga county was set off from Herkimer by act of the Legislature. It included the whole of Oswego and parts of Cayuga and Cortland counties. The territory was divided into eight townships. Soon afterwards a company of gentlemen, consisting of Judge Stevens, Elisha Lewis, Comfort Tyler, John Ellis, Parley Howlett, sr., Asa Danforth, Thaddeus M. Wood, Elijah Rust, William Lard, Medad Curtis, and George Hall, conceived the idea of making a large village at or near the centre of the county. After a full view of the merits of the different localities, they selected Onondaga Hill, by reason of its high and airy location. The valleys were avoided, because they were regarded as very unhealthy. This company purchased parts of farm lots 104 and 119, and employed Judge Geddes to lay them out into village lots, with a suitable site in the centre for a court house and jail. The plan was faithfully carried out, and these buildings, erected soon afterwards, were placed on the spot thus indicated. The site was very capacious, consisting of fifteen acres, with a gentle declivity towards the north, bounded on every side by public streets.

A few years only elapsed before it became apparent that this attempt at a speculation must fail. The "Hollow" improved faster than the "Hill," and the Erie canal eventually killed both. But it is not the only instance illustrating the want of foresight in the shrewdest men. Comfort Tyler, Thaddeus M. Wood, General Danforth and their associates in this enterprise, were men far more sagacious than the generality of our pioneer citizens; but they were not aware of the fact that the marts of commerce, trade and wealth, are always found in valleys and not on mountain elevations.

The people of Onondaga Valley have been their own worst enemies. They not only made no efforts to secure the location of the court house, but actually prevented the laying out of the Erie canal through their village, by placing obstacles in the way of Judge Forman, who was sincerely desirous of running that great artery of trade and prosperity through the place. Had the leading property holders exhibited the spirit of true liberality, the canal would have been carried up to that point from Lodi, and down on the west side of the valley. Thus does selfishness generally defeat its own aims and purposes. Had the canal taken this direction, Onondaga Valley would have occupied the position now maintained by the city of Syracuse.

The first court held in this county was in the corn house of Comfort Tyler, nearly opposite the late residence of General T. M. Wood (now the residence of Morris Pratt), at Onondaga Valley. After this they were held for some time in the parlor of Mr. Tyler's public house, and subsequently in other public places in different parts of the town, to suit the convenience of the litigants.

At that time there was no jail in the county, and the authorities were compelled to take the prisoners to the Herkimer county jail for confinement.

In the year 1804, the county of Oneida had completed a jail in the town of Whitesboro, to which the criminals of this county were transferred, the Legislature having previously passed an act granting this county the right to use the nearest jail. The Whitesboro jail was used until 1810; that year our jail was finished.

In 1801, the Board of Supervisors, then composed of the wisest men in their respective towns, began to take measures to build a court house and jail for this county. Three commissioners, Elisha Lewis, Medad Curtis and T. M. Wood, were selected to superintend this erection, and by a vote, it was determined to locate them on Onondaga Hill. The commissioners did not seem to have much system about building. The buildings were erected by piecemeal and by different persons. The commissioners commenced by contracting with William Bostwick of Auburn to put up the frame and enclose the house. This was done in 1802, and closed Mr. Bostwick's contract. Previous to raising the house, the people of the Hill collected together and made a "bee," for the purpose of cutting away the trees to make room for the new building. The square was at that time covered with a heavy growth of timber. In order to have the use of the court house, a temporary floor and seats were put into it, and the courts held there till the commencement of 1804. The county then began to feel able to finish the court house and jailor's dwelling. The commissioners contracted with Abel House to do the carpenter work inside, leaving out the cells; and with a Mr. Saxton from New Hartford to do the mason work; and E. Webster to furnish the brick for chimneys. The court room and dwelling were completed during that season. After a year or two, preparations were commenced for building the cells of the jail. A contract was made with Roswell and Sylvanus Tousley of Manlius to do the iron work for

a stipulated price of two shillings per pound. I am
not informed who did the wood work, but the cells
were not finished till the year 1810.

This jail was a wood building, fifty feet square,
two stories high, with a square roof pitching four
ways to the eaves. It was not painted. This finishing touch was done by a subscription some years
afterwards, by the people of Onondaga Hill. The
first story was appropriated for the jail and the
dwelling of the janitor, a hall separating them from
each other. The cells were constructed of heavy oak
plank, fastened together with wrought spike. The
doors were made of the like material, with a "dia-
mond" in the centre to pass through the food and
give light to the prisoners. In the rear of the cells
were grated windows. The court room was reached
by a stairway leading from this hall. The Judge's
bench was directly in front of the entrance to the
court room, and was constructed in a circular form.
The whole cost of the building was $10,000, a large
sum apparently for such a structure; but when it is
considered that the work was done mostly on credit,
there will be no occasion for surprise. Besides, the
system of keeping public accounts at that day was
very imperfect. Many of the bills contracted in the
erection of the building were not paid until several
years afterwards.

This court house and jail were used for the purposes designated until the year 1829. The first jailor was James Beebe, a Revolutionary soldier, and father of Mrs. Victory Birdseye of Pompey. His successor was Mason Butts, father of Horace Butts, who was jailor after the removal of the county buildings to Syracuse. John H. Johnson also acted as jailor there for several years.

Syracuse having in 1825-26 grown to be the largest town in the county, the propriety of removing the county buildings to that place began to be agitated. The people on the Hill strongly resisted the measure, and in the first mentioned year succeeded in getting a bill through the Legislature, providing for their retention at that place; but through the influence of the Syracuse Company, Governor Clinton was induced to veto it, and it was thus defeated. But the project did not sleep. In 1827-28, a law was enacted authorizing the Supervisors of the county to erect a court house and jail within the corporate limits of the village of Syracuse. In obedience to the requirements of this act, the Supervisors, in the summer of 1828, met in the village of Syracuse, at the public house kept by James Mann (now the Syracuse House) to take into consideration the selection of a site for the proposed buildings, and also to make the necessary preparation for erecting the same. At that meeting there was a great deal of discussion upon the question, and a wide difference of

opinion existed among the members relative to the
site of the buildings. On taking a vote, it resulted in
placing it midway between Syracuse and Salina, in
consideration of the village of Salina presenting to
the county a full and unincumbered title to the
property, consisting of not less than three acres,
and $1,000.

As an inducement to locate it in the centre of the
village, Messrs. Townsend and James offered the
county, free of expense, all that block of land on which
the Onondaga County Bank and Bank of Syracuse are
now located, with the exception of one lot on which
the First Presbyterian church then stood, on the corner of Salina and Fayette streets. This offer was refused; but as the sequel proved, it would have been
much the best bargain, for this property is now worth
at least ten times as much as the court-house lot was
recently sold for, besides being a much more convenient site for the county buildings. But the site having been fixed it could not be changed.

At this meeting, measures were also taken for the
erection of the county buildings by the appointment
of three men, styled building commissioners, consisting of John Smith, Thomas Starr and Samuel Forman, with power to cause plans and specifications to
be made, and to contract for the erection of the buildings. The County Treasurer was also empowered to
borrow $20,000 in two annual installments of $10,000

each. After the plans were submitted, the commissioners decided to build the jail of stone, fifty feet square and two stories high, with a hall and stairs in the centre. The south half was designed for the jailor's dwelling, and the north half for strong stone cells, and the second story, over the cells, was appropriated for cells for debtors, witnesses, etc. The court house was to be built of brick, sixty feet square, with large columns on the west side, and two stories high. The first story was divided by a hall into four apartments in each corner, for the use of the grand and petit jurors and other purposes. The court room occupied all of the second story except the landing of the stairs and two petit jury rooms in each corner. The Judge's seat was in the south side, opposite the landing of the stairway. These were the county buildings the commissioners decided upon, and invited bids for their erection. In the spring of 1829, the bids were received according to the specifications and plans. John Wall obtained the contract for the building of the jail, which was erected by him early in the year 1829. The cells in this jail were of the strongest kind. Since it was taken down, they have been placed in the basement of the new court house on Clinton square.

L. A. Cheney and Samuel Booth obtained the contract for doing the mason work of the court house, and David Stafford obtained the contract for doing the carpenter work. It was put up that year and enclosed.

In the following year, Mr. Wall made a bargain with the commissioners to complete the edifice, and during that year it was finished ready for the occupation of the courts.

The estimate for these buildings proved to be some thirty per centum short of their expense, the total cost of them having been upwards of $27,000.

The jail was abandoned in 1850, after the erection of the penitentiary and the removal of the jail prisoners to that institution. The materials were used in the erection of the work-shops at the penitentiary and the new court house.

Attempts were made from time to time to change the site of this court house, but they all failed until after the destruction of the building by fire, on the morning of the 5th of January, 1856. At a meeting of the Board of Supervisors, April 28, 1856, it was decided by a vote of twenty-four to one, "that the site of the court house for Onondaga county be, and is hereby, changed to the lot in Block 81, on the corner of Clinton square and Clinton alley."

The plan of the building, as presented in the report of the committee, consisting of T. C. Cheney, Elizur Clark and Bradley Cary, was then adopted; and Messrs. Slocum, Johnson and District Attorney Andrews were directed to execute the papers for an exchange of sites with Colonel Voorhees. The next day Timothy C. Cheney, Luke Wells and D. C. Greenfield were appointed a committee to superintend the erection of the building, and Horatio N. White, architect. At a subsequent meeting of the Board in June, the proposals for the erection of the building, advertised for by the commissioners, were opened and the contract awarded to Messrs. Cheney & Wilcox, at $37,750, the contractors to have the materials of the old court house and jail. Mr. Cheney thereupon resigned his place as commissioner, and Elizur Clark was appointed to fill the vacancy. Portions of the work were afterwards sub-let—the cut stone work to Spalding & Pollock, the carpenter and joiner work to Coburn & Hurst, and the iron work to Featherly, Draper & Cole. The building is now in process of construction, and will be completed on the first day of October, next.

In the year 1821, Judge Forman, who then resided in Syracuse, conceived the idea of manufacturing salt by solar evaporation. Mr. Forman, with Isaiah Townsend of Albany, went to New Bedford for the purpose of examining works that had been previously erected there. He met in that noted sea-faring town Stephen Smith, with whom he counseled upon the subject. Upon Mr. Forman's statements in regard to the strength of the water, its purity and abundance, Mr. Smith consented to embark in the enterprise of erecting similar works here. This gentleman, together with William Rotch, jr., Samuel Rodman and James Arnold of New Bedford, formed the " Onondaga Salt

Company." Of this company, Mr. Smith was the controlling agent, and Henry Gifford superintended the construction.

Subsequently to the formation of this company, Judge Forman proceeded to Albany and procured the passage of a law by the Legislature, authorizing the company to take possession of the grounds and erect the necessary works. He also endeavored to induce William James and Isaiah and John Townsend to form another company and embark in the manufacture of coarse salt; but they declined. He then applied to Henry Eckford, the celebrated naval architect of New York, who consented, and with other gentlemen, established "The Syracuse Salt Company." Judge Forman was appointed the agent of this company and Matthew L. Davis, secretary.

Mr. Eckford was then owner of the "Walton Tract." Before the works of this company had far advanced William James and Isaiah and John Townsend of Albany and James McBride of New York became the proprietors.

At that period, the Salt Springs were termed the "Old Federal Springs." The water was pumped by hand labor by men perched on high stagings, and collected into rude reservoirs for distribution.

The companies thus formed immediately set about the execution of their plans. The first thing done was to cut away the trees, clear the grounds (the

position between the " Genesee turnpike " and the Erie
canal was an almost impassable swamp), preparatory
to the erection of the vats. It was essential that a
greater supply of water should be procured. Accordingly the two companies, at their joint expense, erected
the first great reservoir, pumps and aqueducts at
Salina; the machinery propelled, as it now is, by surplus water from a branch of the Erie canal. The
starting point for the vats was just north of Church
street.

After these works were fairly under way, the
Onondaga Salt Company broke ground west of the
creek, near the dwelling subsequently occupied for
many years by Joseph Savage. Here the first growth
of trees was still standing, and yielded nearly a hundred cords of wood to the acre. The building of vats
was prosecuted with great diligence and energy; about
two million feet of lumber being consumed annually
for several years.

In 1826, Mr. Gifford covered twenty acres of ground
on private account; but he was unable to procure
water for three years. This investment was continued
by Mr. Gifford until the land was sold by the State,
a year or two since.

Such, in brief, was the origin of the coarse salt
manufacture. There are now in existence upwards
of 23,000 vats, or " covers," occupying about 380 acres,
in which is invested a capital of $1,161,000.

It may not be out of place here to make a brief allusion to Stephen Smith. Mr. Smith in early life was particularly noted for his persevering industry in the pursuit of knowledge. He was a son of Abraham Smith of New Bedford, with whom he learned the trade of a blacksmith, but did not follow the occupation. At the age of twenty-one, he went to New York, found employment in a celebrated commercial firm there and became a partner in a ship-chandlery establishment, which, during his absence in Europe, became unsuccessful. In 1801, he went to England and France on an agency. He made several voyages as supercargo to India and China. Subsequently he went on different occasions to Italy, Spain and Portugal.

The war of 1812 and ill health detained him at home, and he then embarked in the manufacture of salt from sea water at Yarmouth on Cape Cod. It was while prosecuting this enterprise that Judge Forman met him and induced him to come to Syracuse, as before stated. Mr. Smith continued to reside here until his death, which occurred in 1854. He was a man of strong mind, a close observer of passing events, liberal views and unbending integrity. No man stood higher in the community than Stephen Smith. The monument at his grave marks the last resting place of "God's noblest work, an honest man."

The first furnace erected west of Oneida county

was built by Nicholas Mickles, father of Philo D.
Mickles, who emigrated from New England to lay the
foundation of a fortune in this then frontier county.
It is usually called the "Old Furnace," and has long
been a landmark on the road to Onondaga Hill. Judge
Forman was associated in this enterprise with Mr.
Mickles, and they did a heavy business for many
years in the manufacture of kettles for the western
country and for the salt works. During the war of
1812, they had a heavy contract with the government
for supplies of cannon balls and shells. These missiles of death were transported by wagons to Salina,
whence they were taken by water to Oswego and there
distributed to various points along the frontier. Mr.
Mickles was a man of intelligence and probity and
highly esteemed.

In every community there are men with characteristics so marked as to attract particular notice and
comment. Syracuse has not been wanting in this
respect. I propose to terminate these random
"Reminiscences" by adverting to one of them, who
was well known to many persons now residing in this
vicinity. I allude to James Sackett.

Mr. Sackett originally emigrated from New
England and settled in Skaneateles; but he removed
to Syracuse in 1826, long before which he acquired
the sobriquet of "Old Sackett," by which he was
ever afterwards known. He was very eccentric in

his habits and conversation. He acquired a large property by the purchase of land warrants of Revolutionary soldiers, and locating the lots in this section of the State. He was very fond of horses, of which he raised the finest breed in this county. He had a habit of rounding off his sentences with the very expressive but rather impolite phrase, "G—d d——n you!" Always a bachelor, he never made more than one attempt to obtain a wife. The lady he selected, and who resided in an adjoining county, was first made acquainted with his intentions by hearing an individual hallooing at her father's gate. She went out to ascertain what was wanted. Mr. Sackett sat in his buggy. On her inquiring his errand, his response was: "I have made up my mind to marry you; will you have me, G—d d——n you?"

She replied: "Mr. Sackett, this is a short notice; I will take ten days to consider."

"Ten days, ha! to consider on marrying Mr. James Sackett; ten days, G—d d——n you! ten days, ha!" and Mr. Sackett drove away, never calling again.

In 1824, he contracted with a man to build him a house about 22 feet by 40. It was to be set on his block on Salina street, opposite the Empire. That block was owned by him, and nothing was on it except at the south end, where were two or three little buildings. It was a pretty field for a residence. The

contractor did not come and put up the house as he
agreed. He then contracted with another builder to
put up the same kind of a house. It was immediately
done. While the second contractor was finishing the
first house, the first contractor came with the second
house. Although Mr. Sackett was under no obliga-
tion to receive the house, he said to the builder:
"Here, put it up at the end of this one." Of course,
he had a house 22 by 80 feet. He had a rough board
fence put around the lot, which was entered by a
gate swinging on a post in the centre. After his
house was finished and he had resided in it a few
years, the crickets had taken joint occupancy with
him. They were rather noisy, and disturbed the old
man. Mr. Sackett was a timid man; so he undertook
to expel them. He succeeded very well, with the
exception of one old chap that bid him defiance.
This fellow was located behind the chimney, where
he kept up a perpetual song. But he was not out of
the reach of harm. One Monday morning, masons
were seen at work taking down the chimney, which
was razed to the ground, and this noisy old chap
driven from his quarters, and the chimney rebuilt so
as to exclude him thereafter.

Mr. Sackett had also singular tastes in the matter
of dress. He wore a frock coat reaching down to his
heels, a wide brimmed hat, with a large veil over his
face. Such an outfit on a tall, slim, fleshless man

like Mr. Sackett made him an object of notice to every person. He always hired masons to fill his ice house, so that the work should be well done. In doing odd jobs, he would hire more men than were necessary, and would often discharge them all before the work on hand was completed. He usually traveled about the country in an old, rickety buggy, with a patched top of various colors, drawn by a splendid horse. Wherever he went on foot, he carried an old umbrella, with a large white patch on the top. But with all his oddities, he was a well disposed man, and correct and prompt in business matters. He died worth an estate valued at $150,000.

FIRST PRESBYTERIAN CHURCH. From a recent photograph.

CHAPTER XIII

FIRST PRESBYTERIAN CHURCH

The original site of the First Presbyterian church was on the northeastern corner of Salina and Fayette streets, where the retail dry goods store of D. Mc-Carthy & Company now stands. The church edifice was a plain, wooden structure, clapboarded and painted white, with green outside blinds, two story, and surmounted with a spire of moderate height, as were all steeples of an early day. The inside was finished with pine, painted white throughout, the division of the pews being capped with cherry. The gallery front was of an elliptical form. The pulpit was situated in the west end of the building, and the choir was for a time placed in the gallery just above, but subsequently removed to the east end. This edifice was the only one in the block upon which it was situated, enclosed by Washington, Fayette, Warren and Salina streets, and so continued for many years. A portion of the remainder of the square was occasionally used for the purpose of the peripatetic shows of that day. This spot was called a common or goose pasture.

This church building, though at first located somewhat out of the village, afterwards, with the growth of the village, became centrally located; and it was often used for important public meetings, as there were no public halls in which the people could be accommodated. Suspended in the belfry was the bell, which in those days sounded the alarm of fire, the call to church and the funeral knell. It was then the custom to strike upon the bell the number of years of the age of the deceased as soon as the spirit had departed, as was generally observed in all country villages. The Fourth of July gatherings were for many years held in this building. It was also customary to read from the pulpit notices of important meetings and transactions, and, among others, was read annually for many years from the pulpit of this church, the necrological record for the previous year. These death notices were usually read on the first Sunday in January.

The certificate of the incorporation of this church society, as recorded in the County Clerk's office, was executed and recorded December 22, 1824, before David S. Colvin, a Commissioner, etc. This document says that at a meeting of the members of the Presbyterian Society in the village of Syracuse, in the town of Salina, December 14, 1824, held at the school house, Moses D. Burnet and Miles Seymour were chosen to preside; and that the society was named "First Presbyterian Society in the village of Syracuse." These seven Trustees were elected by "pluralities of voices" : Joshua Forman, Moses D. Burnet, Heman Walbridge, Miles Seymour, Rufus Moss, Joseph Slocum and Jonathan Day.

Another record in the County Clerk's office shows that at an election "holden" at the Presbyterian meeting house, January 10, 1827, the society was reincorporated, "the incorporation being dissolved by means of a neglect to exercise the powers necessary for its preservation." The following were chosen Trustees: Jonathan Day, Moses D. Burnet, Joseph Slocum, George Hooker, Stephen W. Cadwell, Elbert Norton and John Wall. The acknowledgment to this certificate of reincorporation contains the following clause: "I certify that on the 26th day of January, 1827, came before me Frederick Phelps and Edward Chapman, to me known to be the within grantors, and acknowledged that they executed the within. David S. Colvin, a Commissioner, etc." It might be added that at the annual meeting of this church society, held January 1st, 1894, a resolution was passed, authorizing an application to the Court to change the name to The First Presbyterian Society of Syracuse.

According to the first church manual, published

by J. M. Patterson in 1835, the church edifice was built in the summer of 1825, and dedicated in January of 1826. The Rev. Dirck C. Lansing, D. D., of Auburn Theological Seminary, who had formerly been the first pastor of the "United Church of Onondaga Hollow and Salina," from 1810 to 1814, preached the dedication sermon. The church was organized April 6, 1826, by a committee from the Onondaga Presbytery, consisting of the following gentlemen: Ministers, Hezekiah N. Woodruff, Hutchins Taylor, Ralph Cushman, Washington Thatcher; Elders, Dr. Joseph W. Brewster, William Eager, Harry Moseley. Frederick Phelps and Edward Chapman were elected Elders, and Pliny Dickinson, Deacon, at that time. The society consisted, at its formation, of the following twenty-six members: Frederick Phelps, Edward Chapman, Pliny Dickinson, Rufus Moss, J. W. Hanchett, Jonathan Day, Archibald L. Fellows, Agrippa Martin, Benoni Stilson, Samuel Mead, Anna Phelps, Florilla Chapman, Melinda Kasson, Harriet Newton, Margaret Hanchett, Theodosia Wall, Deborah Webb, Olive Pease, Catharine Marble, Nancy Toogood, Eliza Parsons, Eve Van Buren, Elizabeth Cummings, Julia Northam, Mary A. Huntington, Sarah Norton.

When the church edifice was dedicated, in January, 1826, Dr. Lansing brought with him the Rev. John Watson Adams, at that time engaged in theo-

J.W. Adams

logical studies at Auburn Seminary. Mr. Adams was then thirty years of age. The society invited the young clergyman to preach a few sermons, with a view to settlement, at a salary of $600 per year. Mr. Adams accepted the invitation, and the result was that he was ordained and installed pastor of the church June 28, 1826. He was the first pastor of this church, and he sustained this relation uninterruptedly till his decease, April 4, 1850, in the fifty-fourth year of his age.

Dr. Adams, for he had been honored with the degree of D. D., is remembered with the kindest feelings by his congregation and associates, as he was a man of scholarly attainments, warm friendships, in spite of the occasional coldness of his exterior, and a preacher whose views of divine truth were lucid, comprehensive and sound. The character of this remarkable man, combined with acumen and strength of intellect and the higher qualities of moral virtue, a peculiar native diffidence and self-distrust. In his labors among the people of this city, where the whole life of his manhood was spent, he was successful and highly useful, fully meeting, in this regard, the anticipations and predictions of his earliest friends.

Dr. Adams commenced a history of Onondaga County, and he was for several years engaged upon the work, with a view of ultimate publication; but his parochial duties and other uncontrollable circumstances interposed, and the idea was abandoned. His material, however, was used and acknowledged by Joshua V. H. Clark in writing "Clark's Onondaga."

In the early days, when the Calvinistic teachings prevailed more extensively than in these progressive days, the people were bound by strict religious observances. At a meeting of the First Presbyterian Church and Society, held March 31, 1835, certain rules and regulations were unanimously adopted and ordered to be printed as an appendix to the articles of faith of the church. The first rule was: "We regard the Sabbath as holy time, and all profanations of it, by walking or riding out for pleasure, journeying. or engaging in other secular employments, unless when compelled so to do by the paramount claims of mercy, as a violation of our covenant engagements. Therefore, resolved unanimously, that the Session of this church be requested to make such violations a subject of discipline."

There were some exceptions to this prevailing custom, as is shown in the following entry from the Sunday school minute book, under date of March 16, 1834: "Last night was the great conflagration of our village. Blocks 93 and 94, and the one on the opposite side of the canal, being the great centre of business, were entirely consumed. All are engaged in saving their property, and there is no church or Sabbath school."

A form of covenant was adopted, March 31, 1835. After the great powder explosion, a relief meeting was held in the church, August 23, 1841, at which $2,800 was raised at once for the benefit of the victims. On January 5, 1846, steps were taken for the erection of a new church edifice; and on June 28, 1846, the building was commenced on the opposite side of Fayette street, on the site now occupied by the present church edifice. The original church site was a gift from the Syracuse Company. Many thought at the time that it was too far away from the village, and much complaint was made of the mud encountered in going to the services. At that time, thirty-three feet on the north side of the canal, where most of the people had settled, could have been purchased for thirty dollars per foot; but the trustees thought the price too high. The new and present site was purchased at a cost of $10,000, and the following building committee was appointed: Henry Gifford, Elias W. Leavenworth, Thomas B. Fitch, Zebulon Ostrum and Albert A. Hudson. The services of the celebrated architect, Lefever, were solicited, and plans were submitted by him of the noble edifice which has so long ornamented the centre of the city. The church was erected at a cost of about $40,000; and $10,000 has been since expended upon it. The new edifice was completed and first services were held therein November 24, 1850. It was dedicated two days thereafter.

The old church property was purchased by Henry A. Dillaye, who erected upon that site a handsome five-story block, at that time by far the finest building in Salina street. The block covered the entire lot, and it was then thought to be too far from the centre of business to be profitable for leasing; but the investment proved to be a good one. The building was burned in 1855, and was rebuilt the following year. It was soon afterwards purchased by Dennis McCarthy for a dry goods store.

The old church edifice was torn down in April, 1850, and just as the last timbers were removed the venerable and beloved Dr. Adams passed from earth. The church society removed to Market Hall, April 7, 1850, while the new edifice was being built.

The Rev. Charles McHarg, of Cooperstown, N. Y., received a call to become pastor of this church in June, 1850; he began his pastorate in September and was installed December 18. In October, 1851, Mr. McHarg resigned; his pastoral relations were dissolved November 24, and his labors with the church were closed December 8. His resignation was reluctantly accepted by the church, for his character, fine culture and commanding abilities had rendered him a favorite with the congregation and the community.

From December, 1851, to May, 1854, the church was without a settled pastor. A call was extended February 27, 1854, to the Rev. Sherman Bond Can-

field, which was accepted by him. On May 1, 1854,
Mr. Canfield began his pastorate; and September 26
he was installed. His resignation, made in October,
1870, ill health impelling to this action, was accepted
October 22. His death, March 5, 1871, occurred in
St. Louis, Mo., and his funeral services were held in
the church of which he had been pastor for over six-
teen years. Dr. Canfield was highly educated, a man
of great logical power, sturdy in his opinions, inclined
to be conservative, and at times very eloquent; he
was of reserved and somewhat cold exterior, but in
private circles genial and warm-hearted, especially to
young men.

In May, 1861, the meeting of the General Assembly of the New School Presbyterian Church of the
United States was held in this church, the Rev. Dr.
J. B. Condit being moderator. On January 26, 1870,
a petition was made by some of the members to leave
the church and organize the Fourth Presbyterian
Church. This organization was perfected that same
year, about sixty members joining the new society,
among them being E. T. Hayden, who had served
continuously since July, 1833, as Deacon or Elder.
From October, 1870, to November, 1872, the pulpit
was supplied by the Rev. Dr. J. B. Condit and the
Rev. Dr. E. A. Huntington, both of Auburn Theological Seminary, and others.

The Rev. Dr. Nelson Millard, of Peekskill, N. Y.,

was called to this pastorate May 17, 1872; and he was installed November 19, following. During that summer the church had been thoroughly repaired, and the main auditorium and Sabbath school room elaborately frescoed. Dr. Millard was an eloquent, forcible, fearless preacher, and he was greatly respected by his congregation. In December, 1883, he received a call from Norwich, Conn. He is now pastor of a leading church in Rochester. Three meetings of the church society were held expressive of the desire of the church to retain the pastor; but the call to Norwich was accepted by Dr. Millard January 13, 1884, on which date the pastor officiated for the last time.

From that time to September, 1885, the pulpit was supplied mainly by the Rev. Dr. Wellesly P. Coddington of the Syracuse University. During July and September of 1884, extensive repairs were made to the edifice and the organ. A call to the pastorate was extended to the Rev. Dr. George B. Spalding, of Manchester, N. H., June 29, 1885, which was accepted, September 1, following; and the new pastor was installed, October 1, 1885. Dr. Spalding continues as pastor of this church, and he is a worthy successor of the eminent divines who preceded him.

THE STATE ARSENAL.—From a recent photograph.

CHAPTER XIV

THE OLD STATE ARSENAL

The old State arsenal, located in Onondaga Hollow (now called Onondaga Valley), is one of the most important historic landmarks of this county; and it is fast mouldering into decay, through neglect and abandonment. It was erected on the hill, half a mile east of Onondaga Valley, at the side of the old Seneca turnpike road, leading from Onondaga to Manlius. It is a stone structure, originally of imposing appearance, two stories and a half high, upon whose roof there rested, some fifty years ago, two huge wooden cannon which indicated the purpose to which the building had been dedicated. But one of the cannon fell to decay, and it was followed by the other emblem of war. The roof and parts of the walls have also suffered from neglect and the lapse of many years.

The property whereon this building stands was deeded to the State of New York by Cornelius Longstreet, father of Cornelius T. Longstreet, in 1809. The building was erected in 1810, and it was occupied

(223)

soon after its completion by stores which were sent
there by the Secretary of War.   It was built by New
York State and occupied by the United States.   The
stone for its construction was obtained from the
quarries near by.   The building occupies a small
square of ground, somewhat removed from the high-
way, but it possesses the right of way.

In the early days, Onondaga was one of the most
important military posts in New York State. Accordingly, in 1808, an act was passed authorizing the Governor of the State to deposit five hundred stand of
arms at Onondaga for the defense of the frontier and
such quantities of ammunition and military stores as
in his opinion would be necessary in case of an invasion.   The Governor was also authorized and empowered to provide, at the expense of the State, a
suitable place for keeping the arms and military stores
in good order and fit for immediate service, and to
appoint keepers of such places of deposit.

The arsenal was built under the direction of the
Governor, and it was used for a number of years as a
large deposit of arms and ammunition.   As a military
storehouse it was abandoned a few years after the
war of 1812, when the necessity for its maintenance
had passed away.   The last time the arsenal was in
State use was during the war of the Rebellion, when
Brigadier-General John A. Green of the National
Guard stored a quantity of State arms there, and by
this act maintained the State's right of possession.

Jasper Hopper, who came to Onondaga in 1802, when he was appointed clerk of the County of Onondaga, was appointed keeper of the military stores at the arsenal. He located at the east end of Onondaga Hollow and kept the office there in his dwelling house for several years. Afterwards he removed the office to the west end of the Hollow, and kept it there till its removal to Onondaga Hill. In those early days, Onondaga was a very important post, and the one to which all the surrounding posts in the central part of the State were required to make their report.

Mr. Hopper was also a United States Commissary for the procuring and distributing of rations to the army on its marches to and from the frontier. It might also be added, to show the importance of Onondaga Hollow in those early times, that Mr. Hopper was Postmaster for a period of nineteen years, under every administration without distinction of party, during a time when the office was an important one, being a distributing office for the county and posts adjacent.

The name of Nicholas Mickles should be mentioned in this connection. He established the Onondaga Furnace, and carried it on till his decease which occurred at Onondaga Hollow in 1827. This old furnace stood on the west side of the west road from Syracuse to Onondaga Valley, just north of where the Onondaga Hill road turns westward, on land now embraced in Elmwood Park. During the war of 1812, Mr. Mickles was employed by the Government to cast shot and shell for the army and navy. Elisha and Dioclesian Alvord were the consignees of this shot and shell, and they shipped the ammunition to Oswego and Sacket's Harbor, where the Government forts were located.

An account of this old arsenal would not be complete without some reference to the celebrated order of sending an armed vessel from Oswego to Onondaga Hollow. As the accounts of different authorities differ, it is safe to say that the most reliable account is that given by Joshua V. H. Clark in his history entitled "Clark's Onondaga." This history was published in 1849, and it is the basis of all the other histories of this county, so abundantly rich in the history of the Indians, the pioneers and the early settlers.

Mr. Clark says: "It was with regard to the Government property at this place, that Secretary of War Armstrong committed a most laughable mistake, which was noticed at the time in most of the public prints in the Union. A large amount of shot and shell was lying at the Onondaga Furnace which was wanted by the fleet on Lake Ontario. Secretary Armstrong directed one of the Naval Commanders then at Oswego, to proceed forthwith with one armed vessel via the Oswego river, to Onondaga Hollow, and remove the Government property from that place to Oswego. The obstructions at Oswego Falls were found to be quite too formidable to allow of the execution of the Secretary's order, and the project was abandoned. The joke was too good to be kept a secret, and its publication created much merriment at the Honorable Secretary's expense."

An effort has been repeatedly made by the Onondaga Historical Association to have what remains of this old building preserved and put in proper condition, as the sole relic of early war history in this locality. But nothing has so far been done in the matter, though steps are now being taken which will doubtless be successful.

A few years ago, William Kirkpatrick and Major Theodore L. Poole, in behalf of the Onondaga Historical Association, started a project to erect a monument to the memory of Captain Benjamin Branch, who was buried, in 1814, on the south side of the old Seneca turnpike road, at the top of the hill above Hopper's Glen. But the monument has never been erected. A letter from the Adjutant-General's office in Washington, dated July 9, 1889, and written to Major Poole, gives this account of Captain Branch: "The records of the office show that Captain Benjamin Branch, United States Light Artillery, died October 14, 1814, at Onondaga Hollow, N. Y. Captain Arthur W. Thornton, United States Light

Artillery, was at that time absent from the company, sick, at the same place; but he died in 1836, in Florida. There is no record of the death of any other man of the United States Light Artillery in October, 1814, when a detachment of the company passed through Onondaga. From the data furnished it cannot be determined who the other deceased soldier, herein referred to, is."

The burial plot for this soldier was purchased by Captain Arthur W. Thornton from Amasa Cole, the same day that Captain Branch died. It is a beautiful site, overlooking the whole valley. The company of Light Artillery was encamped on the green at Onondaga Hill. Captain Branch came from an old Virginian family, some members of which are still living in Virginia.

THE ONONDAGA ACADEMY. From a recent photograph.

CHAPTER XV

THE ONONDAGA ACADEMY

The Onondaga Academy, occupying a beautiful
and picturesque location in Onondaga Valley, has a
history which is clearly identified with the earliest
history of Syracuse; and this academy has always
been ranked among the best in the State, graduating
a long list of young men and women who afterwards
attained distinction and honor. It was intended to
be a rival of Hamilton College, and it was founded
by the same man who obtained the charter for
Hamilton College. But through continual lack of
funds, a disadvantage which it encountered from its
very beginning, it never rose above the rank of an
academy. Its first Principal and the President of
its first Board of Trustees, was the Rev. Caleb Alexander, a Presbyterian Clergyman, who was an able,
cultivated, ambitious man, but one who failed to
retain the full confidence of his associates.

In 1801, when Mr. Alexander was forty-six years
old, he was appointed as a missionary for Western

New York, under the auspices of the Massachusetts Missionary Society. It was his duty to visit the churches and the Indians and to labor among them. But he continued in the work for a short time only, for in 1803 he organized the Fairfield Academy, at Fairfield, Herkimer county, of which he became Principal, a school that prospered and one that is to-day of considerable influence. When that academy was seven or eight years old, the people of Fairfield wished to broaden its basis, in order that it might be made a college.

Mr. Alexander went to Albany, in order to procure a charter for such an institution, but instead of carrying it to Fairfield, he took it to Clinton, a more promising town near Utica, and where the rival Oneida Academy, munificently endowed by Dr. Kirkland, was located. The Clinton people were glad to get the charter; and thus Hamilton College came into being. It was stipulated that Mr. Alexander should be the first President of Hamilton College, in return for obtaining the charter, but he failed in his purpose. He was paid $5,000 as compensation for his services to the Clinton people, though the Fairfield people said it was the price of his treachery. That was in 1812. The same year he went to Onondaga Hollow, then a town of considerable importance in the State, and began his plans to found an institution that would outrank those with which he had been recently connected.

From Jasper Hopper's minutes of a preliminary meeting, held in Onondaga Hollow, now known as Onondaga Valley, August 15, 1812, it is learned that upon application made by the Rev. Caleb Alexander, subscription papers were prepared for establishing an academy for the instruction of youth, to be located not more than one hundred rods from the Seneca turnpike road. The subscriptions were in shares of $25 each, and were payable to John Adams and Joshua Forman, in three yearly installments and not to be binding unless $4,000 was subscribed for the purpose.

The sum of $2,000 was subscribed at that meeting, Joshua Forman heading the paper with $500. A similar paper pledged the subscriber to contribute to a fund for the endowment of the academy, the aggregate to be not less than $3,000. This contribution was to be in money, in land or in mortgages upon land, the interest to be paid annually. Shares in this fund were to be twenty dollars each. Joshua Forman headed the list with $750. At the close of the meeting the endowment fund had reached $3,425.

The papers were circulated for some weeks subsequently, and each fund was increased to something over $4,000, as appears in the application for the charter. As these subscription papers were not preserved, it is not known who were all of the contributors to the academy funds. The charter names twenty-two trustees as follows: Joshua Forman, John Adams,

Thaddeus M. Wood, Nicholas Mickles, Joseph Forman, Joseph Swan, William H. Sabin, George Hall, Cornelius Longstreet, Caleb Alexander, Dirck C. Lansing, William J. Wilcox, Levi Parsons, Judson Webb, Jasper Hopper, Gordon Needham, James Geddes, Daniel Bradley, Benjamin Sanford, Jacob R. DeWitt, Oliver R. Strong, Jacobus DePuy. More than one-fourth of these original trustees were graduates of eastern colleges.

A charter was applied for as soon as the funds were subscribed, but it was not granted until April 20, 1813, after considerable correspondence between the subscribers, the Board of Regents and Governor Tompkins. The institution was endowed by the State with a gift of land from the Literary Fund of the Board of Regents. In the meantime the school had been opened by Mr. Alexander in September, 1812, in the Lancastrian school house which had been erected in Onondaga Valley in 1809. That building is still standing.

The courses of study arranged by Mr. Alexander give evidence that the Onondaga Academy was designated for a high grade college. In addition to the Lancastrian department, as it was called in those days —which required the older and more capable pupils to act as monitors in taking charge of the younger ones, resulting in what is now known as the system of monitorial government—there were to be the regular Freshman, Sophomore, Junior and Senior classes; and the studies prescribed for each class were closely modeled after the Yale College curriculum.

One of the important features of the Lancastrian system of education was object teaching, as now used in kindergarten schools; and another feature was teaching the rudiments of handicraft, now known as manual training, and in some instances teachers were trained somewhat after the manner of the present normal school methods. The kindergarten features were dropped after two or three years, but the system of governing through the agency of monitors, commonly called "spies" by the pupils, was not entirely extinct as late as 1862.

In October, 1813, orders were given for the erection of an academy building, seventy-four by thirty-four feet. Building operations were commenced that winter, the contractors being two brothers, Moses and Aaron Warner; but the house, which was made of stone, was not ready for use until the spring of 1815, and not entirely completed until the middle of 1816.

A belfry was added at an additional cost of $30, and the tin on its roof shone like silver, being visible many miles distant. It became a favorite trysting place for the students, and many names and initials are carved upon its woodwork. The belfry was constructed to receive a bell which had been bought in Albany and brought to Onondaga Valley on a freight wagon. The bell was presented to the Academy by Joshua Forman, and the same old bell is still in service.

That belfry, which possesses many associations dear to the graduates of this historic academy, came near being fatal to the building, for one night it was found to be in flames. Two young men, mischief-loving fellows, boarded at the time with Lewis H. Redfield, learning the printer's trade and attending school. They saw the fire and heroically put it out. These young men were Willis Gaylord Clark, the renowned poet, and his brother, Lewis.

The first meeting of the Board of Trustees, after the granting of the charter, was held in the old school house April 24, 1813. Mr. Alexander was chosen President. Joseph Swan was chosen Treasurer, and he was the only one of the original twenty-two trustees that remained in the Board continuously from that time till the dissolution of the Board in 1866, and during a large part of that time he held the office of Treasurer, Secretary or President. Jasper Hopper was the first Secretary. Thaddeus M. Wood, a remarkably bright, though pugnacious, attorney, was one of the most active of the Trustees, and his aggressive personality impressed itself upon the policy of the young academy. It might also be added that much of the legal difficulties which hindered the progress of this academy in the early days, causing

several of the principals to sue for their salaries, was
doubtless due to Mr. Wood's fondness for indulging
in a law suit.

A committee was appointed at that first meeting,
consisting of Caleb Alexander, William H. Sabin and
Thaddeus M. Wood; to prepare a code of by-laws for
the government of the Board and of the school. The
rules are similar to those adopted by almost all the
early colleges in the country. They were very rigid,
and the strictest religious observances were commanded from the students. But in spite of the monitorial system of self-government there was very little
discipline, as the principal lived a mile away, man-
aging his farm (the Lemuel Clark place). Students
were detected in all sorts of offenses and brought to
trial. The first case recorded is that of Robert C.
Owen, whose offense was card playing. He was convicted and expelled. Who his accomplices were in
the game is not now known. It may be that Joseph
Smith, the founder of Mormonism, played with him;
for Joseph was at that time living at the house of William H. Sabin, as a sort of choring boy, and he was
much given to card playing and kindred amusements.

The dormitory plan for rooming the students,
adopted in almost all colleges, prevailed in the young
academy. When Mr. Alexander had shown himself
a poor disciplinarian, his salary was cut down from
$500 to $350, and finally his resignation was accepted

by the Board of Trustees. This was probably in
August, 1817, but the Secretary unfortunately omitted
the date from the minutes in which the event was
recorded. Mr. Alexander was at the next meeting of
the Board, elected President as usual, but in 1818 he
was defeated, and he never again attended the Board's
meetings. His seat as a trustee was retained till 1825,
when it was declared vacant by non-attendance.

Mr. Alexander was born in Northfield, Mass., July
22, 1755. He was graduated at Yale College in 1777.
How it happened that he came to Onondaga Hollow
is not known. Possibly it was through the influence
of the Presbyterian pastor there, the Rev. Dirck C.
Lansing, who married his daughter. Mr. Alexander
died in 1828. His son, William H. Alexander, founded
the Alexander Iron Works of Syracuse, which business was continued by his son, William H. Alexander,
under the firm name of Alexander, Bradley & Dunning. That business is now carried on by William
D. Dunning.

Although the statement does not appear in the
records, possibly by design, there is abundant evidence
to show that the academy, as conceived by Mr. Alexander, was intended for a boys' school.

The courses of study, the rules and regulations,
the penalties, the absence of all allusions to sex and
the general sentiment of that day regarding the proper
sphere of woman all go to show that girls were not

expected to share in the benefits of the Onondaga
Academy. Although the movement for the advanced
education of young women was not then thought of
in this country, yet here in this valley, as early as
1816, girls were admitted to study in an institution
modeled after Yale College and intended as a rival to
Hamilton College. Mr. Alexander, a rigid, old-school
teacher, opposed the project, and so strenuously that
a compromise was effected. On September 14, 1815,
a committee was appointed to purchase a lot and build
a female academy and boarding house adjacent to
Onondaga Academy. The sum of $2,000 was named
as the limit of cost, and Mr. Alexander was directed
to solicit funds for the purpose among the "friends
of science," and he was to be relieved of a part of his
duties of instruction and allowed his traveling expenses. Nothing more was recorded of this project
except an item some years afterwards to the effect
that Mr. Alexander had sued the board for his traveling expenses and an allowance of $1.50 a day. The
first teacher employed in the female department was
Miss Otis of Troy; and she was succeeded by Miss
Ann Maria Tredwell, who afterwards became the wife
of Lewis H. Redfield. The distinction between the
male and female departments was retained till the
academy came under the control of the Presbytery of
Onondaga, but after the first twenty years it was
merely a nominal one.

After Mr. Alexander's resignation, the school was managed temporarily by the usher, Philo Gridley, who had been employed to reside in the building and preserve order, until the Rev. Samuel T. Mills was appointed principal. Then came Sylvanus Guernsey, probably in 1821; the Rev. Jabez Porter, who taught only a few months; and then, in 1824, Samuel B. Woolworth was appointed principal. During the principalship of Mr. Woolworth the courses of study were greatly revised, the old puritanical, inquisitorial code of government was set aside; and simple, sensible rules were adopted. During his six years of service he revived the reputation of the school in all parts of the country, and brought in a class of students that have made their mark in society.

The Rev. Edward Fairchild was the next principal from 1830 till 1831; J. L. Hendrick from 1831 till 1845. Mr. Hendrick was a man of many traits, eccentric, careless in his manners, good-natured, jolly, quick-tempered. More anecdotes are remembered of him than of any other of the principals. For the first two or three years of his term he was continually quarrelling with the trustees. There were quarrels about stoves, quarrels about stove-pipes, about the division of room rent fees, about his salary, about a garden for the principal. But all these matters were adjusted, and Mr. Hendrick became very popular. During his principalship the academy regained much of its lapsed prestige.

The Rev. George Thompson was principal from 1845 till 1847. About this time the academy was virtually passed over to the Presbytery of Onondaga, under the agreement that all appointments to the Board of Trustees or to the faculty should be made on the nomination of the Presbytery. The next principal was the Rev. Clinton Clark. The administration of Mr. Clark was signalized by the complete reunion of the male and female departments. James M. Burt was the next principal in 1847. He had a stormy term of three or four years, in which the whole community was scandalized by the rumor that some of the students had indulged in dancing and music. John Dunlap was the next principal in 1851.

Plans were made in 1852 for a new building, which was completed in 1854. In that year Mr. Dunlap was succeeded by Mr. Bennett; and then came in rapid succession Mr. Lindsley, Mr. Kellham, Mr. Phelps and Benjamin F. Barker, though probably not exactly in this order, for the records are confusing. Theodore D. Camp was principal from 1859 till 1864. He was succeeded by Jacob Wilson, during whose administration the academy was transferred to the Onondaga Free School District to be managed by a Board of Education chosen by the people. This was in 1866.

The last meeting of the academy trustees was held on the 12th of May, 1866, and the proposition to turn over the property of the corporation to the new school

district on condition that the latter assume the debt
of $2,500 upon it was adopted unanimously. The
trustees were glad to be relieved of their duties.

William P. Goodelle was principal from 1866 to
1868, excepting about one month in 1867, when Isaac
Bridgman was principal; then came Wheaton A.
Welch from 1868 to 1874; Mr. Harrington in 1875;
O. W. Sturdevant from 1875 to 1887; E. D. Niles till
1892; and A. W. Emerson till 1893. The present
principal is David H. Cook.

The Onondaga Academy has graduated about 7,000
persons, a large portion of whom have led prosperous
and honored and eventful lives. A large number of
the residents of Syracuse received their early education in this institution, and their commencement
exercises were for many years a great social event,
attracting many of the graduates and a large number
of the residents of this city. The academy has passed
through many vicissitudes of fortune, encountering
adverse criticism, neglect on the part of its trustees
and faculty and graduates and students, surviving
many periods of financial discouragement, and yet
presents at the present time a healthy and prosperous
appearance. It ranks to-day among the best academies
in the State.

CHAPTER XVI

FIRST SETTLER IN THIS COUNTY

Ephraim Webster, the first white person who made a permanent settlement in Onondaga county, was a very remarkable man. It was through his friendship and influence that Asa Danforth and Comfort Tyler, the pioneers in settling Syracuse, were permitted to settle in Onondaga Hollow in 1788. Many things have been written and told of him, but much of his history, preserved in tradition and print, is unfortunately more romantic than real. It is known that Mr. Webster wrote out the story of his life, abounding in adventures among the Indians; and there has been some conjecture as to what became of this manuscript. The story that was commonly reported, and which has been handed down in tradition, is that the author intrusted his manuscript to a young law student in Onondaga Hollow for the purpose of having it published in New York city; and that the young man, after returning from New York city, told Mr. Web-

(241)

ster that he had lost it while passing down the Hudson river.

There are several people now living in Syracuse who are the descendants of Ephraim Webster; and there are some old people among them who can well remember the generation that followed this early pioneer. The story which comes from them, and it bears strong marks of probability, is that Mr. Webster either sold or gave his manuscript to James Fenimore Cooper, the great novelist, who used it in writing the celebrated Leather-Stocking tales. The life and character of Ephraim Webster are very similar to those of Natty Bumppo, the hero of Cooper's Indian stories. In speaking of his hero, Mr. Cooper says in his preface to " The Deerslayer:" " He is too proud of his origin to sink into the condition of the wild Indian, and too much a man of the woods not to imbibe as much as was at all desirable, from his friends and companions;" though he also adds that "in a moral sense this man of the forest is purely a creation."

Mr. Webster not only won the friendship of the Onondaga Indians, some time after they had ceased to be man-eaters, and the gratitude of the early settlers of this county, as was shown in the large grants of land given him, but he was very serviceable to the government of this State not only but also to the United States. The dates of Webster's birth and death and the dates of the writing of the Leather-

Stocking tales, the character and life of Webster and of Cooper, add strong probability to the statement that Webster was Cooper's guide through the forests of New York State and that he furnished valuable material to America's great author. Webster was born, according to the old family Bible, June 30, 1762, and died October 16, 1824. In "The Pioneers," the first of the series written, the Leather-Stocking is represented as already old and driven from his early haunts in the forest by the sound of the axe and the smoke of the settler. "The Deerslayer" should have been the opening book, for in that work he is seen just emerging into manhood. "The Pioneers" was published in 1822; "The Deerslayer" in 1841.

Mr. Webster is known to have been an eloquent man, for it was through his persuasive tongue that he frequently escaped death at the hands of the suspicious and jealous Indians. The following sketch of his life is from a manuscript in the possession of the Onondaga Historical Association: "I was born in the town of Hemsted, in the State of New Hampshire, and when I attained my twenty-first year, as the war was then raging between the colonies and the mother country, I enlisted into the army of the former for eighteen months and joined the regiment of Colonel Jonson, also from New Hampshire. We marched immediately for Lake Champlain, and on arriving in the vicinity of Ticonderoga the corps to which I belonged was divided into two bodies and stationed on each side of the lake which was here about three miles wide."

Here follows the story of one of Webster's feats, when, in company with another soldier, he swam across the lake to carry dispatches to the other portion of the troops.

"When the term of my first enlistment expired, I returned home and spent three months and then again enlisted under old Colonel Jonson and continued in the service till the close of the war. During the last part of my service I was stationed at Greenbush, and while there I formed an acquaintance with a Mohawk Indian by the name of Peter Yarn. Being desirous of learning the Indian language, after receiving my discharge I returned home with him, whose residence was on West Canada Creek. Here I spent three months without speaking a word of English during the time. Being now able to converse with the Indians in their own language. when the spring was fairly set in I went to the mouth of Onondaga Creek and commenced a very brisk trade with the Onondagas for furs and other articles of native merchandise. After three weeks' traffic, having accumulated a pretty good stock in trade I went to Albany, employing several of the Onondagas to accompany me to assist in transporting my goods.

"While in the city I learned from several persons

of importance, one of whom was General Schuyler,
that the British agents at Maumee and other western
posts were striving to induce the western tribes to
continue a warfare against the country and had also
sent an agent to the Six Nations to induce them to
unite in hostilities; and as to the agents that our
government had sent to treat with these western tribes,
they had slain one, bribed the second and frightened
the third away.

"Under these circumstances after some hesitation
I was inclined to enlist as an agent of the government under disguise to visit these western tribes and
ascertain how far they had been tampered with by
British emissaries. Having become somewhat of a
favorite among the Onondagas and neighboring tribes,
twelve hundred, principally Mohawks and Oneidas,
volunteered to accompany me, who pledged themselves
to bring me back in safety, or to fight in my defence
as long as a warrior remained. Partly under the pre-
tence of holding a grand council with the western
tribes and partly that of a general hunt, we visited
the different posts along the western frontier without
molestation or suspicion and remained nearly six
months in the country. As I could speak the Indian
tongue fluently and was dressed in the Indian style,
my companions had no difficulty in concealing my
true character by representing me as having been
captured by the French while a young child and

afterward purchased by the Mohawks and adopted into their tribe.

" In this borrowed character, by being constantly on my guard, I passed without suspicion and thus I had an opportunity of discovering the machinations of the English, which I communicated from time to time to my employer. At the end of six months, however, I was taken sick with a western fever and returned home with my companions. When the English discovered that their trickery had been discovered and communicated to our government, they were highly indignant against me and offered fifteen hundred guineas for my person or my scalp. They, however, no longer hesitated but signed the treaty of peace which included the western tribes that were in their particular interest. I now returned to my old station at the mouth of the Onondaga Creek, and resumed my business of trafficking in furs.

"The second year after my return, a Mr. Newkirk came into the country with two men in his employ, bringing with him two barrels of New England rum, five barrels of whiskey, a quantity of blankets, some red yarn, several dozen hawkbells, a large stock of small white beads. I soon discovered that he was a man of intemperate habits, his favorite beverage being hot flip, made in a cup manufactured from an ox-horn. As I discovered that his habits would soon make a finish of him if persisted in, I was anxious to talk with him on the subject. It was, however, a considerable time before I could find him sufficiently sober to listen to me, and then he very abruptly replied that 'God Almighty owed him a debt of fifteen hundred dollars, and he was determined to settle the account as soon as possible.'

"He continued about three months after this and died alone in his cabin in a fit of what would now be called delirium tremens, his men having left him some days before. With a slab of cedar shaped somewhat in the form of a shovel l dug a grave in a sand knoll near by, placing a slab at the bottom, two at the sides, with another to lay over the body, when the Indians, who had taken the liberty of staving the head of one of the casks of rum and drinking to their heart's content, gathered around in great numbers and manifesting their feigned sorrow in a manner that beggared all description, whooping, singing and weeping and dancing, they tumbled into the grave faster than I could drag them out, till finding it impossible to proceed any farther, while they were present, I finally hit upon the plan of advising them to go and get another drink.

"Approving of the suggestion which was so much to their own taste I was soon left alone, and in a short time I had completed my melancholy task. I continued still to reside at my old station and for several years carried on a successful trade in furs, ginseng

and other Indian commodities, till I was called again
into the service of the State by assisting in surveying
the military tracts, in which are now the counties of
Cayuga, Seneca and some other places. After this I
returned once more to Onondaga and settled on the
mile square of land that was confirmed to me for my
services among the Indians."

These words complete the main portion of the manuscript but to it has been added this paragraph: "Mr.
Webster lived several years on the above-mentioned
mile square as a prosperous farmer but still keeping
up a traffic with the Indians for furs and other articles
particularly for ginseng, which he prepared and sent
to the Chinese market. In the summer of 1822 or '23
he took a journey to the country of the Senecas with
a view of purchasing their annual stock of this article
when he was taken sick and died in his seventy-third
year. He was buried on the western bank of the
Tonawanda in the town of Pembroke, where his dust
still slumbers without even a stone to mark the spot."

The dates in this concluding paragraph are evidently incorrect, and doubtless arose from the fact
that the exact date of Webster's death was for some
time in doubt. It was in his sixty-third year that he
died. The old family Bible gives the date of his death
as October 16, 1824, which is doubtless correct. The
date also in the opening paragraph is evidently incorrect, as a reference to the history of the Revolutionary

war will clearly show, as compared with the old family Bible substantiated by a document referred to in the next paragraph. It is not surprising that at that early day a man who had lived so long among the Indians should have been somewhat remiss in his memory of dates.

From a paper in Webster's handwriting it is learned that his father, Ephraim Webster and Phebe Parker were married by Ebenezer Hay, December 21, 1752. His parents' children are thus given: Samuel, born at Chester, Rockingham county, New Hampshire, December 29, 1753; Phebe, born at Chester in 1756; Asa, born at Chester, April 25, 1785; Susanna, born at Hamstead in the same county, May 16, 1760, and died April 2, 1795; Ephraim, born at Hamstead, June 30, 1762; Parker, born at Hamstead, April 5, 1765; Mary, born at Hamstead, April 3, 1768; Sarah, born at Hamstead, April 20, 1770; Moses, born at Hamstead, October 27, 1772; Ebenezer, born at a place whose spelling looks like Neberry Coos, April 13, 1775, and died, he and his mother, May 1, 1775. There is a Newbury in Merrimack county, New Hampshire. Ephraim Webster was married the second time, to Sarah Wells of New Chester, January 8, 1778, at New Salisbury. There is a Salisbury, Merrimack county, New Hampshire, where the great Daniel Webster, son of Ebenezer Webster, was born in 1782. The statesman Daniel and the pioneer Ephraim were distant relations.

Ephraim Webster's children by his second wife were:
Ebenezer, born at " Neberry Coos," October 2, 1778;
John, born at " Neuburry Coos," September 8, 1780;
Henry, born at New Chester, March 11, 1784; Betsy,
born at Chester, May 31, 1786 and died July 12, 1788.
Ephraim Webster died at New Chester, August 18,
1803. aged seventy-three years, having been born May
24, 1730.

When Colonel Jonson raised his regiment in New
Hampshire in the fall of 1777, young Ephraim, then
15 years old, enlisted and marched immediately to
Lake Champlain, arriving at Fort Ticonderoga, which
General Lincoln vainly attempted to recapture from
the British. The surrender of General Burgoyne at
Saratoga, which occurred soon after, put a stop to
further campaigning, and Webster's regiment returned
to winter quarters. When the term of Webster's first
enlistment expired, he returned home where he spent
three months and then again enlisted under Colonel
Jonson, continuing in the service of the Revolutionary Army till the close of the war in 1783.

During the last year of the service, he was stationed at Greenbush, near Albany, and there formed
the acquaintance of a Mohawk Indian, whose name
was Peter Yarn. Webster, then 21 years old, did not
return home. There is a well authenticated story to
the effect that he had became disappointed in love ;
and believing that he had been deceived by one, he

lost confidence in all, and determined that he would forever abandon civilized life. He accompanied the Indian to his home on West Canada creek in Oneida county, and there learned to speak the Indian language. He finally located at Oriskany, where he became a successful trader, dealing in furs and other articles of native merchandise.

Webster was present at the great council, held at Fort Stanwix (now Rome) in 1784, at which a treaty was made between the Six Nations and the United States. The confidence which the young man had gained from the officers of the government and from the Indians is shown in his having been dispatched for the Senecas, who were slow in coming to the council meeting. He remained two years at Oriskany, and during that time made several excursions with the Indian hunters to Onondaga.

He became intimate and quite a favorite with the Onondagas and was invited by them to come and trade with them. Accordingly in the spring of 1786, he went to Onondaga with a boat load of goods, brought from Schenectady by water. A trading house was erected on the east bank of the Onondaga creek, then a stream of considerable size, near where it empties into the lake ; and there the stock of goods was exposed for sale. This spot was known by the Indians as " Webster's Camp," and it afterwards became known to the early white settlers as " Webster's

Landing." When he had accumulated a good stock of furs from the Indians, he would take them to Albany or New York.

Webster was generally accompanied in his trading expeditions by some white man ; but the most prominent traders with whom he became associated were Asa Danforth, Asa Danforth, jr., and Comfort Tyler, whom he met at their home in a small clearing in the town of Mayfield, in Montgomery county. A warm friendship sprang up between Webster and the elder Danforth, both of them having served in the Revolutionary war. The result was that Danforth with his family and Tyler settled in Onondaga Valley, May 22, 1788. This was the first permanent settlement by the white people, men and women, in this county. The ruins of the old Danforth home, located in the most fertile and picturesque part of the county in the immediate vicinity of Syracuse, are still standing.

And now the settlement at Onondaga Valley, then called Onondaga Hollow, began to grow. Other men with their families, many of whom became distinguished throughout the State, settled there. When the town of Onondaga was cut off from the town of Manlius in 1798, Webster was made the first Supervisor.

Webster was made a Lieutenant of militia whereof Asa Danforth was Lieutenant-Colonel Commandant, April 11, 1798, and Captain of militia, whereof Elijah

Phillips was Lieutenant-Colonel Commandant, January 22, 1801. He was also made Inspector of beef and pork for Onondaga county, April 8, 1803. He became a Justice of the Peace at Onondaga Valley in 1805. Webster made his home at Onondaga Valley, at a point up the Onondaga creek, easily reached by boat from Onondaga lake. He used the place called " Webster's Landing " for trading purposes only, that location being exceedingly unhealthy.

During the controversy with the Indians in the western part of this State, which so soon followed the Revolutionary war and which was instigated by the British, between the years 1788 and 1794, Webster was employed by the State to gain intelligence in the vicinity of the Miamis. He was fully successful in his mission, reported to the satisfaction of those by whom he was employed, and received suitable reward. He was often with the Onondaga Indians at Oswego, while the fort was retained by the British, and rendered valuable service to the State. He would dress as an Indian, and he eluded every effort by the British to discover his real identity.

So highly was he esteemed by the Onondagas, that he was early granted by them a mile square of land in the most fertile part of Onondaga Valley, extending westward from Onondaga creek and southward from a line a short distance north of what afterwards became the old Seneca turnpike road. This land, containing 640

acres, was finally granted to Webster by the Legislature in 1795 for the services he had rendered the State.
But Webster lost this property through indorsing the
paper of his friends. The Onondagas, to again show
their great esteem for him, gave him 300 acres,
bounded on the north by lands owned by Joseph
Bryan, Samuel Wyman and Abiel Adams, and on the
east, south and west by the Indian residence reservation. This gift was confirmed by a grant from the
State, January 14, 1823, according to the copy of the
document in the County Clerk's office, but in July 13,
1823, according to the deeds of this property afterwards recorded.

Webster established his homestead on the 300 acre
grant. The house was a very substantial building,
65 by 20 feet, two stories high, having hickory beams
and oak joists, mortised in the plate above and below,
and it was clapboarded with pine. The house now
owned by Munroe Mathewson, about half a mile beyond the poor house at Onondaga Hill, is very similar
in appearance and construction.

After Webster's death, the widow continued to live
there ; and after her death, the house became the
property of Mrs. Samuel A. Beebe, and then of her
son, Arthur Beebe, by whom it was transferred to
George W. Hunt. The house was located two miles
south of Onondaga Valley and one mile south of
Dorwin Springs. It was completely destroyed by fire
early Sunday morning, May 3, 1891.

Ephraim Webster was a kind, social and obliging man, mild in disposition, of excellent character, good, practical judgment and of an intelligence far above the average. He was absolutely without fear. He was often heard to speak of his wanderings among the Indians as the happiest days of his life. When he settled among the Onondagas he married an Indian woman, who died shortly afterwards. He married another Indian woman from whom he was divorced, as mentioned in a previous chapter. But he did not live with her "near twenty years" as stated in "Cheney's Reminiscences," since the old family Bible, now in possession of the Webster family, gives the date of his marriage to Hannah Danks as Nov. 19, 1796. When the white people began to settle around him, he married Miss Hannah Danks by whom he had several children. But Webster led an unhappy life with the Danks woman as his wife.

It is known that he left Onondaga for Tonawanda creek in Genesee county, and that he was buried in the Indian burying ground just west of the Council House where the Six Nations held their meetings. This was October 16, 1824. There is a quit claim deed recorded in the County Clerk's office, dated December 30, 1824, in which Lucius Halen Webster, a son of Ephraim, transferred to his mother his interest in the 300 acre patent from the State. When Webster went away, he did not intend to return. In the early part of the century, probably in 1803-4, he visited his old home in New Hampshire which he had not seen since he had left the army. It was supposed by his father's family that he had died.

Webster's body was removed from Tonawanda to the white cemetery on the Lewiston road, west of Alabama Centre in Genesee county, the transfer being made in October, 1831. That is the final resting place of the man who made an excellent character for Cooper's "Leather-Stocking Tales."

Ephraim Webster, by his second Indian wife, had a son Harry, who inherited much of his father's ability and character and who was Head Chief of the Onondagas. Harry Webster's sons were George, Richard and Thomas. Thomas Webster is now a chief among the Onondagas. The children of Ephraim and Hannah Webster were Alonzo, Lucius Halen, Iantha, Amanda and Caroline. The children of Alonzo, who was called Deacon, were Alonzo M., Hetty A., Ephraim, Orris, Rosetta Amanda and William. The children of Lucius Halen, a horse doctor, were Emeline, Caroline, Ephraim and Lucius Halen. The children of Iantha, who married Richard Beebe, were Samuel, Charles, Edwin, Wallace, George and Elizabeth. Amanda, who married Abiel Adams, had one child, Udora. Caroline, the youngest child of the pioneer, married Samuel A. Beebe, a brother of Richard Beebe. These Beebe brothers were both farmers and prominent men in Onondaga Valley. Samuel was at one time Supervisor. Arthur Beebe, the attorney of this city, is the only child of Samuel and Caroline, and he lived many years in the old Webster homestead. Hannah, the widow of Ephraim Webster, married Samuel Wyman, whose farm adjoined hers; and she died January 29, 1837.

Lucius Halen, generally called Halen, was Webster's eldest child by his wife Hannah; and he was named after Dr. Isaac Halen of Philadelphia. Dr. Halen was a great friend of Ephraim Webster and the two carried on quite a business in selling ginseng to the Chinese market. Ephraim would collect the root from the Indians and send it to Dr. Halen, who would ship it to China. It was while collecting this ginseng in the western part of the State that Webster was taken sick and died. After his death, and after the property had been divided by giving each child forty acres, Harry Webster commenced six ejectment suits in 1836 to recover possession of the 300 acres of land which his father had left; but his suits, which ran along for two years, were unsuccessful.

CHAPTER XVII

A CELEBRATED BOTANIC INFIRMARY

One of the early landmarks of this city, and one that was widely known throughout the State, was the Botanic Infirmary of Dr. Cyrus Thomson, located in Geddes, on the old turnpike road—now known as Genesee street—on the south side of the Erie canal. The Infirmary was a large, three-story, brick building, whose principal feature was the ten large stone columns, constructed after the Ionic style of architecture and made of stone brought from Vermont. Those stone columns were a great curiosity in the early days, as they were the first stone that were imported into this county; and it was considered a great waste of money, as Onondaga stone was abundant. It is said that an old inhabitant, who came from Vermont, when inebriated through strong drink and pining for his mountain home, would embrace those stony pillars with much warmth of affection, saying they reminded him of his childhood days as they too came from Vermont.

(258)

THE BOTANIC INFIRMARY IN 1844.—From an old wood cut.

There is some dispute among the old inhabitants of this city as to who built this old landmark. The records in the County Clerk's office show that Andrew Phares was granted by the State, September 19, 1827, a patent to lot 6, block 35 and block 69, "of the village of Geddesburgh." This landmark now stands on lot 6 of block 35. On January 3, 1829, Mr. Phares transferred the entire property to John Dodge, Asa Phillips, Amos P. Granger, James Harris, administrator of Gordon Newton, deceased, Elijah W. Curtis and James Tuttle for $1,600. Mr. Phillips "of the town of Granby, Oswego county," sold his interest to John Dodge "of Salina" for $100, December 13, 1829. Mr. Tuttle "of Camillus" sold his interest to Mr. Dodge "of Salina" for $22.55, April 3, 1830. Messrs. Harris, Granger and Curtis sold their interest to Mr. Dodge "of Elbridge" for $300, June 4, 1831. This left the entire property in the name of Mr. Dodge, who was then evidently living in Elbridge. All of these men were prominent and influential.

In October, 1831, Mr. Dodge gave a mortgage for $3,000 on the property to Jirah Durkee of Watervliet, Albany county. This mortgage was assigned to Rutger B. Miller, August 13, 1832, and by Mr. Miller to Chauncey Rowe, December 6, 1833. The mortgage was foreclosed November 22, 1834, in the suit of Mr. Rowe against John Dodge, William H. Alexander, Silas D. Camp, James Johnson, Barnhardt Nellis,

William T. Richardson, the president, directors and company of the Bank of Auburn, Ralph Clark, Charles Williams, George Brinley, William C. Stimson, Henry Bassett, the president, directors and company of the Steuben county bank, and Lemon Smith. The next record in the County Clerk's office shows that the property was sold at public sale, held at the Syracuse House July 16, 1835, by Chester Hayden, Master in Chancery, to Cyrus Thomson for $3,350.

By some of the old inhabitants, it is said that John Dodge built the building, and that he raised the mortgage with this object in view ; and that his purpose was to use the building for a hotel and general stores in supplying the canal trade. But Thomas G. Alvord, who has been closely identified with what is now Syracuse since 1833, and whose memory is excellent, says he knows that Dr. Cyrus Thomson built the building, since he himself was present when it was being built. Mr. Alvord says that the firm of Clark & Alvord, composed of Elizur Clark and Thomas G. Alvord, sold a large amount of lumber to Dr. Thomson, and he thinks this lumber went into the building. According to Mr. Alvord, this old landmark was built by the Doctor in the early '40's for an infirmary, but it was not so used many years, as the business was not very successful. The building was used for a hotel, after Dr. Thomson had ceased to use it for an infirmary.

Dr. Cyrus Thomson is remembered as a very

eccentric man, rough and uneducated, though possessing considerable natural ability, shrewd, a close observer, and fond of telling amusing anecdotes. He was the son of Samuel Thomson, the founder of the Thomsonian system of medicine, and was born January 20, 1797, in Alstead, New Hampshire, where his father was also born. His father and grandfather were farmers in his younger days, and he was raised as a farmer boy.

When he became 21 years old, he had saved $40, and concluded to try his fortune in the far West. He started for Ohio, a distance of 600 miles, on foot, in the company of four other men. He located in Ohio, and in the following year returned to Boston ; but shortly afterwards started again for Ohio. In January, 1820, he arrived at Fabius, Onondaga county, where he called upon Ephraim Rue who had been practicing after his father's system for three years. Young Cyrus and Rue got into trouble in their irregular practice of medicine, and February 8, 1821, they were subjected to a trial and were imprisoned. But Cyrus succeeded in procuring bail of $1,600. His father advised him to remain at the seat of his persecution and continue his practice.

Cyrus Thomson and Miss Maria Mayo were married in Bridgeport, Madison county, March 27, 1823, and shortly afterwards they settled in Geddes, Onondaga county. The Doctor observed of this county:

"Perhaps no other county in the Union is better adapted to the wants and prosperity of mankind than the county of Onondaga." A letter from his distinguished though eccentric father, dated Madison county, New York, July 26, 1823, says that Samuel Thomson of Boston, Mass., authorized Cyrus Thomson to act as his agent in selling his medicines and to become a member of the Friendly Medical 'Botannack" society; the agreement lasting two years.

The young man was very successful in making money through what was termed his irregular methods of practicing medicine. He was frequently arrested and fined, but always made it a point to prescribe for such patients only as were likely to recover, saying it was the best way to elude the law as he could then show that few if any of his patients died from his treatment.

This botanic treatment, called the Thomsonian system, was founded by Samuel Thomson, who claimed to have " discovered the fatal error of Allopathy—the doctrine that irritation, fever and inflammation are diseases." Samuel wrote in his book published in 1825 : "Our life depends on heat ; food is the fuel that kindles and continues that heat ; heat I found was life, and cold was death, and that all constitutions are alike," meaning in regard to their anatomy and physiology, their powers and their wants.

The usual medicines prescribed by Dr. Cyrus

Thomson were lobelia, or Indian tobacco ; hot drops No. 6, composed of undistilled whiskey, gum of myrrh and cayenne pepper ; and sweating. The treatment was very heroic ; and, if the patient's constitution was strong enough, it was almost sure to drive from the stomach almost every form of disease. The Doctor distilled his own herbs, which were many and all found by him in this county. His reputation extended far and wide, and many sick people came to him for treatment.

The Doctor's principal practice, and the one in which he made his fortune, was in selling his medicine through his agents and in traveling about the country, prescribing for all forms of disease. There are many of the older people who can well remember this eccentric Doctor, and his invariable prescription of "hot drops No. 6." Many people were doubtless benefited by this kind of medicine, which was very severe in its effects upon the body, but it would hardly be popular in these more enlightened days. As already stated, the Doctor had accumulated sufficient money in 1835 to purchase the land, which is finely located ; and in the course of a few years he erected the building for an infirmary. The building was covered with signs in large letters. One of those signs read : " The Lord has caused medicines to grow out of the earth and why should man despise them ? "

When the canal was enlarged a part of the eastern

side of the building was cut off, thus giving the Doctor a claim for damages against the State. Testimony was taken June 30, 1858, on an award of $2,203.57 given November 9, 1852. The claimant had appealed to the Canal Board, and April 12, 1854, the case was sent back. The next award was $4,000. On April 2, 1860, a total award of $6,520, including interest of $2,520 for the nine years, was given the Doctor, who, during all this time, had left the eastern side of his building unfinished and open, exposed to all kinds of weather.

Dr. Thomson received his diploma to practice as a Thomsonian Botanic physician in this State from the Thomsonian Medical Society of the State of New York June 14, 1837. The Doctor became one of the rich men in his day, owning considerable real estate, bonds and mortgages; but he allowed his property and his business to slip from him, when he found that his sons, Cyrus and John, would not continue his calling. In the early part of the '60's he almost ceased to practice medicine, refusing the many urgent appeals made upon him. His wife died March 23, 1836, and the following year he married Miss Emeline Morse, with whom he lived twenty years. His third wife is still living.

In 1865 he transferred an undivided half of the property in question to Maria E. Thomson, his daughter by his second wife, and in 1867 he transferred the other undivided half to his son, John Thomson.

THE BOTANIC INFIRMARY.—From a recent photograph.

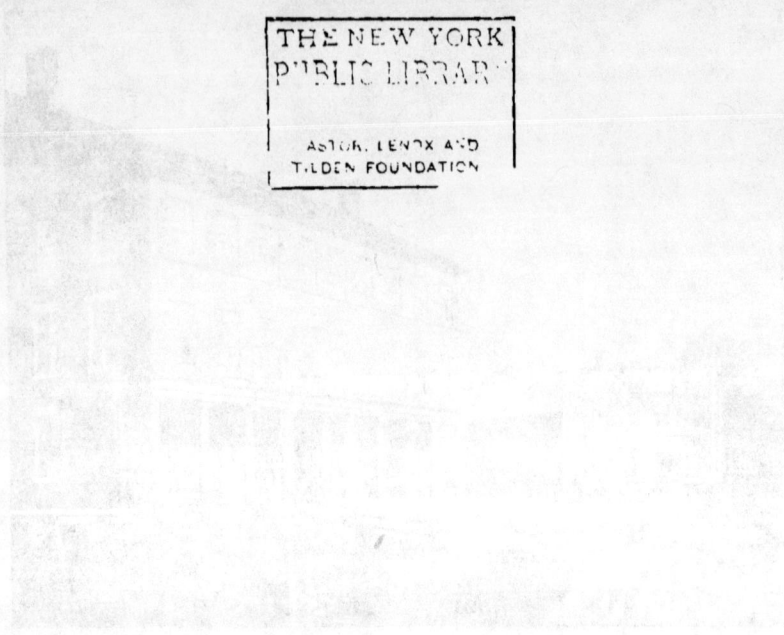

Maria, who married Robert Brown, transferred her interest to John, April 13, 1868. John died September 19, 1868, leaving the property to his wife, Sarah M. Thomson, who purchased the inherited interest from her son, Frank H. Thomson, when he became of age.

Dr. Cyrus Thomson died August 13, 1867, at Bardolph, Ill., where he had gone on a visit to his son Cyrus, who is still living. The doctor is remembered as a most eccentric individual, but he knew how to coin money by humbugging the people. The Thomsonian system, which once enjoyed great prosperity, is no longer practiced, except in a limited manner by irregular practitioners.

One of the Doctor's books was entitled "Learned Quackery Exposed; or Theory According to Art, as Exemplified in the Practice of the Fashionable Doctors of the Present Day," and compiled by Cyrus Thomson and published by Lathrop & Dean, printers, Syracuse, 1844. Among the expressions found in the pamphlet are the following: "Whenever an individual presumes to differ from the opinions of the Medical Faculty of the present day, he is sure to be persecuted and ridiculed and misrepresented. But all this persecution has no other effect than to open the eyes of the people to their situation.

"Truth is abroad in the world, and the spirit of inquiry has gone forth, and the day has arrived when men of learning and genius are neither afraid nor

ashamed but are proud to avow themselves Thomson-
ians, of the Thomsonian school, which has extended
its influence through every section of our country
from Maine to Georgia, and from the Atlantic to the
western wilds. and will continue to spread 'till the
name of Thomson is resounded throughout the world
from the equator to the poles.' The vegetable remedies, which the God of nature has scattered with a
lavish hand over every hill and valley of our country
must and will eventually entirely supersede the use
of mineral poisons. Thousands have been hurried to
an untimely grave by the use of these poisons, when
simple vegetable remedies would have relieved and
cured them almost immediately.

"According to this system, the stomach is the
grand reservoir from which all parts of the body are
nourished, and by proper food well digested, warmed,
enlivened and invigorated. While the stomach is in
a well-regulated state, the whole man is in perfect
health. When through cold, carelessness in diet, or
whatever course, the stomach becomes disordered, the
food is not properly digested, and the whole man
becomes diseased. Now, a medicine is wanted to
create an internal heat to remove obstructions, to expel
the cold from the system, and restore the digestive
powers, and then the stomach resumes its office, the
food nourishes and strengthens the body and the man
regains his health and strength.

"Shall man, when he is acting for the good of his fellow man, be persecuted because the course he is pursuing in the practice of medicine is well calculated for the relief of suffering humanity? No; forbid it Heaven! Forbid it Justice! Let the spirit that is abroad in the land, the elder brother of freedom, * * * put an end to the reign of the Medical Faculty and invest all their gloomy subjects with the rights and illuminations of the Thomsonian system of practice.   If this pamphlet shall produce the effect to open the eyes of one man or woman and start a train of thought which shall lead him or her to flee from the lancet and the poison of the apothecary shop, the author will feel himself amply repaid for the trouble and expense of presenting it to the public."

The pamphlet consists mostly of poetry, showing how the medical faculty is killing mankind by administering calomel, mercury, arsenic, opium, physic, blisters and lance.   There is a long poem on "Three Crafts," described in long metre to the tune of "False Are the Men of High Degree." The burden of the song is this:

> " The nests of college birds are three.
> Law, Physic and Divinity ;
> And while these three remain combined.
> They keep the world oppressed and blind. "

There are many examples given of the fate which befell those who persecuted the Thomsonian practitioners. The following verse is the lament of a

"learned M. D." who tried very hard to have a
Thomsonian indicted by the Grand Jury for not prescribing the drugs used by the "regular faculty" man:

"Where'er I have met them, I've found a repulse,
Too dreadful to mention: I'm almost convulsed:
I thought I should conquer, the laurel should wear,
But the thought of my fortune I hardly can bear.
I found me afflicted with a sore disease,
Which took off my child, my wife did not please.
She often distrusted my honor before;
She caught me too sleek by the meal on the floor."

And then there is "A Remarkable Vision" which
came to Dr. Cyrus Thomson "while in silent repose
upon his bed." The apparition, clothed in a long
white garment, said his name was Deception, the
representative of many who kill their patients by
deadly weapons, such as arsenic, mercury, quinine,
opium, nitre, lancet and knife. The dream caused
some serious reflections in the Doctor's mind. He
said to himself: "If arsenic, mercury and nitre are
in their nature poison, can they in the hands of a
physician be medicine? If when taken by accident,
these things kill, will they cure when given designedly?
Does not mercury go to the same part of a man when
taken by accident as when given by the doctor?"

There is another long poem called "A new Song,
composed by the Friendly Botanic Society." The
following verses describe the principles of the Thomsonian system:

" 'Tis now my object to unfold,
   In a brief way to you,
My system, or the gen'ral rule,
   Which you must keep in view.

" See when the patient's taken sick,
   The coldness gained the day,
And fever comes as nature's friend,
   To drive the cold away.

       *   *   \#   *   *

" The body now has lost its fire,
   The water bears the sway ;
Quick must the air be rarified,
   Or it will turn to clay.

" Then place the patient in a room,
   A lively fire prepare;
And give him Nos. one and two,
   As warm as he can bear.

" And place his body o'er a steam,
   With hot stones from the fire,
And keep a blanket round him wrapped.
   To shield him from the air.

 · The body now receives the heat,
   To overpower the cold :
If there be inward fire,
   Life will the vic'try hold.

" But if there is no inward heat,
 , For you to kindle to,
Then all your labor is in vain,
   You must bid him adieu."

There is an ode to Lobelia, a seed which the Creator has

> "strewed on hills and plains,
> To ease mankind of gripes and pains."

The pamphlet closes with "Lines on the Thomsonian System," written by a patient at the Infirmary. This eulogistic poem concludes thus:

> "The spark is struck that shall illume the world,
> The sacred banner of the Truth unfurled.
> Thomson appears—upreared by nature's hand,
> A second Luther—sent by God's command;
> Poor and unlearned, untutored from the farm,
> To pluck from trampled herbs, a healing balm,
> Though 'all the powers of darkness' storm and rage,
> A ruthless war against the system wage,
> 'Tis vain—the day is past—Truth's sacred light
> Shall banish error to the shades of night."

THE JERRY RESCUE BLOCK.—From a recent photograph.

CHAPTER XVIII

THE JERRY RESCUE

The rescue of the fugitive slave Jerry, in the fall of 1851, was probably the most stirring event in the history of Syracuse. This city was at that time a busy, active place of some twenty-five thousand inhabitants. The citizens were intelligent, cultured and very patriotic. Public meetings in the Town Hall for the consideration of public questions were common. To be sure, in the early days of the immediate emancipation movement, those who came to Syracuse to propound abolition had met with a reception which literally made them feel "at home;" cabbages and more offensive missiles had been showered upon the speakers by an excited audience, and the meetings had been broken up. But far sooner than in most places, William Lloyd Garrison and his friends, on the one hand, and Gerrit Smith and his friends, on the other, persuaded the people in Syracuse to listen quietly to their pleading. Some converts were soon made, especially by the less radical wing,

(271)

led by Gerrit Smith. When the Rev. Samuel J. May, the ardent abolitionist and admirer of Garrison, took charge of the Unitarian Church in 1845, he found the ministers and many of the members of the orthodox Congregational Church, as well as the Unitarian, were decided abolitionists; and several members of the Presbyterian, Methodist and Baptist Churches openly favored the great reform.

When the "underground railroad" was started, Syracuse became a favorite "station." Two colored clergymen, the Rev. J. W. Loguen and the Rev. S. R. Ward, were at the head of this movement. They found a ready and willing helper in the Rev. S. J. May. Mr. Loguen's house, located at the northeastern corner of East Genesee and Pine streets, was used as the stopping place for the poor fugitives on their way to Canada. Several of the leading bankers and business men always stood ready to contribute funds and ask no questions. Hotel keepers complained because Southerners were learning by experience that Syracuse was not a safe place to visit with a retinue of slaves. The trustiest negro was apt to be persuaded by some one of his moral duty to escape from bondage during the night; and next morning his master would leave, swearing to go to some other town next time he had to stop in the North. Not a few negroes preferred remaining in Syracuse to continuing on to Canada. The Syracuse directory for 1852 gives the names of ninety-seven negroes at the end of the book in a separate list headed "Colored Persons." There were probably more than this in the city, and the greater part were escaped slaves.

Such was the condition of the city when, on the 18th of September, 1850, Millard Fillmore, President of the United States, signed the Fugitive Slave Bill. The "monstrous" provisions of this law caused great indignation among the abolitionists of the North, and in many cases the resentment spread to the less radical members of the more liberal communities.

In a few places public indignation meetings were held. What place could be more fitting for such a meeting than Syracuse? All the city papers printed a notice, calling "the citizens of Syracuse and its vicinity, without respect to party," to meet in the City Hall on the 4th of October at early "candle lighting," "to make an expression of their sense of the act of the present Congress," known as the Fugitive Slave Law. This notice was signed by nearly twenty names, some of them being those of men never identified with the abolition movement.

On the day appointed, the City Hall was filled to overflowing with men whose party scruples had at least been overcome by their sense of justice. The Mayor of the city, Alfred H. Hovey, presided, and the following prominent citizens were elected vice-presidents: E. W. Leavenworth, Horace Wheaton,

Jason Woodruff, Oliver Teall, Robert Gere, Lyman Kingsley, Hiram Putnam and Dr. Lyman Clary, who was the only one among them previously known as an active abolitionist. A set of thirteen resolutions was passed with but one dissenting voice.   J. H. Broad, a young Democrat and a lawyer, made a speech in favor of upholding the law; but the speech was received in silence.

The resolutions referred to the Fugitive Slave Law as "a most flagrant outrage upon the inalienable rights of man and a daring assault upon the palladium of American liberties;" they called upon the people to read the law "in all its details, so that they may be fully aware of its diabolical spirit and cruel ingenuity, and prepare themselves to oppose all attempts to enforce it;" they "recommended the appointment of a vigilance committee of thirteen citizens, whose duty it shall be to see that no person is deprived of his liberty without due process of law." The names of the vigilance committee as announced were: C. A. Wheaton, Lyman Clary, V. W. Smith, C. B. Sedgwick, H. Putnam, E. W. Leavenworth, Abner Bates, George Barnes, P. H. Agan, J. W. Loguen, John Williams, the Rev. R. R. Raymond and John Thomas.

The meeting was adjourned till the 1st of October. During the week the "Friends of the Union" had opportunity to get themselves together if they could, but the public sentiment against the new " Law " was too strong. The second meeting was even more strongly enthusiastic than the first. Resolutions were passed declaring it to be "the dictate of prudence as well as good fellowship in a righteous cause that we should unite ourselves in an association pledged to stand by its members in opposing this law, and to share with any of them the pecuniary losses they may incur under the operation of this law;" and also that "such an association be now formed." Besides this, a petition for the repeal of the act was signed by a large number of people and sent to Congress.

In justice, it must be said that there was a sparsely attended meeting of the " Friends of the Union " men afterwards. This was presided over by Major Moses D. Burnet, but this counter-convention proved a failure and its officers deserted it.

The leaders in the abolition movement in the central and western parts of New York, most of them, belonged to the Liberty Party, at whose head stood Gerrit Smith. This party differed from the Anti-Slavery Party, whose stronghold was in the New England States, in that it claimed that slavery was unconstitutional; while the Anti-Slavery Party admitted its constitutionality, but preferred the destruction of the Union and the constitution to the continuance of slavery. This difference of point of view between the two parties, which were really working for a common end, often caused much bitterness of feeling.

When, however, the Anti-Slavery Party, in the spring of 1851, was denied a place of meeting in New York city, it was glad to accept the invitation of the Syracuse abolitionists to hold its meeting in this city. The convention was held on the 7th, 8th, and 9th of May, and was very successful.   Gerrit Smith and the Rev. Samuel J. May welcomed the society.   The resolutions unanimously passed by the society were as radical as usual.   One of the resolutions read: "That as for the Fugitive Slave Law, we execrate it, we spit upon it, we trample it under our feet."

The Liberty party itself had several local meetings in Syracuse during the spring.   The doctrines of this party, as announced in the resolutions adopted at its national convention in Buffalo on September 17, 1851, were: "That righteous civil government enacts no laws, enforces no laws, obeys no laws, honors no laws for slavery."   Resolutions were also then passed, declaring it right to oppose the execution of the Fugitive Slave Law.

There were a number of people in Syracuse, however, who pretended, at least, to admire law and order above all things, and to fear to hurt the rights of the South.   These "Friends of the Union" became alarmed at the great activity shown by the abolitionists, and to offset it they invited Daniel Webster to deliver an address.

Mr. Webster came on the ninth of June, and spoke to a large audience from the balcony in the *Courier* building, overlooking the square in front of the City Hall. He ended with these words : "Those persons in this city who mean to oppose the execution of the Fugitive Slave Law are traitors! traitors! traitors! This law ought to be obeyed, and it will be enforced ; in this city of Syracuse it shall be enforced, and that too in the midst of the next Anti-Slavery convention, if there shall be any occasion to enforce it."

There still existed the association, formed by many of those present, at the indignation meeting of October 4th, 1850. A rendezvous had been fixed upon, and it was agreed that anyone who might know or hear of a person in danger should toll the bell of an adjoining meeting-house in a particular manner. Two or three times in the ensuing twelve months the alarm was given, but the cause for action was removed by the time the members reached the rendezvous, excepting in one case, when it was thought advisable to send a guard to protect a threatened man to Auburn or Rochester. At last the time came.

Among the escaped slaves then living in Syracuse was a man named Jerry. His last name is in doubt. Some say it was McHarg ; some say it was McHenry. He was generally called simply Jerry ; and he was officially known as Jerry. In the winter of 1849–50 he entered the cabinet store of Charles F. Williston, who became the Democratic Mayor of the city in 1856, and was given employment in turning lathes. He was then about thirty years old, large of frame and very powerful. It was said that he had escaped from his master's plantation in Missouri. Jerry afterwards engaged in the cooper trade in the shop of F. Mack in the First ward. He was here alone one morning quietly at work when he was seized from behind, handcuffed and taken before the United States Commissioner, J. F. Sabine, upon the pretense that there was a warrant against him for theft. He there learned that he was arrested under the fugitive slave act. The Commissioner's office was in the old Townsend block, located in West Water street, between South Salina and Clinton streets.

Jerry was arrested on the first of October, 1851. The city was filled with visitors. An unusually good county fair, then at its height, had attracted hundreds of the farmers from the regions round about. And to crown it all the Liberty Party State Convention was in session at the Congregational church. A building now known as Convention Hall, located on the north side of East Genesee street, directly west of the *Courier* building, is standing on the site.

At the convention the State officers for the fall elections had just been nominated, when the ringing of the bell in the Congregational church brought everybody to their feet. The meeting was at once

adjourned, and the delegates went in a body to
Commissioner Sabine's office. Every church bell in
the city, save that of the Episcopal church, rang out
the alarm. The entire city was aroused, and the
people flocked to the Commissioner's office.

Meanwhile the trial was going on. Jerry had been
arrested by the United States Deputy Marshal Henry
W. Allen, on a warrant issued the day before for the
apprehension of a colored man known as William
Henry (in the warrant named Jerry), on the claim of
John M. Reynolds of Marion county, Missouri, represented by James Sear of Newark, Knox county,
Missouri. James R. Lawrence, United States Attorney
for the District of Northern New York, and Joseph W.
Loomis appeared as counsel for the claimant ; and
Leonard Gibbs of Washington county, who had been
attending the Liberty party convention, appeared in
behalf of the alleged fugitive.

Mr. Sear testified that he knew Jerry (pointing to
the alleged fugitive); became acquainted with him in
1820, when he first knew John M. Reynolds, and knew
Jerry till 1845; knew Jerry's mother, and if living she
was with John M. Reynolds or his father-in-law,
William Henry, in Marion county, Missouri; knew
Jerry's mother after his birth.

The sympathy of the crowd inside and outside the
Commissioner's office was clearly with Jerry; while
the case, as it stood, seemed to be clearly against him.

After the case had been adjourned at half past two for half an hour, that a larger room might be obtained, Jerry, acting upon the impulse of the moment, threw himself into the crowd, rushed down the stairs and into the street, and started on a run for liberty. The Marshal and his deputies tried to follow, but their path was made difficult. Although the crowd opened to let Jerry through and closed again when the officers tried to pass, the handcuffs so impeded the captured man's motion that he was overtaken before having run many blocks. Jerry was seized just as he was about to get into a carriage that would have carried him to liberty. After a scuffle which left his body bare and bleeding, with nothing left to cover him but his pantaloons and part of his shirt, he was thrown into the cart of a truckman, who had been pressed into the service. One of the Deputies sat on his body to keep him down; and thus he was driven through the streets to the police office and thrust into the back room. This police office was in the building, located on the northwestern corner of West Water and Clinton streets—a building now known as the Jerry Rescue block.

An excited crowd, a few ready to aid, the vast majority incensed against the officers, had followed them to the place where they arrested Jerry and back again to the police office. The ill treatment of the poor black man caused indignation in every breast.

Jerry was in a perfect rage, a fury of passion. The
Rev. Mr. May, at the request of the Chief of Police,
went into the little room where he was confined, and
after some difficulty succeeded in quieting him.

Meanwhile, the vigilance committee was preparing
for action. Soon after Jerry was taken to the police
office, Thomas G. White invited a few brave spirits
into the counting room of Abner Bates to settle
upon some plan of action for rescuing Jerry. The
men adjourned to meet at Dr. Hiram Hoyt's office at
early candle-light, and to bring with them as many
good and true and brave spirits as they could vouch
for. It was about dusk when one by one, and far
enough apart to disarm suspicion, some twenty or
thirty men sauntered into the office of Dr. Hoyt.

"It was agreed," writes the Rev. Samuel J. May in
his "Recollections of the Anti-Slavery Conflict," "that
a skillful and bold driver in a strong buggy, with the
fleetest horse to be got in the city, should be retained
not far off to receive Jerry when he should be brought
out; then to drive hither and thither about the city,
until he saw no one pursuing him; not to attempt to
get out of town, because it was reported that every
exit was well guarded, but to return to a certain point
near the centre of the city, where he would find two
men waiting to receive his charge. With them he was
to leave Jerry, and know nothing about the place of
his retreat.

"At a given signal, the doors and windows of the police office were to be demolished at once, and the rescuers to rush in and fill the room, press around and upon the officers, overwhelming them by numbers, not by blows, and so soon as they were confined and powerless by the pressure of bodies around them, several men were to take up Jerry and bear him to the buggy aforesaid. Strict injunctions were given, and it was agreed, not intentionally, to injure the policemen. Gerrit Smith and several others pressed this caution very urgently upon those who were gathered in Dr. Hoyt's office. And the last thing I said, as we were coming away was: 'If anyone is to be injured in this fray, I hope it may be one of our own party.'"

But this was not all that was being done towards a rescue. The court room overlooked the Erie canal on one side, while close by the door was a bridge. On either side of the canal, in front of the building, was a large open square; and this was filled with excited men, while many a woman could be seen here and there in the crowd as well as filling the windows of all the buildings overlooking this exciting scene.

The bridge spans made a most excellent place from which to address the multitude, and the abolition orators made the most of their opportunity. Samuel R. Ward, the colored preacher, spoke with all the earnest sarcasm, if not with quite the skill, of an Antony. He reminded the people that there was a

law on the statute books which flew into the face of
one of the first principles of the Declaration of Independence. Nevertheless, it was a law and all patriotic
citizens must obey it, though they might be ashamed
to hold up their heads afterwards; it controverted the
golden rule which they had all learned at their mothers'
knees, but it was a law and they must bow before it;
yonder locked in a room and awaiting the judgment
of his captors, was a man who had committed no
greater crime than to wish to breath the same air of
freedom with themselves. Yet the law said he might
be loaded with chains and carried away like a dog;
and the law was paramount. C. C. Foot of Michigan
and others addressed the crowd in similar strains.

The officials who had the arrest in charge became
alarmed during the afternoon, and tried to get the
militia out to keep order. Marshal Allen commanded
the Sheriff of the county, William C. Gardiner, to bring
the militia to his aid. Sheriff Gardiner could not do
this, but instead ordered Captain Edward R. Prendergast to get his company in order, ready for action if
needed. But there had, as yet, been not the slightest
breach of the peace, and the crowd had been remarkably well behaved, considering the excitement. The
news that the militia had been called out caused a general murmur of indignation in the city. This reached
the ears of Colonel Origen Vandenburgh, who at once
countermanded the orders of the Sheriff, which the

latter had no right to give. It might be added that Colonel Vandenburgh was the moving spirit in originating the scheme of the " underground railroad " in New York city. The police of the city, with the exception of a few who had been pressed into service of the government, were in sympathy with the general feeling. The United States officials, few in numbers as they were, were at the mercy of the crowd.

At 5 o'clock the examination of the prisoner was resumed. Hervey Sheldon and David D. Hillis appeared, to assist Mr. Gibbs in behalf of the alleged fugitive, and J. R. Anderson appeared to assist Messrs. Lawrence and Loomis for the claimant. The testimony of Mr. Sear was resumed; but before any progress was made Commissioner Sabine consented to hear the claim of the defense, that the prosecution should produce evidence that persons were legally held to service in Missouri. The excitement of the large and increasing crowd outside the office was becoming intense, and a number of windows in the office were broken by stones thrown against them. At 7 o'clock the Commissioner adjourned the court till 8 o'clock the following morning.

The crowd outside had become so excited that it was clear nothing but the rescue of Jerry could satisfy it. The rescuing party from Dr. Hoyt's office had just arrived on the scene, blackened like negroes and otherwise disguised; and they were armed with clubs, axes, rods of iron or whatever they could find. The windows were broken in, and the casements were attacked with axes and bars of iron; but so firm were the fixtures that progress was slow. Finally a timber about ten feet long and four inches thick was used as a battering ram. By the application of this powerful instrumentality, the casements were soon stove in, and nothing remained to the rescuers but to enter and overpower the police, who were retained to guard the outer door of Jerry's prison. The assailants now rushed through the apertures into the office, led by J. M. Clapp, Peter Hollenbeck, James Davis and others. At this moment, Ira H. Cobb and L. D. Mansfield, who had remained in the police office to look after Jerry, turned off the gas, and left the room in darkness. The partition between the rescuers and the victim was a strong one, and the door was locked. The axes and iron bars and other weapons were again used. Marshal Fitch partially opened the door and pointed his pistol at one of the rescuers. He received a blow on his arm from a rod of iron which broke the bones; and the pistol and arm fell down together. The Marshal, distracted by pain and fear, leaped out of the north window of the room onto the side of the canal, and thus escaped. The other officers opened the door and thrust Jerry into the arms of his friends, and thus escaped injury to their persons.

Jerry was received at the door by Peter Hollenbeck

and William Gray, both colored men and the latter a
fugitive slave. His body was mostly naked, being
covered only by tattered pantaloons and shirt, which
hung on him in rags. He was suffering from a
wounded rib and other bruises received by the harsh
treatment of his captors. His powerful frame was
perfectly helpless because of his shackles.

Jerry was taken in a sort of triumphal procession
through the great crowd of people to the Syracuse
House and thence to the railroad depot; but the mass
of humanity was so dense that the carriage to take
him off could not come to him. Several rescuers now
ran in opposite directions through the crowd, crying:
"Fire! fire! fire!" In a short time Jerry was left
alone with a few brave men, who lifted him, groaning
with pain, into a carriage. It was a long and wander-
ing ride that he took that night. He was finally taken
to a colored man's house in the eastern part of the
city, where his shackles were with some difficulty
removed. He was then clad in female attire and
taken to the house of Caleb Davis in Genesee street,
his rescuers not being willing to trust his colored
friends.

Jerry was too ill to be moved for several days.
Only five or six people knew of his whereabouts. It
was generally supposed that he was in Canada. Some
abolitionists got so incensed with Mr. Davis for his
denunciations of the perpetrators of the outrage on

law and liberty that they wanted to make it warm for him. A liberal reward had been offered for Jerry's apprehension, and in some way a faint suspicion was aroused in the minds of those most eager for his arrest, that he was still in the city. The roads were all watched. Four days or so after the "Rescue," Jerry was able to go forward.

The "article" could not, for obvious reasons, be forwarded by daylight, and night would not suffice to reach the St. Lawrence river. One night Jerry was hidden under some straw in a covered wagon, and driven rapidly towards the north. Some hint of his escape reached the ears of the "Patriots," and the wagon was instantly pursued by two or three others. There are numerous toll gates in the north part of Syracuse, along the Cicero plank road. Before the first wagon, they all opened like magic; but the drivers of the pursuing buggies never before encountered such stupid and sleepy gate-tenders. Two hours before Jerry left the city, Caleb Davis had driven over the route and left some money at every toll gate. Under such unequal conditions, the chase was very soon given up.

The next morning at day break, the fugitive and his friend drove into the barnyard of a Mr. Ames, a well-to-do farmer in the town of Mexico. Mr. Ames was a Quaker and an Odd Fellow. It was because he was an Odd Fellow and had been written to by a brother in the lodge that he received his visitors kindly, gave them provisions and shelter and speeded them on their journey, though, as he said, he was an old Hunker Democrat and had no sympathy with their kind of people. So the day was passed in the haymow, and a very liberal supply of food was furnished by the kind-hearted women of the family.

At dark, Jerry was driven to the house of a Mr. Clark, near Oswego. After some trouble and a delay of several days, the captain of a small vessel agreed to set sail after dark. By him Jerry was taken to Kingston, where he soon was established again in his trade as a cooper. In Kingston Jerry married; and according to all accounts he lived a happy and comfortable life there for four years, when he was taken ill and died.

As to just what sort of a man Jerry was, it is hard at the present day to learn. His friends, the abolitionists, praised him in the highest of terms. The "Patriotic" papers made him out the most worthless of negroes. Said the Syracuse *Journal* at that time: "We notice in all sections of the country the papers represent that Jerry was a very bad fellow, that he was a thief, etc., and had been in the penitentiary four times in this city. This, if true, would have very little to do with the merits and demerits of the Fugitive Slave Law or Jerry's rescue. It could not be expected that a man brought up thirty-five

years in the midst of slaves, where all the command-
ments of the Decalogue are set at naught, would have
a very nice sense of morals. Yet Jerry was not so
bad as many represent. His commitments to the
penitentiary all grew out of difficulties in regard to
the woman he was living with. He was never charged
or convicted as a thief or a robber."

If the more morally earnest men and women of
Syracuse took a high-minded satisfaction in the influence the "Rescue" would have upon the treatment in
the North of the escaping fugitives, the less intellectual
women were not above getting pleasure in trying to
torture the defeated United States officials in a very
feminine way. They carefully packed up Jerry's
shackles and sent them by express as a present to
President Fillmore. They presented James R. Lawrence, counsel for the Government in the Jerry case,
with thirty pieces of silver—three cent pieces—as the
price of betraying innocent blood. Many more similar
acts they performed.

The news of Jerry's rescue traveled throughout
the entire country; it became a National affair. In
the course of a week all the newspapers in New York
State and many beyond had published some account
of the "Jerry Rescue." By far the greater number
severely censured the entire proceeding, though but
one paper in Syracuse, the "Copperhead" *Star*, took
this stand. There was great indignation aroused.

The Albany *Argus*, the chief Democratic paper, said: " The recital of the outrages upon the law and its ministers at Syracuse will be read with mingled astonishment and shame. They are a reproach to the city where they were permitted, a burning disgrace to the State at large. This is the first instance of forcible resistance to the execution of the laws of the Union that has occurred in this State. It is the first instance where an armed mob has attempted, with or without success, to overcome a judicial tribunal by violence, to trample on the law."

The Washington *Union* seriously recommended that the city be placed in a state of siege by the army, and be declared out of the Union until it repented of its sins and manifested a disposition to return to its duty.

On the 15th of October, it began to look serious for the men who participated in the rescue of Jerry. Five men were arrested and taken to Auburn to be tried before Judge Alfred Conkling; and there was every indication that more arrests were soon to follow. The men arrested were Moses Summers, Stephen Porter, James D. Davis and two colored men: William Thompson and John Brown. A process was also served on Ira H. Cobb, but he was ill and unable to answer it.

The warrants on which these men were arrested charged them with "having aided and assisted a negro man named Jerry, alleged to be a fugitive from labor," to escape from Deputy Marshal Allen. The prisoners were therefore commanded "in the name of the President of the United States of America" to appear before the court. On the afternoon of that same day the case was opened. For the Government appeared James R. Lawrence, United States District Attorney, and for the prisoners, John G. Forbes, D. D. Hillis, and Q. A. Johnson. Bail to the amount of $2,000 each was provided for the three white prisoners, and to the amount of $500 for the colored men. George Barnes, W. E. Abbott and R. R. Raymond signed the bonds. On the 16th, Prince Jackson and Harrison Allen, two more negroes, were arrested and brought before the court.

Judge Conkling decided that it was "proper to presume that there is no testimony tending to fix upon the defendants the guilt of any higher offence" than that of "having unlawfully aided in the escape of an alleged fugitive from labor." The prisoners were held for the Grand Jury of the next United States District Court, to be held at Buffalo on the second Tuesday of November. Bonds to the amount of $2,000 for each of the four white men were signed by ex-Governor W. H. Seward, Lyman Clary, Oliver T. Burt, Henry Gifford, R. W. Washburn, George Barnes, W. E. Abbott, Abner Bates, John Ames, Hiram Putnam, E. W. Leavenworth, C. B. Sedgwick,

Samuel Mead, Hiram Hoyt, Daniel McDougall, Charles A. Wheaton, R. A. Yoe, Charles Leonard and Alanson Thorp. Similar bonds of $500 each, for the four colored men, were signed by ex-Governor Seward.

After the examination of the prisoners was over, Mr. Seward invited all the party who came from Syracuse in behalf of the prisoners, to his beautiful residence, and there entertained them delightfully.

The following is a list of the witnesses introduced for the Government by James R. Lawrence: B. L. Higgins, Joseph Williamson, Joseph F. Sabine, George A. Green, John W. Jones, Thomas M. Masson, Henry M. Baker, Emery Ormsby, Sylvester House, Henry Shattuck, Charles Woodruff, Edward Prendergast, Oliver C. Stuart, Henry W. Allen, Benjamin P. Kinney, William Baldwin, Paige Newton, Charles P. Cole, Alonzo Torrey, George Blair, Willard Johnson.

At the Buffalo United States District Court, true indictments were found against the prisoners held over by Judge Conkling, and also against W. L. Crandell, L. H. Salisbury, J. B. Brigham and Montgomery Merrick. These men all gave bail to appear before the United States District Court at Albany in January. Nothing of importance developed at the Albany court, and the cases were transferred to the United States District Court at Canandaigua.

At the time of the sitting of the court, Gerrit

Smith went to Canandaigua and addressed a large crowd in the open air, using such forcible arguments that no jury could be empanelled on which there were not several who had formed an opinion against the law. So Judge Hall let all the "Jerry Rescue Cases" fall to the ground forever.

At these various court sessions, only the cases of Enoch Reed, W. L. Salmon and J. B. Brigham, who had also been indicted, came to trial. The two latter were acquitted, and Reed died while waiting for an appeal from a conviction.

The men indicted were hardly fair selections. Most of them had nothing to do with the rescue beyond a little active sympathy. Although Gerrit Smith, Charles A. Wheaton and the Rev. Samuel J. May had published in the papers an acknowledgment that they had assisted all they could in the rescue of Jerry, the attorney did not see fit to bring any of them to trial.

H. W. Allen, the United States Deputy Marshal, and James Sear, the agent of the claimant, were arrested on warrants, charging them with attempting to kidnap a citizen of Syracuse. An indictment was found against Mr. Allen by the Grand jury of Onondaga county, but the prisoner was discharged by Judge Nelson before whom the trial came, on the ground that he had acted under the United States laws.

In answer to a call, signed by 800 citizens of

Onondaga county, a meeting of those who "respected law and order" was held in the City Hall, October 25, 1851. The meeting was called to order by Harvey Baldwin, and Moses D. Burnet was elected the presiding officer. The following vice-presidents were elected: B. Davis Noxon, Johnson Hall, Phares Gould, Miles W. Bennett, James Lynch, Lewis H. Redfield, Israel S. Spencer, Harvey Loomis, J. Stanford, John G. Forbes, Thomas Spencer, Rufus Stanton, Otis Bigelow, Hervey Rhoades, Daniel Kellogg and E. S. Phillips. The following secretaries were elected: W. H. Watson, Stephen D. Dillaye, Cornelius L. Alvord, Benjamin L. Higgins and E. C. Adams. The following committee on ordinances was appointed: George F. Comstock, John F. Wyman, W. M. Watress, Stephen D. Dillaye and Thomas T. Davis.

The resolutions adopted stated that the "citizens of Syracuse and of the county of Onondaga deeply regret the commission of the outrage upon the law, and would express our unqualified abhorrence of the monstrous transactions," and "we repel the accusation that any number of the citizens of Onondaga were engaged in the affair." This meeting was all the "law and order" people did to prove their strength in Syracuse.

For eight or ten years thereafter, on the first of October, there was held in this city a celebration of the Jerry Rescue. At first these celebrations were

largely attended ; but year by year the interest in
them died out and they were discontinued. In the
speeches delivered on those occasions, Syracuse was
declared the leader in the cause of resistance to
"oppression and unconstitutional slave law ;" and
ever since the civil war, Syracusans have been wont to
ascribe to the Jerry Rescue the beginning of effective
resistance to slavery in the North.

There was not another attempt made to execute the
Fugitive Slave Law in this part of the State. There
was perfect safety here for fugitive slaves. And
furthermore, the strength of the anti-slavery party
was increased not only here but far outside, by the
successful outcome of the affair. Syracuse was almost
the only city of any size in the North, where the
leaders of the anti-slavery faction had in their ranks
many of the leading business men, lawyers, physicians
and clergymen. But the distinguishing characteristic
of the "Jerry Rescue" is that the leaders carried
through the rescue, even in spite of the likely
acquital of Jerry ; because they wished to work a
moral effect upon the community. It was the work
of enthusiasts in the cause of "freedom to the negro,"
rather than of sympathizers with a negro about to be
returned to slavery.

CHAPTER XIX

MERCHANTS IN EXCHANGE STREET

As one approaches the city from Onondaga lake, coming along North Salina street, he is reminded by the old-fashioned buildings, now almost deserted, that a village which once gave prosperity to many enterprising merchants has almost passed away. The most picturesque of these old landmarks and the one that affects the imagination most vividly in portraying the commercial importance of Salina, when that village contained most of the wealth within the present limits of Syracuse, is the one lo ated in the middle of Exchange street, between North Salina and Park streets, and now adorned by a sign which shows that it was once used as a brewery by Dalton & Fleming.

This building was erected close to the Oswego canal, a short branch of which runs directly in the rear of the building, and then passes through an underground outlet into the canal, a short distance away. The construction of the building, which is made of brick, three stories high and containing three

THE WILLIAMS BUILDING.—From a recent photograph.

stores, shows that it was admirably adapted for carrying on a mercantile business. From the many signs painted on the north side, facing the canal, it is evident that grape wine was once manufactured there.

This brick block was erected in 1828, by Williams & Company, a mercantile firm composed of Coddington, Gordon and Frank Williams, the first two being brothers and the latter a cousin, who occupied the middle store. The store nearest North Salina street was occupied by Williams & Allen, and the one nearest Park street was occupied by Richmond, Marsh & Clark, composed of Thomas Richmond, George Marsh and Elijah Clark. Ira H. Williams, a brother of Frank, clerked for Williams & Company, and subsequently bought out the firm. He afterwards took into partnership John P. Babcock, the firm name being Williams & Babcock. This firm afterwards moved into Wolf street, where Ira H. Williams carried on business till about 1878, when he died ; John P. Babcock having died some years previously. Williams & Allen went out of business in the early ⋅ '40's, and they were succeeded by another mercantile firm composed of John O'Sullivan Lynch and his brother James, who continued in business for about ten years. Richmond, Marsh & Clark went out of business about the same time with Williams & Allen, and their store remained vacant for a number of years.

It should be stated that in 1825, when the middle

section of the canal was opened and when the cutting
of the lateral canal to the salt works in the same year
gave still further stimulus to the community, Free
street, between North Salina and Park streets, which
contained almost all the large mercantile houses in
the village of Salina, was entirely destroyed by the
cutting through of the Oswego canal. After the matter
had been discussed in the village a few years, a meeting
was held, April 28, 1828, and it was resolved to lay
out Exchange street, between Canal (now North
Salina) street, and Salt (now Park) street, fifty feet
wide and twenty-four rods long. William H. Beach,
Mathew VanVleck and John G. Forbes were appointed
appraisers. The street was named Exchange street,
as it was an exchange for the business portion of Free
street, which street extended from Lodi to Wadsworth
(now Seventh North) street.

This portion of Free street was simply placed nearer
to Wolf street, and parallel with Wolf street, so that
the business houses might be on the south side of the
canal. Exchange street then became the principal
thoroughfare for the village of Salina.

The only business of any importance at that time
not located in Exchange street was that conducted by
Thomas McCarthy, father of the late State Senator
Dennis McCarthy, who settled in Salina in 1808, and
won the foremost position as a merchant and salt
manufacturer. That store was located at the corner

of Free and Park streets, the canal having made a slight bend to the north before reaching it, thus leaving it on the south side of the canal.

Dean Richmond, who eventually became one of the leading railroad presidents in the country, was a merchant in Exchange street. Ichabod Brackett, who came to Salina about 1800 and who died in 1832, built a dwelling and store combined on the corner of Exchange and Park streets. Samuel P. Smith was a cabinet maker, probably the first of any prominence in Salina, and his store was also in this street and near Salina street.

Some of the other merchants were Noah Wood, whose son, Marshall Wood, continues to keep a store in Wolf street, Hezekiah Barnes, Jeremiah Stevens, Hunter Crane, Felt & Barlow and Crane & Risley. Almost all these merchants dealt in groceries, dry goods, boots and shoes, hardware, etc., such as are generally found in country stores; and nearly all of them were interested in the manufacture of salt. It will be remembered by all the old Salt Pointers, who were always ready for a fight and rather liked it than not, that Frederick Ganier kept a very fine restaurant in this street, in the golden days when Salt Point contained many rich young men.

Noadiah M. Childs, who is still living, was a merchant, prior to 1841, in the old block, built by Williams & Company. He was afterwards, when occupying the

Alvord building, in partnership with Miles W. Bennett, the firm name being Bennett & Childs. Almer Pierce, now living in Park street, was a merchant in the Williams building in the '60's. In 1869 the building was used as a brewery by William Kearney and John Fleming, under the firm style of Kearney & Fleming. That firm continued in business about two years, when Mr. Kearney sold out his interest to Richard Dalton. The firm of Dalton & Fleming continued the brewery business some three or four years. Dr. J. H. Turk, at one time the keeper of the pest house, was the next occupant of the building, he using it for making grape wine. H. A. Moyer, the wagon manufacturer, afterwards used the building, which had been purchased in 1876 by John Greenway for $2,600, as a storehouse. The two western stores were occupied in 1885 by D. H. Gowing, who continues there his business of manufacturing Rennet's extract used in the making of cheese.

In 1840, a salt company was formed by Dean Richmond, Ashbell Kellogg, Hamilton White, Horace White, Thomas T. Davis, Henry Davis, Lewis H. Redfield, John Wilkinson, Frank Williams, Gordon Williams and Coddington B. Williams. The purpose of this company, composed of these influential and rich men, was to form a monopoly and control the entire salt industry. The company started by giving fourteen cents a bushel for the salt, when the market price was eight or nine cents; and it took the entire product. The plan was to ship the salt to the West, and sell it at large prices in the rapidly growing States, far removed from the sea coast. The western head-quarters was Columbus, Ohio; and the company was there represented by Dean Richmond. The salt was shipped west and exchanged for wheat, which was shipped to the eastern market. But the company lost heavily on the salt and on the wheat. The country had not recovered from the disastrous panic of 1837; and there was a great stringency in the money market

Among the principal creditors of this salt syndicate were the directors of the Bank of Pontiac in Pontiac, Mich. Those were times when " wild cat " banks and " wild cat " business ventures prevailed extensively in the western States. The great depression in money matters caused all the banks in Michigan to fail. The Bank of Pontiac had as its principal asset the Pontiac railroad, which is now called the Detroit, Pontiac and Milwaukee railroad. The State of Michigan had loaned its credit in building this railroad. The salt company took the railroad in payment for its salt sold in that State. These heavy losses in the west wiped out the entire capital of the salt syndicate ; for not only did the banks in Michigan fail, but also in Indiana and Illinois and the surrounding States. The State Bank of Indiana was the only bank that stood up under the financial depression, though the State

Bank of Illinois had an existence, with large discounts on its money.

As the men who composed this salt syndicate of Salina were stockholders and directors in the Onondaga County Bank, the Bank of Salina and the Bank of Syracuse, the failure of this salt syndicate came near causing the failure of these earliest three banks. Thomas G. Alvord, acting as attorney for the three banks, spent the winter of 1841-42 in Lansing, Mich., and negotiated with the Legislature of that State for the purchase of the Pontiac railroad. The State had loaned a large part of its stocks to build the road, when the "wild cat" banks collapsed. Mr. Alvord succeeded in buying the railroad, which had cost $136,000, for $33,000. The road was then leased to Gordon Williams, and it was afterwards sold to him. It might be added that Dean Richmond afterwards went to Buffalo and engaged in the commission business; and that, like John Wilkinson, he eventually became a railroad king.

THE STATE SALT BUILDING.— From a recent photograph.

CHAPTER XX

THE SALT INDUSTRY

The old State building, located on the southeastern corner of North Salina and Exchange streets, and occupied for many years by the Superintendent of the Onondaga Salt Springs, is by far the most important landmark in the city of Syracuse ; for it was in that building the State government exercised parental control over the salt industry, to which this city owes its beginning and much of its prosperity and from which came a revenue that more than paid half the cost of the whole undertaking of building the Erie and Champlain canals.

The building was erected by the State government in 1828, when Exchange street was opened. The Salt Superintendent's office was in the extreme corner of North Salina and Exchange streets, and the Salt Inspector's office was in the southwestern corner of the building, opening into North Salina street. The Oswego Canal Collector had his office directly over the Superintendent's office, the entrance being in

(303)

Exchange street. There was another office on the ground floor, to which entrance was had from Exchange street, and was occupied by the Salt Inspector, but afterwards by Enos T. Hopping and Thomas G. Alvord as a law office.

This office was occupied by Mr. Hopping from 1830 till 1840. The partnership extended from 1835 till 1838. Mr. Hopping was appointed Brigadier-General of Volunteers by President Polk at the outbreak of the Mexican war. He died in 1844, in the Camp of Instruction at Mier on the Rio Grande, and his remains were brought to Salina, where they were buried with great honor. Mr. Alvord, who continues in the manufacture of salt and who is widely known as "Old Salt" for the great services he has rendered in protecting this industry, became Lieutenant-Governor of this State.

The property on which this building was located was originally purchased from the State by Elisha and Dioclesian Alvord in 1807, about the time of the laying out of Salina by James Geddes. In 1813 the Alvord brothers made a division of their property, and this property fell into the possession of Elisha, father of ex-Lieutenant-Governor Alvord. Mr. Alvord sold the property, which included the Alvord building, and extending from what is now the Oswego canal, along North Salina street, through Exchange street and half through the next block towards Wolf street, to William Clark in 1825. Mr. Clark conducted a mercantile business in the Alvord building. He sold to the village of Salina his interest in Exchange street, when that street was opened in 1828, and sold to the State, in the same year, the property where the State building is now located. The building continues in the possession of the State, but the Superintendent's office has been removed to the stone building in North Salina street, between Willow and Noxon streets.

In the upper part of this building on the third floor there was a public hall. The celebrated Hunters' Society, organized in 1836–37 for the purpose of aiding the "Patriot" war in freeing Canada from Great Britain and annexing it to the United States, for which project there was much sympathy in those days, held its meetings in that hall. About twenty-five or thirty men from Salina joined in the Canadian rebellion. The commanding officer of the regiment, which had its beginning in Salina, was General Von Schultz. and he was assisted by Colonel Martin Woodruff and Captain Stephen Bulkley. The regiment proceeded to Ogdensburg by the way of Oswego, crossed over the St. Lawrence river and occupied the windmill just below Prescott as their fort. They were attacked by the British army and defeated in the celebrated Windmill battle. The officers were hung at Port Henry in Kingston. Some of the "Patriot" soldiers were pardoned, and some ran away and escaped.

The first Superintendent of the Onondaga Salt Springs was William Stevens, whose appointment dated from June 20, 1797. He remained in office till his death in 1801, and was succeeded by Asa Danforth, after whom the village of Danforth was named, who was in office for five years. He was succeeded, April 8, 1806, by Dr. William Kirkpatrick, the father of the present William Kirkpatrick, and he continued in office till 1808, when, for the two following years, he became a member of the Tenth Congress. Then for one year each, 1808–10, T. H. Rawson, Nathan Stewart and John Richardson held the office. Dr. Kirkpatrick was reappointed Superintendent in 1811, and continued in office till 1831, an unbroken term of twenty years.

Then followed Nehemiah H. Earll till 1836; Dr. Rial Wright, father of the present Chief of Police, Charles R. Wright, till 1840; Thomas Spencer till 1843; Dr. Rial Wright for a second term till 1845; Enoch Marks till 1848; Robert Gere, father-in-law of Congressman James J. Belden, till 1852; Hervey Rhoades till 1855. Vivus W. Smith, the father of ex-Postmaster Carroll E. Smith, was made Superintendent in 1855, and continued as such to and including the year 1864.

It was during this period, in 1862, that the greatest yield was had from the salt springs in any one year in their history, the amount being 9,053,874 bushels.

It was also during this period that the superintendent's office was removed to its present location. George Geddes, son of James Geddes, after whom the village of Geddes was named, was the next Superintendent, continuing in office till 1871. Then came John M. Strong, the present Canal Collector, till 1874; Archibald C. Powell, with a temporary four months' occupancy by Calvin G. Hinckley, till 1880; N. Stanton Gere, the son of Robert Gere, till 1883. The present incumbent, Peter J. Brumelkamp, was appointed Superintendent in 1883.

Prior to 1797, the year in which the first Superintendent was appointed, when the manufacture of salt had reached 25,000 bushels, each person was a squatter, planting his kettles at the place most convenient to the shallow hole from which he first dipped, and afterwards pumped by hand, his salt water. From the very beginning of the use of salt water there had been local strife and contention about " prior rights." In order to settle these disputes, and at the same time to encourage and promote the manufacture of salt at the Onondaga Salt Springs, the first known sources of salt in the United States away from the sea coast, the State government created the office of Salt Superintendent.

The salt springs, known as the Onondaga Salt Springs Reservation, were purchased by the State from the Onondaga Indians by the treaties of 1778 and 1795.

This reservation includes the greater part of the present city of Syracuse; and of this large amount of land, comprising about 10,000 acres, almost all of which, excepting what is used in the manufacture of salt, has been sold to individuals, the State continues to reserve the right to any salt well which may be found on the premises.

In the early days of the salt industry, and for many years thereafter, the pioneers, however hardy and venturesome, were deterred from settling at "Salt Point"—the name by which Salina has always been known—in consequence of the low, wet, marshy lands, where the salt water was found, which were the hot beds of the most deadly miasmatic diseases. To each man brave enough to settle at "Salt Point," the State government gave for a term of years a salt lot, a store and house lot, a seven acre pasture lot and a fifteen acre marsh lot; and the manufacturer of salt was allowed to cut his wood from any part of the dense forests on the Reservation.

Most of the early settlers came from Connecticut; and they were either themselves soldiers of the Revolution or the sons of Revolutionary sires. They were as a rule, men of small means, unable to seek a market far from home. In return for the salt, they received from the farmers all kinds of farm produce. In this way almost every salt manufacturer became a country merchant. Free street, and afterwards Exchange street, where almost all the stores were located, would become filled with farmer's sleighs; and the village of Salina would frequently contain more strangers than the taverns and private houses could well accommodate.

On account of the marshy grounds and the poor roads through the forests, transportation was mostly confined to the winter months, when the snow would allow of better traveling. But gradually, as the forests became cleared and better roads were made, the trade of the merchants extended also into the summer months. As the salt industry increased and became more prosperous, the natural water-ways through the inland lakes and the numerous rivers afforded the venturesome trader an excellent means of transportation in batteaux and river boats. As early as 1799, salt was sold by Elisha Alvord in Detroit, while the stockaded town was still in possession of the British.

The canal with its enlarged and greater reach of territory, causing many thriving towns to grow up in the wilderness, greatly benefitted the "Salt Pointers," who became rich merchants and built for themselves beautiful homes on the fine elevated lands in Salina. And now that the low lands have been improved by drainage and cultivation, Salina will compare favorably, as a healthy location, with any other portion of the State. Then came the railroad, built shortly before the civil war, which has superseded the canal

and batteaux, as they superseded the wagon and
sleigh; and to-day three-fourths of all salt sent to
market goes by rail.

The Salina steam pump house receives the brine
from the DeWolf and Marsh groups, and forces it up
into the tower, whence the brine is distributed to the
various manufacturers of fine and coarse salt. The
first settlers obtained the salt water by dipping it
from shallow pits. As the demand for salt increased,
the pits were made larger and deeper, and the pump
took the place of the dipper and the pail. A well,
curbed with wood, was built nearly opposite this State
pump house, just across the side-cut canal; and it was
fourteen feet long, ten feet wide and twenty-five feet
deep. The salt boiler would climb a ladder to the
platform, elevated high enough to stand upon and
work with the handle of the pump, adjust his trough
and pump his required supply of salt water; and
returning to his work he would dip the brine from
his reservoir into his kettles. The hand pump was
followed by horse power, which has been followed by
steam power. The history of the progress of the
manufacture of salt may be read in the depth and
number of the wells which have been and now are on
the Reservation.

Engraved by J.C. Buttre

Joshua Norman

CHAPTER XXI

THE FOUNDER OF SYRACUSE

The biographical sketch of Joshua Forman, which appears in "Clark's Onondaga," is here reproduced in its entirety, since it is probably the most authentic account of this distinguished man's life and since the valuable history written by Joshua V. H. Clark has long since been out of print :—

Joshua Forman.—To give anything like a perfect biographical notice of this distinguished individual, would require a person more familiar with his public acts, more intimate with occurrences which transpired at the period in which he was most active, and one who knew better the public worth and private excellence of his character than the author. But as he, for a period of more than a quarter of a century, was a leader in the affairs of this county, and became identified with all the majestic projects of State policy, we cannot pass him by without an attempt to do justice to his merits.

Joshua Forman was born at Pleasant Valley, in

(311)

the county of Duchess and State of New York, the
6th of September, 1777. His parents were Joseph and
Hannah Forman, who, previous to the Revolution,
resided in the city of New York. Upon the breaking
out of the war and the approach of the British to that
city, Joseph Forman with his family retired to
Pleasant Valley, where the subject of this sketch was
born. At an early age he evinced a strong desire for
learning, in which he was encouraged by his friends.
In the fall of 1793, he entered Union College, at
Schenectady, and in due time graduated with honor.
Directly after his collegiate cause was completed, he
entered the law office of Peter W. Radcliffe of Pough-
keepsie, where he remained about two years. He then
went to the city of New York and completed his law
studies in the office of Samuel Miles Hopkins. Soon
after the close of his professional course, he was married
to Miss Margaret Alexander, a daughter of the Hon.
Boyd Alexander, M. P. for Glasgow, Scotland. In the
spring of 1800, Mr. Forman removed to Onondaga
Hollow, and opened a law office on the east side of the
creek, where he began early to manifest his public
spirit and enterprise. At the time he settled at
Onondaga Hollow, the village was mainly situated on
the east side of Onondaga Creek, and he, being desirous
of building up the village and of extending its
boundaries, soon located his father and his brothers,
John, Samuel and Daniel W., near the west end of

the present village, on the north and south road
passing through the same, and rapidly built up the
western part. This left a space in the middle, comparatively unoccupied. Here, Judge Forman soon
after erected a large hotel and afterwards a fine
residence for himself, which was occupied many
years after Judge Forman left the Hollow, by his
brother-in-law, the late William H. Sabin. He was
also mainly instrumental in procuring the location of
the academy, church, and two or three stores in the
same vicinity, before he removed from Onondaga,
thereby connecting the whole into one tolerably
compact settlement.

By his integrity and straightforward course in the
practice of his profession, he soon became distinguished as a lawyer, and by his talents and gentlemanly deportment he became familiarly known
throughout the country.

In 1803, William H. Sabin joined him as a partner
in the practice of law, and for several years they did
an extensive business. The subject of the Erie canal
became a theme of deep interest to several of the
leading men of Onondaga, and to none more so than to
Judge Forman. Conversations were held by those who
were friends to the project, and measures were early
taken to bring the great question before the public.
Mr. Forman's talents as a public speaker, and as a man
of influence and character, eminently distinguished

him to be the individual who should be foremost in
moving in the matter. Accordingly in 1807, a union
ticket was got up, headed by John McWhorter,
Democrat ; and Joshua Forman, Federalist. This
ticket was carried with trifling opposition. It was
headed "Canal Ticket," and as such received the
cordial support of a large majority of the electors of
Onondaga county.

As was anticipated by the friends of Judge Forman
and the great work which he was designated to advocate, he brought forward the ever memorable resolution in the House of Assembly, which alone would
render his name immortal, directing a survey to be
made "of the most eligible and direct route of a canal,
to open a communication between the tide waters of
the Hudson and Lake Erie."

Mr. Forman had studied the subject of canals as
constructed in foreign countries. His mind had been
applied intently to their construction, utility and cost,
and these labors had been brought to bear and have
weight upon the subject now under investigation. He
had well considered all the advantages that would
accrue to the United States and the State of New York,
if this important work should be completed. He had
prepared an estimate of the cost of construction based
upon statistics of the Languedoc canal.

While discussing this subject in Albany, during
the session, Judge Wright and General McNeill, of

Oneida, became converts to the plan through the instrumentality of Judge Forman; and Judge Wright agreed to second the resolution about to be offered whenever it should be brought up. Judge Forman had no confidence that the general government would assist New York in the construction of a canal, but the resolution framed and offered by him was so worded as to give President Jefferson an opportunity to participate in the measure if he would. Fired with the novelty and importance of this project, and somewhat piqued at the manner of its reception by the members of the House, the advocate took pains to prepare himself thoroughly upon the subject, and when the resolution was called up, he addressed the House in a forcible and eloquent speech in its favor. Fortunately the resolution was adopted, and for this he was for years called a "visionary projector," and was asked a hundred times if he ever expected to live to see his canal completed ; to which he uniformly answered, that "as surely as he lived to the ordinary age of man, he did ; that it might take ten years to prepare the public mind for the undertaking, and as many more to accomplish it, nevertheless it would be done."

Had not Joshua Forman brought forward the subject as he did, it is not easy to conceive who would have had the moral courage to meet the ridicule, of proposing in earnest, what was considered so wild a

measure. Had it not been for this timely movement,
the subject might have lain idle for years, so far as
Legislative action was concerned. But by it, the ice
was broken, and an impetus given to a direct canal, by
the discoveries made under it, and to Joshua Forman
must ever be accorded the high consideration, as the
first legislative projector of the greatest improvement
of the age.

During all the times of darkness, discouragement
and doubt, he boldly stood forth the unflinching
champion of its feasibility, utility and worth, till the
day of its completion.

On the occasion of the grand canal celebration, first
of November, 1825, Judge Forman was selected by the
citizens of Onondaga county, and as President of the
village of Syracuse, to address Governor Clinton and
suite, on their first passage down the canal accompanied by various county committees along the line. He
had but three hours to prepare his address, and it
thus appears in the Syracuse *Gazette* of November 2,
1825 :—

"Gentlemen : The roar of cannon rolling from Lake
Erie to the ocean, and reverberated from the ocean to
the lakes, has announced the completion of the Erie
Canal, and you are this day witnesses, bearing the
waters of the lakes on the unbroken bosom of the
canal, to be mingled with the ocean that the splendid
hopes of our State are realized. The continued fete

which has attended your boats, evinces how dear it was to the hearts of our citizens. It is truly a proud day for the State of New York. No one is present who has the interest of the State at heart, who does not exult at the completion of a work fraught with such important benefits, and no man with an American heart, that does not swell with pride that he is a citizen of the country which has accomplished the greatest work of the age, and which has filled Europe with admiration of the American character.

"On the Fourth of July, 1817, it was begun, and it is now accomplished. Not by the labor of abject slaves and vassals, but by the energies of freemen, and in a period unprecedently short, by the voluntary efforts of its freemen, governed by the wisdom of its statesmen. This, however, is but one of the many benefits derived from our free institutions, and which marks a new era in the history of man—the example of a nation whose whole physical power and intelligence are employed to advance the improvement, comfort and happiness of the people. To what extent this course of improvement may be carried, it is impossible for any mere man to conjecture ; but no reasonable man can doubt that it will continue its progress, until our wide and fertile territory shall be filled with a more dense, intelligent and happy people than the sun shines upon in the whole circuit of the globe. It has long been the subject of fearful apprehension, to the patriots of the Atlantic States, that the remote interior situation of our western country (for want of proper stimuli to industry and free intercourse with the rest of the world) would be filled with a semi-barbarous population, uncongenial with their Atlantic neighbors.   But the introduction of steamboats on our lakes and running rivers and canals to connect the waters which nature has disjoined, (in both which this State has taken the lead, and its example has now become general,) have broken down the old barriers of nature, and promise the wide-spread regions of the west all the blessings of a sea-board district.

"But while we contemplate the advantages of this work, as a source of revenue to the State, and of wealth and comfort to our citizens, let us never forget the means by which it has been accomplished; and after rendering thanks to the All-Wise Dispenser of events, who has by his own means and for his own purposes brought about this great work, we would render our thanks to all citizens and statesmen, who have in and out of the Legislature sustained the measure from its first conception to its present final consummation.   To the commissioners who superintended the work, the board of native engineers, (a native treasure unknown till called for by the occasion,) and especially to his Excellency, the Governor, whose early and decided support of the measure, fearlessly throwing his character and influence into the scale, turned the poising beam and produced the first canal appropriation, and by his talents and exertions kept public opinion steady to the point. Without his efforts in that crisis, the canal project might still have been a splendid vision—gazed upon by the benevolent patriot, but left by cold calumniators to be realized by some future generation. At that time, all admitted that there was a high responsibility resting on you, and had it failed, you must have largely borne the blame. It has succeeded, and we will not withhold from you your due meed of praise.

"Gentlemen, in behalf of the citizens of Syracuse, and the county of Onondaga, here assembled, I congratulate you on this occasion. Our village is the offspring of the canal, and with the county must partake largely of its blessings. We were most ungrateful if we did not most cordially join in this great State celebration."

Judge Forman having concluded his address, Governor Clinton replied in a very happy and appropriate manner; in the course of which he adverted to the important views presented in the address, and observed that they were such as he had expected from an individual who had introduced the first legislative measures relative to the canals, and had devoted much thought and reflection to the subject. His Excellency also adverted to the prosperous condition of Syracuse, and of the county, and concluded by expressing his congratulations on the final accomplishment of this great work.

As one of the committee from Syracuse, Judge
Forman attended the ceremony of mingling the waters
of Lake Erie with those of the Ocean, off Sandy
Hook. He had now passed through all the stages in
the progress of the great work, from its first
announcement in the legislature to its final consummation in uniting the waters of Lake Erie with the
Atlantic Ocean. His efforts in this great undertaking
will ever be an enduring monument of his wisdom,
and to future generations will his fame extend.

It is not to be supposed that Judge Forman had
employed all his time and talents upon this single
object. As a lawyer, he became distinguished ; and,
on account of his integrity and legal acquirements,
was appointed First Judge of Onondaga County
Common Pleas in 1813. He filled the station with
credit and ability for ten years ; in fact, he elevated
the character of this tribunal to the pitch which gained
for it the high reputation which it has since enjoyed.

He took an early and active interest in the establishment of churches in this county. "The First
Onondaga Religious Society," at Onondaga Hill, in
1806, and the "Onondaga Hollow Religious Society,"
in 1809, owe their early organization mainly to his
efforts. The Onondaga Academy, founded in 1814,
owes its existence to the interest he manifested in the
cause of education and to his fostering care. He was
also one of the most active in promoting the organi-

zation of the First Presbyterian Society in Syracuse, in 1824, and was one of its first Trustees.

In 1807 he took a lease of the Surveyor-General for a term of years, of a part of the reservation lands at Oswego Falls, for the purpose of erecting a grist mill in that wilderness country, at which time not a house was owned by an inhabitant between Salina and Oswego. This was the first mill erected on the Oswego river in modern times, and it greatly facilitated the settlement of that region.

In 1808, he founded the celebrated Plaster company of Camillus, for the purpose of more effectually working the extensive beds in that town. In 1813, Judge Forman built the canal and excavated ground for the pond at Onondaga Hollow, where he erected a grist mill, which was then considered one of the best in the country.

In 1817, while there was yet a strong opposition to the Erie Canal, and its friends were in the greatest anxiety, and even doubt as to the final result, Judge Forman furnished a series of articles, which were published in the Onondaga *Register*, signed X, in defense of the work. These papers were written with great ability, and are said by competent judges to be inferior to none that had been written upon that subject.

In 1821, Judge Forman obtained the passage of a law, (drawn by his own hand,) authorizing the lowering of Onondaga lake, and subsequently the lake was

lowered about two feet. The great difficulty had been
caused by the high water in the Seneca river, rising to
a certain height, which obstructed the channel of the
Onondaga outlet ; and such was the nature of the
obstructions, arising from the narrowness and crook-
edness of the passage, that when the Seneca river
subsided to its proper limits, the water of Onondaga
lake was retained, and in rainy seasons did not fall so
as to make dry ground around it till late in summer,
which was the cause of much inconvenience to the
people living in the vicinity of the lake. To obviate
this, the lake was lowered, and by it the lands around
Salina and Syracuse were improved, leaving bare a
beach about the lake, in some places of several rods in
width. For the cause of philanthrophy and humanity
this was a most important measure. The country
around became more healthful, and although previously infested with a fatal miasma in August and
September, from that time to this, the country about
Syracuse and Salina, has been considered as healthy as
any other section in the State.

In 1822, Judge Forman procured the passage of a
law authorizing the erection of fixtures for the purpose
of manufacturing coarse salt by solar evaporation,
with a three-cent per bushel bounty on salt so manufactured, for a given number of years. He went to
New Bedford in company with Isaiah Townsend, to
make inquiries relative to solar evaporation of salt

water, from persons interested in this mode of manufacturing salt from sea-water on Cape Cod. They engaged Stephen Smith to come on to Syracuse with them to manage the salt fields, he having had experience in this mode of manufacture. Mr. Smith was appointed agent of the Onondaga company, and Judge Forman of the Syracuse company, and these two proceeded to make the necessary erections for the manufacture of coarse salt.

At this time the Salina canal terminated at the mill on the southern border of the village of Salina, and there was no water to be had, available for purposes of carrying machinery in the immediate vicinity of the principal salt spring. With a view of accomplishing this object, Judge Forman accompanied Governor Clinton to Salina, pointed out the ground, and proposed to have the Salina canal extended so as to communicate with Onondaga lake; and the following year this plan was carried out, the canal was continued to the lake, and arrangements made for the erection of pump works. This grand improvement in the elevation of brine, was made at the expense of the Syracuse and Onondaga Salt companies, under the direction of Judge Forman. Afterwards the State bought the fixtures, aqueducts, etc., as they had reserved the right to do. To no individual so much as to Judge Forman are we indebted for a modification of our salt laws, and for the substitution of water

power, for hand labor, in the elevation of brine, for
the reservoirs, and all the apparatus connected with
those improvements, and for the introduction of the
manufacture of coarse salt by solar heat. These were
measures in which the public were deeply interested,
which particularly absorbed his attention, and which
have greatly improved and increased the manufacture
of salt in the town of Salina.

Judge Forman was emphatically the founder of the
city of Syracuse. He came to this place when there
was but a small clearing south of the canal, and lived
in a house which stood in the centre of Clinton street;
since removed. When he came to Syracuse, it was
deemed a doubtful and hazardous enterprise. His
friends earnestly desired him to withdraw. But at no
time did his courage, energy or faith fail him. He
foresaw and insisted that it must eventually become a
great and flourishing inland town, and in spite of
much determined opposition, and amidst a variety of
obstacles and almost every species of embarrassment,
he persisted in his efforts, till he had laid broad and
deep the foundations of this flourishing city.

The most prominent obstacles were found in the
rival villages in the vicinity, which were likely to be
affected by the building up of a larger one in their
midst, and in the extensive swamps and marshes which
everywhere in this region prevailed, and in the consequent unhealthiness of the locality.

His work being accomplished, circumstances required his removal from this scene of his usefulness,
and the theatre of his labors. In 1826, he removed to
New Jersey, near New Brunswick, where he superintended the opening and working of a copper mine,
which had been wrought to some extent prior to and
during the Revolution. Soon after his departure from
Syracuse, the State of New York became sadly convulsed and deranged in its financial affairs. Our
banking system was extremely defective—reform was
demanded by an abused and outraged community. All
saw and admitted the evil, but no one was prepared
with a remedy. At this crisis, Judge Forman came
forward with a plan for relief, and upon the invitation
of Governor Van Buren he visited Albany, and submitted his plan to a Committee of the Legislature
then in session. At the suggestion of the Governor,
he drew up the bill which subsequently became a law,
and is known as the Safety Fund Act, the great objects
of which were, on the one hand, to give currency and
character to our circulation, and on the other, to
protect the bill-holder. At the special request of
Governor Van Buren, Judge Forman spent most of
the winter in attendance in the Legislature, in perfect-
ing the details of this important act.

This plan operated well for many years, and the
Safety Fund banks of this State sustained themselves
under some of the severest and heaviest revulsions

which the monied institutions of the country have ever experienced. And it may be safely affirmed that no system in practice on this side the Atlantic has better stood the test of experience, or secured so extensively the popular confidence as this. The Safety Fund system was exclusively the plan of Judge Forman, and although modifications have since been made, and others projected, in our banking laws, it may be questioned whether the system has been materially improved.

In 1829–30, Judge Forman bought of the government of the State of North Carolina an extensive tract of land, consisting of some three hundred thousand acres, in Rutherfordton county. He took up his residence at the village of Rutherfordton, greatly extended its boundaries, established a newspaper press, and was considered the most enterprising individual in that part of the State; became quite distinguished as a public man, and noted for his exertions to elevate the character, and improve the mental and moral condition of the inhabitants in that region.

In 1831, after an absence of about five years, Judge Forman visited Onondaga. He was everywhere received with unqualified demonstrations of joy and respect, and every voice cheered him as the founder of a city and a benefactor of mankind. The citizens of Syracuse, through their committee appointed for that purpose, consisting of Stephen Smith, Harvey

Baldwin, Amos P. Granger, L. H. Redfield, Henry Newton, John Wilkinson and Moses D. Burnet, availed themselves of the opportunity to present to him a valuable piece of silver plate as a tribute of the high respect and esteem which was entertained for his talents and character, and in consideration of his devotedness to their interests in the early settlement of the village. The plate is in the form of a pitcher, and bears this inscription: "A tribute of respect, presented by the citizens of Syracuse to the Honorable Joshua Forman, founder of that village. Syracuse, 1831."

At the ceremony of presenting the plate, mutual addresses were delivered; on the one hand, highly expressive of the affection and regard of a whole community, to a distinguished individual, who had toiled and exhausted his more vigorous energies for their welfare; and on the other, the acknowledgment of past favors at the hands of his fellow-citizens and coadjutors, thankful that he had been the humble instrument of contributing to their prosperity, hoping that the bright visions of the future importance of Syracuse, which he had so long entertained, might be realized, he bade her citizens an affectionate farewell.

On his return to his home in North Carolina, Judge Forman took with him this token of the gratitude of his fellow-citizens, and it remained with him till the year 1845, when he presented it to his daughter, the lady of General E. W. Leavenworth, of Syracuse, then on a visit to her father who was in feeble health, remarking, that it constituted a part of the history of Syracuse, and that after his death there it should remain.

While his health permitted, Judge Forman's business was principally that of making sales of the lands he had purchased in North Carolina.

In 1846, this venerable man re-visited his former friends and acquaintances of his earlier years, and found in each full heart an honest welcome. To all it was apparent that the advances of time had made sad inroads upon his physical and mental powers. Seventy winters had shed their snows upon his devoted head. He had heard much of the growth and prosperity of his cherished city, and of his beloved Onondaga. He had fixed his heart upon again treading the soil of his revered county. He had earnestly desired to return to the land of his fathers before his course on earth should be closed, to witness the result of those wonderful improvements in the accomplishment of which he had taken so deep an interest and so active a part, and to see the fulfillment of those predictions which had sometimes acquired for him the name of a visionary projector and enthusiast, and once again for the last time to behold in the body the few surviving friends of his earlier years. He could not bid adieu to the world in peace, till this last and greatest of his earthly wishes should be gratified.

On this occasion a public dinner was tendered to him by P. N. Rust of the Syracuse House. A large number of the most distinguished gentlemen of the county were present, together with the few gray-headed pioneers, who still lingered in the land. Nearly all the company were the personal friends of Judge Forman, many of them having been sharers or attentive observers of his early and patriotic public efforts, for the social, mental and moral improvement of this county. Few indeed are the instances, where an individual, mantled in the hoary locks of age, after an absence of twenty years, returns to the scenes of his primitive usefulness, with so many demonstrations, on the part of friends and former neighbors, of joy and thankfulness, as in the one before us. It was also a season of peculiar gratification to him. Here he beheld the results of his labors in early active manhood. Here he beheld the progress of a thriving town founded by his fostering hand. Here he received the warm greetings of the friends of his early life, and here he met with them, to bid them a kind, affectionate and last adieu.

Moses D. Burnet presided on this very interesting occasion. A formal address of congratulation, on account of the great success of his early labors, and the remarkable fulfillment of his hopes and predictions, was made by the Hon. Harvey Baldwin, which was replied to, in behalf of Judge Forman, (he being unable to articulate distinctly, on account of a paralitic shock,) by his son-in-law, E. W. Leavenworth.

General Amos P. Granger, Hon. George Geddes, Lewis H. Redfield, and several other gentlemen of note, addressed the party in a very felicitous manner.

The proceedings of this very interesting meeting may be found in the Onondaga *Democrat* of the 3rd of October, 1846, and other city papers of that date.

From Syracuse, Judge Forman retired to his mountain home, in the milder climes of the sunny South, carrying with him the most vivid recollections of the kindness and hospitality of his friends; looking back upon a well spent life, much of which was devoted to the service of his country, without regret; and forward, without a fear to the hour when he will be called away from the scenes of society and earth.

Judge Forman is still living, (1849,) at his home in North Carolina, having bid adieu to the cares and business occupations of life.

The character of this distinguished man may be summed up in a very few words. His mind was of no ordinary cast, and whether we view him as a fellow-citizen, a neighbor, a legislator, a jurist, a judge, or as a man, we find nothing that we cannot respect and admire. Full of life and energy himself, he infused with uncommon facility the same spirit into others, and wherever he was found, in him was the master spirit of every plan. He possessed a mind of uncom-

mon activity, never wearying with the multiplicity of
his labors and cares; it was stored with an unusual
variety of knowledge, extending far beyond the
boundaries of his professional pursuits, and he possessed a rare felicity in the communication of this
knowledge to others. This fund of solid and general
information, upon every variety of topic, and his
forcible and happy manner of communication, joined
with the most social and cheerful disposition, rendered
him on all occasions a most agreeable and interesting
gentleman in conversation, and the delight of every
circle in which he moved. He greatly excelled in the
clear perceptions of the results of proposed measures
of public improvement, and in a capacity to present
them forcibly to others, carrying along with him
individuals, communities and public assemblies, by
his easy flowing language, and a manner at once most
clear, captivating and persuasive. His whole life was
characterized by the most public spirited efforts for
the general good, and the most disinterested benevolence,—always comparatively forgetful of his own
private interest, in his zeal for the accomplishment of
works of public utility. Through the long period of
his stirring and eventful life, he sustained a character
without stain and without reproach, and now standing
on the borders of the grave, is most justly entitled to
the admiration and gratitude of his countrymen.

It was the happiness of the author, in his youthful

days, to spend several months in the family of Judge
Forman, at Onondaga Hollow, and he takes pleasure
in this opportunity of testifying to his domestic virtues
and private worth.

[The remains of Joshua Forman were removed
from Rutherfordton, North Carolina, and placed in
Oakwood cemetery in Syracuse.   The records kept at
this cemetery show that these remains were placed in
the lot of General Elias W. Leavenworth, May—1875.
General Leavenworth's first wife was Miss Mary E.
Forman, daughter of Judge Forman.   This lot is a
beautiful one, finely located, and the grave is marked
by a handsome marble slab.   On the monument, about
which there is a stone canopy, there is written this
inscription: "Joshua Forman.   Founder of the city
of Syracuse, Author of the Safety Fund Banking law
of this State, the first person who offered a resolution
in the Legislature and procured an appropriation for
the construction of the Erie canal.   He was born at
Pleasant Valley, in the county of Duchess, N. Y., on
the 6th day of September, 1777, and died at Rutherfordton, N. C., on the 4th day of August, 1849."]

CHAPTER XXII

THE LEGEND OF HIAWATHA

The legend of Hiawatha, which gives the traditional account of the confederacy of the Iroquois Indians, the most powerful of all the Indian nations in the United States, has become of great importance, especially to the citizens of Syracuse and Onondaga county, where the legend originated, because Longfellow has immortalized it in his beautiful "Song of Hiawatha." Longfellow gave credit to Mr. Schoolcraft for this Indian tradition; and he adds: "The scene of the poem is among the Ojibways on the southern shore of Lake Superior, in the region between the Pictured Rocks and the Grand Sable." Of course, Longfellow, as a poet, could locate the scene of his poem wherever his fancy lead him; but Schoolcraft, as an historian, properly located the scene on the banks of Onondaga lake. Schoolcraft called his legend: "Hiawatha, or the Origin of the Onondaga Council-Fire, an Iroquois Tradition;" and he states that his information was "derived from the verbal

(333)

narrations of the late Abraham LeFort, an Onondaga
Chief, who was a graduate, it is believed. of Geneva
college."

The Rev. William M. Beauchamp of Baldwinsville,
New York, justly regarded as good authority on the
history of the Iroquois Indians, in an article published
in the *Journal of American Folk-Lore*, in 1891, says:
"In any form the tale has been known to the whites
less than fifty years, and the Onondaga version first
had publicity through Mr. J. V. H. Clark, in a
communication to the New York *Commercial Advertiser*. He obtained it from two Onondaga chiefs.
Schoolcraft used these notes before they were included
in Clark's history, and afterwards appropriated the
name for his Western Indian legends, where it had no
proper place. About the same time, Mr. Alfred B.
Street had a few original notes from other Iroquois
sources which he used in his metrical romance of
"Frontenac," along with some from Schoolcraft.
Thus, when Longfellow's "Hiawatha" appeared, I
was prepared to greet an old friend, and surprised at
being introduced to an Ojibway instead of an Iroquois
leader. The change, however, gave a broader field
for his beautiful poem, a gain to all readers, but as he
retained little beyond the name it may be needless to
refer to that charming work.

"Viewed philosophically, all the legends of
Hiawatha may have been useful to the Iroquois, as

harmonizing with and strengthening the best features
of their character in recent days. As a divine man,
coming to earth expressly to relieve human distress,
he presented a strong contrast to Agreskoue, in honor
of whom they feasted on human flesh, when first
known to the whites. Had such a tradition existed,
however, when the French missionaries entered their
land, it would have been produced to show that their
teaching was nothing new. As a mere man, suffering
injuries patiently, steadily keeping in view one great
and beneficient purpose, not only forgiving but
bringing to high honor the man who had injured him
most, he also taught an important lesson, but this
was learned from no Indian sage. This ideal came
from those white men who spoke of a better life."

From "Clark's Onondaga," it is learned that these
distinguished Indian nations were called by the French
"Iroquois," by the English "The Confederates" or
"Five Nations," by the Dutch "Maquas," and by
themselves "Mingoes;" meaning by all "United
People." Their territory proper, extended from
Hudson's river on the east to the Niagara on the
west; from lake Ontario on the north to the Allegha-
nies on the south. When it was that these five Indian
nations, composed of the Mohawks, Oneidas, Onondagas, Cayugas and Senecas, formed their famous
confederacy is a matter of conjecture. The Onondagas
were considered the third nation. They became, from

their central position and numbers, their strength of mind, skill in diplomacy and warlike bearing, the head or leading nation of the confederates. The grand council-fire of the union was usually kept with them. They kept the key of the great council house of the Five Nations; the Mohawks holding the door on the east, as did the Senecas on the west. No business of importance, touching the interests of the Five Nations, was transacted elsewhere but at Onondaga. This nation is divided into eight several tribes or clans, called by themselves, the Wolf, the Bear, the Beaver and the Tortoise. These are called superior clans, and from these may be selected the chiefs of the nation. The inferior clans are the Deer, the Eagle, the Heron and the Eel; from which civil chiefs may not be elected. Individuals belonging to these latter clans are not considered eligible to office. Though there formerly were instances where, by great individual merit as warriors, they have occasionally been selected as war chiefs; considered the lowest class of officers known to their laws. Among the Onondagas the line of descent is emphatically in the female branch of the family. The inference to be drawn from this is that the son is certainly derived from the mother, but may not be from whom he acknowledges as father.

In referring to the Iroquois confederacy, Mr. Beauchamp says: "The true date was probably about A. D. 1600." The account of this Hiawatha legend,

as given by Joshua V. H. Clark, in "Clark's Onondaga" is as follows:—

At what period or for what purpose this league was
originally formed, is a matter wholly speculative, as
the records of history and Indian tradition are alike
uncertain, and throw but feeble light upon the subject. It is supposed, however, that anciently they
were separate and independent nations; and probably
warred with an equal relish upon each other as upon
their neighbors, and perhaps finally united themselves
for purposes of greater strength and security, thereby
enlarging their power and importance at home,
enabling them to prosecute more vigorously their
conquests abroad. Common danger or a desire for
conquest were the motives, rather than a far-seeing
policy, which must have actuated these people to form
a league of consolidation.

By some authors, the time of the formation of the
great league of confederation was about the life of one
man before the Dutch landed at New York. By
others, about an hundred years before that period.
Webster, the Onondaga interpreter, and good authority, states it at about two generations before the white
people came to trade with the Indians. But from the
permanency of their institutions, the peculiar structure of their government, the intricacy of their civil
affairs, the stability of their religious beliefs and the
uniformity of their pagan ceremonies, differing from

other Indian nations in important particulars, we are
inclined to the opinion that their federative existence
must have had a much longer duration. And from
the following tradition, we are inclined to the opinion
that the period is unknown, and the time lost in the
clouded uncertainties of the past.

Hundreds of years ago, Ta-oun-ya-wat-ha, the
Deity who presides over fisheries and streams, came
down from his dwelling place in the clouds to visit
the inhabitants of the earth. He had been deputed
by the Great and Good Spirit Na-wah-ne-u, to visit
the streams and clear the channels from all obstructions, to seek out the good things of the country
through which he intended to pass, that they might
be more generally dissiminated among all the good
people of the earth, especially to point out to them the
most excellent fishing grounds, and to bestow upon
them other acceptable gifts. About this time, two
young men of the Onondaga Nation were listlessly
gazing over the calm blue waters of the "Lake of a
Thousand Isles." During their revery, they espied,
as they thought, far in the distance, a single white
speck, beautifully dancing over the bright blue waters
—and while they watched the object with the most
intense anxiety, it seemed to increase in magnitude,
and moved as if approaching the place where they
were concealed, most anxiously awaiting the event of
the visitation of so singular an object; for at this time

no canoes had ever made their appearance in the
direction whence this was approaching.

As the object neared the shore, it proved in sem-
blance to be a venerable looking man, calmly seated
in a canoe of pure white, very curiously constructed,
and much more ingeniously wrought than those in use
among the tribes of the country. Like a cygnet upon
the wide blue sea, so sat the canoe of Ta-oun-ya-wat-
ha upon the "Lake of a Thousand Isles." As the frail
branch drifts towards the rushing cataract, so coursed
the white canoe over the rippling waters, propelled by
the strong arm of the god of the river. Deep thought
sat upon the brow of the gray-haired mariner; pene-
tration marked his eye, and deep, dark mystery pervaded his countenance. With a single oar he silently
paddled his light-trimmed bark along the shore, as if
seeking a commodious haven for rest. He soon turned
the prow of his fragile vessel into the estuary of the
"double river," and made fast to the western shore.
He majestically ascended the steep bank, nor stopped
till he had gained the loftiest summit of the western
hill. Then silently gazing around as if to examine
the country, he became enchanted with the view;
when, drawing his stately form to its utmost height,
he exclaimed in accents of the wildest enthusiasm,
Osh-wah-kee! Osh-wah-kee!

[Mr. Clark adds in a foot note that this word,
Osh-wah-kee, "being interpreted literally, signifies

from the circumstance here related—' I see everywhere
and see nothing.' From this our English name for
the river Oswego is derived."]

During the observations of the spirit man, (for so
he was afterwards called,) the two men who had lain
concealed, cautiously watching all his movements,
discovered themselves. Ta-oun-ya-wat-ha very civilly
approached them, and after the greetings usual at the
first meeting of strangers, very gravely made inquiries
of them respecting their country and its advantages,
of their fisheries and hunting grounds, and of the
impediments in the way of the prosperity of the nations
round about. To all of which the hunters, (for so
they were,) could give no very favorable answers, but
briefly stated to him the disadvantages they had ever
been doomed to labor under, and the sufferings they
had borne in consequence.

A degree of familiarity and mutual confidence had
by this time become awakened in the bosoms of the
parties, and the greatest freedom of conversation
proceeded without restraint. The hunters provided
for their venerable guest a repast of roast venison, who
received it in thankfulness; they smoked the calumet
together and were refreshed.

Ta-oun-ya-wat-ha disclosed to the hunters the spir-
ituality of his character and the object of his mission,
after which he invited them to proceed with him up
the river, as he had important business to transact,

and should need their services. After a moment's consultation together, the hunters consented to accompany him, and forthwith joyfully attended him to his canoe.

Of the events which immediately succeeded, we have not now time or disposition to speak, only that many of them were truly marvelous, and worthy a place only in the pages of Indian Mythology.

From this, Ta-oun-ya-wat-ha ascended all the lesser lakes and explored their shores, placing all things in proper order, for the comfort and sustenance of all good men. He had taught the people of the various tribes the art of raising corn and beans, which had not before been cultivated among them. He also encouraged them to a more faithful observance of the laws of the Great and Good Spirit. He had made the fishing grounds free, and opened to all the uninterrupted pursuit of game. He had distributed liberally among mankind the fruits of the earth, and had removed all obstructions from the navigable streams.

Pleased with the success of his undertakings, the spirit-man now resolved to lay aside his divine character, and in after years to make his abode among the children of men. He accordingly selected for his residence a beautiful spot on the shore of the Cross Lake, (Te-ungk-too, as called by the natives). [Located near Jordan.] After awhile he totally relinquished his divine title of Ta-oun-ya-wat-ha, and in all respects assumed the character and habits of a man. Nevertheless, he was always looked up to as an extra ordinary individual, as one possessing transcendent powers of mind and consummate wisdom. The name Hi-a-wat-ha (signifying very wise man), was spontaneously awarded him, by the whole mass of people, who now resorted to him from all quarters for advice and instruction. The companions of the spirit-man, at a subsequent council, were rewarded by a seat in the councils of their countrymen, and became eminently distinguished for their prowess in war and dignified bearing in the council room.

After a quiet residence of a few years at his new location, the country became greatly alarmed by the sudden approach of a ferocious band of warriors from north of the great lakes. As they advanced, indiscriminate slaughter was made of men, women and children. Many had been slain, and ultimate destruction seemed to be the consequence, either of bold resistance, or of a quiet relinquishment of absolute right.

During this signal agitation of the public mind, people from all quarters thronged the dwelling place of Hi-a-wat-ha for advice in this trying emergency. After a deep and thoughtful contemplation of the momentous subject, he informed the principal chiefs that his opinion was to call a grand council of all the tribes that could be gathered from the east and from the west, that the advice of all might be received; "for," said he, "our safety is in good council and speedy, energetic action." Accordingly, runners were dispatched in all directions, notifying the head men of a grand council to be held on the banks of the lake Oh-nen-ta-ha. [Onondaga lake.]

This council was supposed to have been held on the high ground where the village of Liverpool now stands. In due time the chiefs and warriors from far and near were assembled with great numbers of men, women and children to hold this important council, and to devise means for the general safety. All the principal men had arrived, except the venerable Hi-a-wat-ha.

The council-fire had been kindled three days, and he had not yet arrived. Messengers were dispatched, who found him in a most melancholy state of mind. He told them that evil lay in his path; that he had a fearful foreboding of ill-fortune, and that he had concluded not to attend the great council at Oh-nen-ta-ha. "But," said the messengers, "we have delayed the deliberations of the grand council on account of your absence, and the chiefs have resolved not to proceed to business until your arrival."

The White Canoe had always been held as a sacred treasure, and, next to the wise man himself, was regarded with awe and reverence. It had been deposited in a lodge, erected especially for its security,

to which none but the most worthy and noted of the
chieftains could have access.   Hither on this occasion
Hi-a-wat-ha repaired, and, in the most devout and
humiliating manner, poured out his soul in silence to
the Great Spirit.   After a protracted absence he
returned with a countenance beaming with confidence
and hope.   Being over-persuaded by his friends, he
reluctantly yielded to their earnest solicitations.   The
White Canoe was carefully removed from its sacred
resting place, and reverently launched upon the bosom
of the river.   The wise man once again took his
accustomed seat, and bade his darling and only
daughter (a girl of some twelve years of age) to
accompany him.   She unhesitatingly obeyed, took her
place beside her venerable parent in the devoted vessel,
and directly they made all possible speed to the grand
council ground.

On the approach of the aged and venerable
Hi-a-wat-ha, a general shout of joy resounded throughout the assembled host, and every demonstration of
respect was paid to this illustrious sage and counsellor.
As he landed and was passing up the steep bank
towards the council ground, a loud sound was heard
like a rushing and mighty wind.   All eyes were
instantly turned upwards, and a dark spot was discovered rapidly descending from on high among the
clouds.   It grew larger and larger as it neared the earth,
and was descending with fearful velocity into their very

midst. Terror and alarm seized every breast, and
every individual seemed anxious only for his own
safety. The utmost confusion prevailed throughout
the assembled multitude, and all but the venerable
Hi-a-wat-ha sought safety by flight. He gravely
uncovered his silvered head, and besought his daughter
to await the approaching danger with becoming resignation; at the same time reminding her of the great
folly and impropriety of attempting to obstruct or
prevent the designs or wishes of the Great Spirit.
" If," said he, " he has determined our destruction,
we shall not escape by removal, nor evade his
decrees." She modestly acquiesced in her kind parent's
suggestions and advice, and with the most patient
submission waited the coming event.

All this was but the work of an instant; for no sooner
had the resolution of the wise man become fixed, and
his last words uttered, than an immense bird, with a
long and pointed beak, with wide-extended wings,
came down with a mighty swoop, and crushed the
beautiful girl to the earth. With such force did the
monster fall, and so great was the commotion of the
air that when it struck the ground, the whole assembly
were forced violently back several rods. Hi-a-wat-ha
alone remained unmoved and silently witnessed the
melancholy catastrophe of his child's dissolution.

His darling daughter had been killed before his
eyes in a marvelous manner, and her destroyer had

perished with her.   The dismayed warriors cautiously
advanced to the spot and calmly surveyed the dismal
scene.   It was found upon examination that the
animal, in its descent, had completely buried its beak,
head and neck up to its body in the ground.   It was
covered with a beautiful plumage of snowy white, and
every warrior, as he advanced, plucked a plume from
this singular bird, with which he adorned his crown;
and from this incident, the braves of the confederate
nations forever after made choice of the plumes of the
white heron as their most appropriate military ornament while upon the war-path.

Upon the removal of the carcass of the monster,
the body of the innocent girl was found to be completely ground to atoms.   Nothing could be seen of
her that would indicate she had ever been a human
being.   At this appearance, the bereaved and disconsolate parent gave himself up to the most poignant
sorrow.   Hollow moans and distressing grief told too
plainly the bitterness of his heart.   He spurned all
proffers of consolation, and yielded to the keenest
feelings of anguish and unbounded sorrow.

He became an object of perfect despair, and threw
himself down upon his face to the earth, dejected and
disconsolate.   The shattered fragments of the innocent
girl were carefully gathered together, and interred in
all the tenderness and solemnity of bitter grief.   Every-
one seemed to participate in the afflictions of the aged

and venerable counsellor, and to sympathize in his sufferings and woe. Still, no comfort came to his soul.
He remained in this prostrate situation three whole
days and nights unmoved. The fears of the assembled
chiefs were awakened lest he might become a willing
victim to his own melancholy and misfortune.

Nothing had been done as yet in the council, and
such had been the causes of delay that many began to
despair of accomplishing anything of consequence.
Some even thought seriously of returning to their
homes without an effort. At length a few of the
leading chiefs consulted together, as to what course it
was most expedient to pursue. It was at once resolved
that nothing should be attempted without the voice
of the wise man should be heard. A suitable person
was thereupon dispatched to ascertain whether he
breathed. Report came that he was yet alive. A
kind-hearted, merry chief, named Ho-see-noke, was
directed by the council to make to the prostrate
mourner a comforting speech, to whisper kind words
in his ear, and if possible arouse him from his reverie.

After a deal of formal ceremony and persuasion,
he gradually recovered from his stupor, and conversed.
After several messages had passed between the assembled chiefs and Hi-a-wat-ha, he arose and manifested
a desire for food. He ate and drank of such as was
hastily prepared for him, and acknowledged himself
strengthened and refreshed.

He was conducted to the presence of the council, a conspicuous place was assigned him, and all eyes were turned towards the only man who could with precision foretell their future destiny. The subject of the invasion was discussed by several of the ablest counsellors and boldest warriors. Various schemes were proposed for the repulsion of the enemy. Hi-a-wat-ha listened in silence till the speeches of all were concluded. His opinion was gravely and earnestly sought by many of the surrounding chiefs.

After a brief reference to the calamity which had so recently befallen him, the wise man said: "This is a subject that requires mature reflection and deliberation. It is not fitting that one of so much importance should be treated lightly; or that our decision should be hasty and inconsiderate. Let us postpone our deliberations for one day, that we may weigh well the words of the wise chiefs and warriors who have spoken. Then I will communicate to you my plan for consideration. It is one which I am confident will succeed, and ensure our safety."

After another day's delay, the council again assembled and all were anxious to hear the words of Hi-a-wat-ha. A breathless silence ensued, and the venerable counsellor began:

"Friends and brothers:—You are members of many tribes and nations. You have come here, many of you, a great distance from your homes. We have

convened for one common purpose, to promote one
common interest; and that is to provide for our
mutual safety and how it shall best be accomplished.
To oppose these hordes of northern foes by tribes,
singly and alone, would prove our certain destruction;
we can make no progress in that way; we must unite
ourselves into one common band of brothers. Our
warriors united, would surely repel these rude invaders
and drive them from our borders. This must be done, ˙
and we shall be safe.

"You—the Mohawks, sitting under the shadow of
the 'Great Tree,' whose roots sink deep into the earth
and whose branches spread over a vast country, shall
be the first nation; because you are warlike and
mighty.

"And you—Oneidas, a people who recline your
bodies against the 'Everlasting Stone' that cannot be
moved, shall be the second nation; because you give
wise counsel.

"And you—Onondagas, who have your habitation
at the 'Great Mountain' and are overshadowed by its
crags, shall be the third nation; because you are
greatly gifted in speech and mighty in war.

"And you—Cayugas, a people whose habitation is
the 'Dark Forest' and whose home is everywhere,
shall be the fourth nation; because of your superior
cunning in hunting.

"And you—Senecas, a people who live in the 'Open

Country ' and possess much wisdom, shall be the fifth
nation; because you understand better the art of raising corn and beans, and making cabins.

" You, five great and powerful nations, must unite
and have but one common interest, and no foe shall
be able to disturb or subdue you.

" And you—Manhattoes, Nyacks, Montauks and
others, who are as the feeble ' Bushes '; and you, Nar-
agansetts, Mohegans, Wampanoags and your neighbors who are a ' Fishing People,' may place yourselves
under our protection.   Be with us, and we will defend
you.   You of the South, and you of the West, may
do the same, and we will protect you.   We earnestly
desire your alliance and friendship.

" Brothers—If we unite in this bond, the Great
Spirit will smile upon us, and we shall be free, prosperous and happy.   But if we remain as we are, we
shall be subject to his frown; we shall be enslaved,
ruined, perhaps annihilated forever.   We shall perish
and our names be blotted out from among the nations
of men.   Brothers: these are the words of Hi-a-wat-ha
—let them sink deep into your hearts—I have said it."

A long silence ensued; the words of the wise man
had made a deep impression upon the minds of all.
They unanimously declared the subject too weighty
for immediate decision. "Let us," said the brave
warriors and chiefs, "adjourn the council for one day,
and then we will respond." On the morrow, the

council again assembled. After due deliberation, the speech of the wise man was declared to be good and worthy of adoption.

Immediately upon this was formed the celebrated Aquinuschioni or Amphyctionic league of the great confederacy of Five Nations, which to this day remains in full force.

After the business of the great council had been brought to a close, and the assembly were on the eve of separation, Hi-a-wat-ha arose in a dignified manner, and said:

"Friends and Brothers: I have now fulfilled my mission upon earth; I have done everything which can be done at present for the good of this great people. Age, infirmity and distress sit heavy upon me. During my sojourn with you, I have removed all obstructions from the streams. Canoes can now pass safely everywhere. I have given you good fishing waters and good hunting grounds. I have taught you the manner of cultivating corn and beans, and learned you the art of making cabins. Many other blessings I have liberally bestowed upon you.

"Lastly, I have now assisted you to form an everlasting league and covenant of strength and friendship for your future safety and protection. If you preserve it, without the admission of other people, you will always be free, numerous and mighty. If other nations are admitted to your councils, they will sow jealousies among you, and you will become enslaved, few and feeble. Remember these words; they are the last you will hear from the lips of Hi-a-wat-ha. Listen my friends; the Great-Master-of-Breath calls me to go. I have patiently waited his summons. I am ready; farewell."

As the wise man closed his speech, there burst upon the ears of the assembled multitude the cheerful sounds of myriads of the most delightful singing voices. The whole sky seemed filled with the sweetest melody of celestial music; and Heaven's high arch echoed and re-echoed the touching strains, till the whole vast assembly were completely absorbed in rapturous ecstacy. Amidst the general confusion which now prevailed, and while all eyes were turned towards the etherial regions, Hi-a-wat-ha was seen majestically seated in his white canoe, gracefully rising higher and higher above their heads through the air, until he became entirely lost from the view of the assembled throngs, who witnessed his wonderful ascent in mute and admiring astonishment—while the fascinating music gradually became more plaintive and low; and finally, it sweetly expired in the softest tones upon their ears, as the wise man Hi-a-wat-ha, and the god-like Ta-oun-ya-wat-ha retired from their sight, and quietly entered the mysterious regions inhabited only by the favorites of the Great and Good Spirit Ha-wah-ne-u.

[Mr. Clark adds in a foot note: "The substance of the foregoing tradition may be found in the 'Notes on the Iroquois,' pp. 271 to 283. It is but simple justice to the author of this work to say that the article in the 'Notes' was framed from a MS. furnished by the author of this to the Editor of the *Commercial Advertiser* of New York, for publication in that paper."]

Such is the traditionary account of the Onondagas of the origin of the very ancient and honorable league first formed by the illustrious Five Nations, given to the author by the late Captain Frost and La Fort, head chiefs of the Onondagas, 6th February, 1845.

This tradition, like all others, proves nothing positively, further than that the Iroquois themselves know little of their own origin, history, or the antiquity of their most prominent characteristics and institutions. These being orally transmitted from generation to generation, and their minds ever deeply imbued with superstition, events are magnified to miracles, distinguished men are deified, and every circumstance of note is mystified and mingled with ignorance, barbarism and extravagance.

Longfellow's beautiful poem, "The Song of Hiawatha," was published in November, 1855. It attracted great attention, receiving unbounded praise and severe criticism. The New York *Tribune* of November 27, 1855, contained a criticism from T. C.

P., of Pennsylvania, copied from the *National Intelligencer* of the preceding day, which called the reader's attention to the "Kalewala," the great national epic of the Finns. The critic added: "My object in writing this present brief notice is to call the attention of the literary public to the astounding fact that Professor Longfellow, in his new poem, "Hiawatha," has transferred the entire form, spirit, and many of the most striking incidents of the old Finnish epic to the North American Indians. The resemblance is so close that it cannot be accidental, and yet the only approach to an acknowledgment of the source of his inspiration is found in the beginning of his first note, where he says: 'This Indian *Edda*, if I may so call it.'"

Mr. Schoolcraft hastened to the defense of Longfellow's Hiawatha, and his letter to the *National Intelligencer*, dated Washington, D. C., December 7, 1855, was reproduced in the New York *Tribune* of December 18, 1855. Mr. Schoolcraft said: "Every author is responsible for what he utters. This truth is particularly apposite at this moment in relation to the Indian oral legends heretofore published by me, which have recently been quoted by a distinguished writer. The appearance of a popular American poem, on American materials, is suited to arouse literary excitement from the banks of the Aroostook to the Rio Grande. Not believing that anything at

all is necessary to vindicate Professor Longfellow's
literary integrity in quoting my Indian legends, any
more than the taste, talent and judgment displayed in
his beautiful, characteristic and truly American
poem of Hiawatha, there is yet something due
from me on the subject from the citations of my
'Algic Researches,' and of the third volume of my
Indian History. No allusion is made to the critical
acumen to which the poem has given birth in the
press. The reference is exclusively to the originality
of the legends quoted by the author of 'Hiawatha,'
and to their veraciousness to the traditions of the
native lore, which I have reported from the North
American wigwams."

The cool, confident manner in which Mr. Schoolcraft, who was then Agent of the Statistics, etc., of
the Indian tribes of the United States, under the
Department of the Interior at Washington, appropriated to himself the credit of being the first to give
an account of the legend of Hiawatha, aroused Mr.
Clark from his generally mild disposition and caused
him to assert his claims to this legend and to bring
Mr. Schoolcraft before the bar of public opinion.

Under date of January 10, 1856, Mr. Clark wrote
the following letter to the New York *Tribune :—*

"The Song of Hiawatha" has become the subject
of much extravagant praise, and a theme for the
severest criticism. Animadversion has had the effect

to awaken a curiosity, and create an excitement that otherwise would have remained dormant; and the "Song" has been read by thousands who, but for this pen-and-ink warfare, would never have looked upon its pages. By this time it has been dispatched by the whole reading public, and it has afforded nearly as much gratification to its traducers as to its admirers.

The legend of Hiawatha was first related to the writer of this by the Onondaga chiefs, Captain Frost (Ossahinta), and Abram LaFort (Dehatkatons), in the summer of 1843. During the winter of 1843-'44, I wrote it out in full, and read the paper before the members of the Manlius Lyceum, and in the month of March following I repeated the same before a literary association at the village of Fayetteville, having at that time not the remotest idea of ever publishing anything in a permanent form relative to the Onondaga Indians.

In March, 1844, I furnished to the New York Historical Society a paper giving the Indian names to localities in Onondaga county and vicinity, at the suggestion of a committee which had been appointed by the Society to secure so desirable an object. Mr. Henry R. Schoolcraft, as chairman of the committee, by letter dated March 12, 1844, acknowledged the receipt of my communication, with the thanks of the committee, saying further: "Permit us to ask a continuance of your researches so far as relates to the

Onondaga tribe," etc. In my communication to the
committee I intimated that I had in my possession
tales and traditions illustrative of Indian character
and history. In a postscript to the letter above referred
to, Mr. Schoolcraft adds: "As I am collecting the
traditions of the Indians, imaginative as well as historical, I should be gratified for any contributions you
may make in this way; send me a copy of the tradition
of 'Green Pond.'" Upon this I sent him a copy of
the tradition requested, it having been previously
published by me in the New York *Commercial Advertiser*, at the instance of my friend, the late Col.
William L. Stone, as other pieces of like character
furnished by me had been before. In a letter from
Mr. Schoolcraft, dated April 19, 1844, in answer to
one from me a short time previous, he further says:
"This letter shows you to be too much at home on the
subject of Aboriginal names to allow us to think of
excusing you from further services of this kind."

In 1845, Mr. Schoolcraft, under the authority and
patronage of the State, visited the several tribes of
Indians in Western New York for the purpose of ascer-
taining their true condition as to property, schools,
resources, manner of living, etc., or in other words, to
take a complete census as far as possible of these
people, and furnish a series of statistics necessary to
form full and comprehensive data, respecting their
circumstances, wants and requirements, as well as

their advancement in the arts, agriculture and civiza-
tion; and if possible to recover from obscurity
somewhat of their mysterious history. On that tour
Mr. Schoolcraft, on various occasions, by letters now
in my possession, solicited information from me. (See
also "Notes on the Iroquois," pp. 192, 468.) In a
letter under date of July 24, 1845, *after* his visit to
Onondaga, he says: "I should feel under many
obligations to you if you would give me some account
from personal observation of the vestiges of ancient
occupancy in your vicinity," and afterward adds, "I
know of no one who is so well qualified to give it as
yourself."

Now it is a well-known fact that persons acting in
the capacity of official agents among the Indians are
always looked upon by them with suspicion and
distrust. Mr. Schoolcraft most emphatically asserts
as much when he says: "The census movement was
consequently the theme of no small number of sus-
picions and cavils and objections. Without any certain
or generally fixed grounds of objection, it was yet the
object of a fixed but changing opposition." (See
"Notes on the Iroquois," pp. 5, 6.) Mr. Schoolcraft
was looked upon with suspicion by the Onondaga
Indians, and by none more so than by Captain Frost
and Abram La Fort, principal chiefs of the Onondaga
Nation. Hence it became essential to the advancement
of his labors that some one more in the confidence of

the Indians should act in concert with the State Agent, in order effectually to secure the whole information desired. Besides, he remarks that "far more time than was at my command would be required to cultivate this attractive field of research." (See "Notes on the Iroquois," p. 192.)

By a reference to the "Notes on the Iroquois," anyone may see at a glance that many items received from me which he considered of value in his researches were adopted in his official report made to the Legislature, and which were retained in his subsequent "Notes on the Iroquois," which were considerably enlarged and improved, though embracing nearly all of the report. For many of these items the customary acknowledgments were made ; for others no sign of recognition was given. The tradition of Hiawatha, which he had previously received from me through the editor of the *Commercial Advertiser*, in manuscript form, was among this latter number, and it is inserted as if gleaned by his own laborious research.

Mr. Schoolcraft's report on the subject of the New York Indians was made to the Legislature in 1846. His enlarged and improved version, the "Notes on the Iroquois," was published in 1847. During the years 1846–'47 and '48, a train of accidental, though urgent circumstances, was thrown around me which eventuated in my bringing out a history of "Onondaga" from materials already in my possession, with

the addition of contributions from sundry individuals
throughout the country. My "Onondaga" was
published in 1849, and my version of the tradition of
Hiawatha is there inserted in volume I. at page 21.
At page 30 is the following note:

"The substance of the foregoing tradition may be
found in the 'Notes on the Iroquois,' pp. 271 to 283.
It is but simple justice to the author of this work to
say that the article in the 'Notes' was framed from
a manuscript furnished by the author of this to the
editor of the New York *Commercial Advertiser*, for
publication in that paper."

I have been thus minute in the foregoing remarks
in order to show substantially the relation that existed
between Mr. Schoolcraft and myself relative to Indian
affairs during his researches among the Indians of
Western New York in the years 1844-'45 and '46, and
to show that I had some knowledge of the tradition of
Hiawatha long before Mr. Schoolcraft's visit of
inspection among the New York Indians in 1845.

What I am about to say would not at this late day
be said were it not for the fact that the tradition of
Hiawatha, (notwithstanding the note in Clark's
"Onondaga," vol. I. at page 30,) has been transferred
from the "Notes on the Iroquois" to Mr. Schoolcraft's
larger work entitled, "History, Condition and Prospects of the Indian Tribes in the United States,"
published in 1853, (see page 314, third part,) and is

there entitled, "Hiawatha, or the Origin of the Onondaga Council-Fire," at which place is appended the following note: "Derived from the verbal narrations of the late Abraham Le Fort, an Onondaga Chief, who was a graduate, it is believed, of Geneva college;" and because the substance of Mr. Schoolcraft's note is reiterated in a note at the end of Mr. Longfellow's poem, "The Song of Hiawatha," at page 299; and because, in a letter dated, Washington, December 7, 1855, "To the Editor of *The National Intelligencer*," copied in the *Tribune* of December 18, Mr. Schoolcraft says: "Every author is responsible for what he utters," and again: "The reference is exclusively to the originality of the legends quoted by the author of Hiawatha."

Now, if Mr. Schoolcraft means (as the books declare) that he had the Onondaga tradition of Hiawatha, as it is related in his "Notes on the Iroquois," and as it is transferred to his larger work, "History, Condition and Prospects of the Indian Tribes in the United States," "derived from the verbal narrations of the late Abraham Le Fort, an Onondaga Chief, who was a graduate, it is believed, of Geneva college," then I say, unequivocally, that he is most egregiously mistaken, and asserts what, upon reflection, he would be unwilling to repeat.

It was on the fourteenth day of August, 1845, at my room in the hotel at the village of Aurora, Cayuga county, on a certain occasion when Mr. Schoolcraft delivered an address before the G. O. I., and after he had visited Onondaga, that I gave him several items of information, some verbal, some written, and some printed from the *Commercial Advertiser*. I then and there referred him to the legend of "The Wise Man Hiawatha, or the White Canoe," the manuscript of which had a short time previously been sent by me to the *Commercial Advertiser* for publication.

I am quite certain that at that time the story of Hiawatha was new to Mr. Schoolcraft. I then referred him to the source whence I derived it. I also at the same time gave him a note to Mr. Francis Hall, one of the publishers of the *Commercial Advertiser*, requesting him to deliver to Mr. Schoolcraft the said manuscript. Mr. Hall subsequently wrote me that he had so delivered it, but that it had not been returned to him.

The legend or tradition of Hiawatha was copied almost verbatim into Mr. Schoolcraft's "Notes on the Iroquois," the different points proceeding in exactly the same order of sequence, the language only in several places being changed, and all without the customary credit. Whether the tradition was improved by the transformation anyone may judge by comparison. (See Clark's "Onondaga," vol. I. pp. 21 to 30, and Schoolcraft's "Notes on the Iroquois," pp. 271 to 283, and his "History, Condition and

Prospects of the Indian Tribes in the United States," (third part, page 314, etc.)

Now, I challenge Mr. Schoolcraft to show that he had any clue to the narrative and details of the Onondaga tradition of Hiawatha, until he had access to my manuscript as received by him from the editor of the New York *Commercial Advertiser*.

As an evidence, I here most distinctly and emphatically assert that the name "Hosee Noke," at page 278 of the "Notes" is an unadulterated fiction of my own, created for the occasion, suggested by a wild, half-crazy, merry-Andrew sort of fellow, an Indian, who always took the lead in all the grotesque dances held at the Onondaga Castle, who bore a similar name, and who was a "Runner," and who is since dead.

Again, the speech of Hiawatha, as it appears at page 280 of the "Notes," is a pure invention of my own, and it is identical, verbatim, with the same speech in Clark's "Onondaga," vol. I. at page 28, which is like the manuscript furnished to Mr. Schoolcraft by me through the editor of the *Commercial Advertiser*. In the "Notes," however, Mr. Schoolcraft has transposed the word Onondaga, and entirely omitted the word Mohawk, which should be in its place, which change wholly destroys the force, truth and beauty of the allusions, for it makes them totally inapplicable as rendered in the "Notes." The Onondagas were always known as "The People of the Hills." Father Hennepin, Lib. II. page 104, styles them the "Iroquois Highlanders," and in early times the Mohawks were styled the "Great Tree," to which the Dutch first made fast the chain of friendship in their intercourse with the "Five Nations." The names of the Senecas and Cayugas are omitted in their proper places in the "Notes," as are also the names of the several other Indian nations.

The version of "Hiawatha, or the Origin of the Onondaga Council-Fire," in the larger work of Mr. Schoolcraft, is merely an abridgement of the story as it appears in the "Notes," though the speech of Hiawatha is retained mainly. Most of the first part of the tradition is entirely omitted in the larger work, with the supplementary addition of the note accounting for the source of its derivation.

The name Hi-a-wat-ha is purely Onondaga. It has no existence or counterpart among the Indians beyond the precincts of the Confederate Nations. Other nations may have their "Quetzalcoatl," their "Maniton," their "Manabozho," their "Mondamni," or other divinities, known by various names and possessed of live characteristics, yet the Iroquois alone have the true Hi-a-wat-ha, the great founder of their league.

Upon the appearance of the tradition of Hiawatha in the "Notes on the Iroquois," in 1847, I called the attention of several of my friends to the fact of its having been previously read before the Manlius Lyceum, and we compared the manuscript copy retained by me with the version in the "Notes on the Iroquois," and found them identical in the delineation throughout, and verbatim in many entire paragraphs, which circumstance could not possibly have occurred had the tradition been "derived from the *verbal* narrations of the late Abraham Le Fort, an Onondaga Chief."

These gentlemen, my friends above referred to, will attest to the facts herein set forth.

For myself I claim no particular merit or distinction for the tradition of Hiawatha, as the source of its origin as it appears in English.

Nor do I wish in the remotest sense to detract a particle from the well-earned fame of Mr. Schoolcraft in regard to his Indian researches. But since the tradition of Hiawatha has become the theme and substance of a purely American poem, which is attracting a world-wide attention, and the origin of the tradition has been wrongfully attributed in a note at the end of the volume, and has been introduced into the greatest Indian work of the age par excellence, as "derived from the verbal narrations of the late Abraham Le Fort, an Onondaga Chief," it is as well that the public should be informed truly of the source.

This letter is signed by Joshua V. H. Clark, and it is dated Manlius, Onondaga county, New York, January 2, 1856.

Homer D. L. Sweet, in his biographical sketch of Joshua V. H. Clark, whose death occurred in Manlius. June 18, 1869, in his sixty-seventh year, says: "Very unfortunately for Mr. Schoolcraft, he replied to Mr. Clark, and imputed motives to him unworthy of a gentleman. Mr. Clark, in a rejoinder, produced the proofs and convicted Mr. Schoolcraft of plagiarism, if not of untruthfulness."

Mr. Longfellow sent a copy of his "Song of Hiawatha" to Mr. Clark, January, 1856, accompanying it with a letter, which was given to the Onondaga Historical Association.

Mr. Beauchamp, in a letter to the Syracuse *Standard*, April 11, 1894, makes reference to another legend of Hiawatha, accidentally found by him in a book published in 1839. This book is entitled: "The History of the New Netherlands, Province of New York and State of New York, to the adoption of the Federal Constitution," written by William Dunlap and printed for the author by Carter & Thorp of New York in 1839. Mr. Dunlap says that he had frequent communication with Ephraim Webster, the Indian interpreter, and he adds: "Mr. Webster was most conversant with the Onondagas, and when I knew him in 1815, cultivated land in Onondaga Hollow, and was looked up to by the Indians as a friend and father."

Mr. Dunlap's account of the origin of the Iroquois confederation is as follows:—

The Indian tradition of the origin of the confederacy as given by him [Ephraim Webster], was as
follows: He said that the happy thought of union for
defence originated with an inferior Chief of the
Onondagas, who perceiving that although the five
tribes were alike in language, and had by co-operation
conquered a great extent of country, yet that they had
frequent quarrels and no head or great council, to
reconcile them; and that while divided, the Western
Indians attacked and destroyed them; seeing this, he
conceived the bright idea of union, and of a great
council of the chiefs of the Five Nations. This, he
said, and perhaps thought, came to him in a dream;
and it was afterward considered as coming from the
Great Spirit. He proposed this plan in a council of
his tribe, but the principal chief opposed it. He was
a great warrior, and feared to lose his influence as
head man of the Onondagas. This was a selfish man.

The younger chief, who we will call Oweko, was
silenced; but he determined in secret to attempt the
great political work. This was a man who loved the
welfare of others. To make long journeys and be
absent for several days while hunting, would cause
no suspicion, because it was common. He left home
as if to hunt; but taking a circuitous path through
the woods, for all this great country was then a
wilderness, he made his way to the village or castle
of the Mohawks. He consulted some of the leaders

of that tribe, and they received the scheme favorably:
he visited the Oneidas, and gained the assent of their
chief; he then returned home. After a time he made
another pretended hunt, and another; thus, by de-
grees, visiting the Cayugas and Senecas, and gained
the assent of all to a great council to be held at Onondaga. With consummate art he then gained over his
own chief, by convincing him of the advantages of
the confederacy, and agreeing that he should be considered as the author of the plan. The great council
met, and the chief of the Onondagas made use of a
figurative argument, taught him by Oweko, which
was the same that we read of in the fable, where a
father teaches his sons the value of union by taking
one stick from a bundle, and showing how feeble it
was, and easily broken, and that when bound together
the bundle resisted his utmost strength.

Mr. Beauchamp's letter, to which reference has been
made, contains a letter to him from Dr. Horatio Hale,
the distinguished philologist, in which Dr. Hale says:
" 'Oweko' does not differ so widely from ' Hiawatha '
that we may not fairly presume to have been a corruption of the latter name, made in passing from one
dialect to another, and finally into English. The
Mohawk form of the name, as you will see in the
'Book of Rites,' p. 128, is Ayonhwahtha. The
strong dental aspirate, represented by ' hth,' heard by
a foreign ear, might easily become a 'k.' We have
many examples of corruption quite as great."

Regarding the words " Oweko " and " Hiawatha,"
Mr. Beauchamp says: " In regard to Mr. Hale's
conjecture on the name, while good, it is hardly
required, as the relator of Webster's story merely
says: ' The younger chief, whom we will call Oweko,
was silenced.' The inference is that he was uncertain
in his recollection of the name, and gave it as best he
could."

Dr. Hale is of the opinion "that the justly venerated
author of this confederation, the far-famed Hiawatha,
was not, as some have thought, a mythological or a
poetical creation, but really an aboriginal statesman
and law-maker, a personage as authentic and as admir-
able as Solon or Washington. The important bearing of
these conclusions on our estimate of the mental and
moral endowments of primitive or uncultivated man
is too clear to require explanation."

Mr. Beauchamp, while not agreeing entirely with
this opinion of Dr. Hale, is inclined to think that it is
in the main correct.

CHAPTER XXIII

SHORT HISTORY OF SYRACUSE

The old town of Salina, now the towns of Salina and Geddes and the city of Syracuse, the greater part of which was originally embraced in the Salt Springs Reservation, was incorporated March 27, 1809, its territory having been a part of the original townships of Manlius and Marcellus. The villages of Syracuse, Salina and Geddes, now forming the greater part of the city of Syracuse, were originally in the town of Salina. The village of Salina was incorporated March 12, 1824. The village of Syracuse was incorporated April 13, 1825; and the first meeting for the election of village officers was held at the old schoolhouse May 3, 1825. The village of Geddes was incorporated April 20, 1832, though a map of the site of Geddes village was made as early as 1807, and several other maps a few years later. Geddes was not formed as a town until 1848. The town included all that part of the town of Salina west of Onondaga lake, not now embraced in the city of Syracuse. Syracuse was

(370)

incorporated by act of Legislature as a city, December 14, 1847, and it included the villages of Salina and Syracuse. An election was held in those two villages January 3, 1848; and by the vote of that election the act of incorporation became a law. The first election in the city of Syracuse was held March 7, 1848, and the first Common Council meeting was held March 13, 1848. The annexation of Geddes and adjacent territory to Syracuse, was authorized by act of Legislature May 17, 1886. The Danforth territory was authorized to be annexed to Syracuse by act of Legislature June 15, 1886. Danforth had been incorporated as a village after the election held December 21, 1874, favoring such action.

The city of Syracuse is situated in the midst of a rich agricultural region, and near the centre of New York state. It is a favorable place for holding conventions, because of its central location; and it is often called "The City of Conventions" and "The Central City." Syracuse is the county seat of Onondaga county. This county was originally formed from the western part of Herkimer county, March 5, 1794, and included all of the Military Tract, the boundaries of which embraced, (besides the territory of the present Onondaga county,) all of what is now included in the counties of Cayuga, Seneca, Cortland, and all of that part of Tompkins county lying north of a line drawn west from the head of Seneca lake to the southwest corner of Cortland county, and all that part of Oswego county lying west of the Oswego river. From this then great county, Cayuga was taken off March 8, 1799; Cortland, April 8, 1808; and a part of Oswego, March 1, 1816. When organized, the county was divided into eleven towns, viz: Homer, Pompey, Manlius, Lysander, Marcellus, Ulysses, Milton, Scipio, Ovid, Aurelius and Romulus. The town of Onondaga was set off from the original townships of Marcellus, Pompey and Manlius, by an act of Legislature, March 9, 1798. A part of Salina was taken off in 1809, and a part of Camillus in 1834.

The first courts in Onondaga county were held in barns and private residences at Onondaga, Levanna, on the shore of Cayuga lake, now in Cayuga county, and Ovid, now in Seneca county. The first court house was erected at Onondaga Hill in 1805-'06. The commissioners appointed to select the site for the court house were Asa Danforth, George Ballard and Roswell Tousley.

The Walton Tract, which plays such an important part in the history of Syracuse, being situated in what is now the heart of the city, and consisting of 250 acres of land of the Salt Springs Reservation, was sold at public auction in June, 1804, and bid off by Abraham Walton for $6,550. The sale was authorized by act of Legislature, and the proceeds were expended in laying out and improving a road running from lot forty-nine,

Manlius, to lot thirty-eight, Onondaga, east and west through the reservation. This road was the old Seneca turnpike. The land had been advertised for sale with the announcement that upon it was a good mill site. The tract was laid out in an irregular form by James Geddes, in order that as much dry land might be secured as possible. But notwithstanding all the precaution of Mr. Geddes, it was found impossible to locate the ground in such a manner as to avoid entirely the swamp, some considerable portion of which was covered with water most of the year; a doleful place, indeed, for the site of a future city.

A portion of the Walton Tract was sold to Michael Hogan and Charles Walton, who, with the original proprietor, held it in common. After some unimportant changes, the tract was sold in 1814, for $9,000, to Forman, Wilson & Company, composed of Joshua Forman, Ebenezer Wilson, Jr., and John B. Creed. The tract was sold by the Sheriff, October 26, 1818, to Daniel Kellogg and William H. Sabin for $10,915. The next owner was Henry Eckford, the celebrated ship builder of New York. He purchased it in 1823. In May, 1824, the Walton Tract was transferred for $30,000 to the Syracuse Company, composed of William James of Albany, who owned five-eights; Isaiah Townsend and John Townsend of Albany, who owned two-eighths; and James McBride of New York, who owned one-eighth. The tract was then deeded in

SHORT HISTORY OF SYRACUSE

trust to Moses D. Burnet and Gideon Hawley. During
all this time, extensive sales had been made of portions
of this tract to different individuals.

The village officers of Syracuse are as follows:

1825.—Trustees—Joshua Forman, President; Amos
P. Granger, Moses D. Burnet, Heman Walbridge,
John Rogers. Assessors—James Webb, Alfred
Northam, Thomas Spencer. Clerk—John Wil-
kinson. Treasurer—John Durnford.

1826.—Trustees—William Malcolm, President; Jonas
Mann, John Wall, Henry Young, A. N. Van
Patten. Assessors—A. N. Van Patten, Stephen
W. Cadwell, Alfred Northam. Clerk—Peter
Van Olinda. Treasurer—John Durnford.

1827.—Trustees—Jonas Mann, President; Archie
Kasson, John Wilkinson, James Webb, Jonathan
Day. Assessors—Stephen W. Cadwell, Barent
Filkins, Humphrey Mellen. Clerk—John C.
Field. Treasurer—Volney Cook.

1828.—Trustees—Henry Newton, President; John
Wall, Amos P. Granger, John Wilkinson, John
H. Johnson. Assessors—Joseph Slocum, Calvin
Riley, Pliny Dickinson. Clerk—John C. Field.
Treasurer—Stephen W. Cadwell.

1829.—Trustees—Stephen W. Cadwell, President;
Joseph Slocum, B. Davis Noxon, Calvin Riley,
H. W. Van Buren. Assessors—Elbert Norton,
James Webb, W. B. Kirk. Clerk—John C.
Field. Treasurer—George Fitch.

1830.—Trustees—William B. Kirk, President; Elbert Norton, Schuyler Strong, Columbus Bradley, H. W. Van Buren. Assessors—R. I. Brockway, David Stafford, Joseph Savage. Clerk—John C. Field. Treasurer—Hiram Judson.

1831.—Trustees—Daniel Elliott, President; B. Davis Noxon, Elijah Dunlap, Columbus Bradley, Roswell Hinman. Assessors—Theodore Ashley, William H. Alexander, Paschal Thurber. Clerk—Hiram A. Deming. Treasurer—Elbert Norton.

1832.—Trustees—Hiram Putnam, President; William Malcolm, David Stafford, jr., Willet Raynor, Columbus Bradley. Assessors—Daniel Elliott, George Hooker, Mather Williams. Clerk—Hiram A. Deming. Treasurer—Elbert Norton.

1833. —Trustees —Henry Davis, jr., President; Columbus Bradley, Stephen W. Cadwell, Lewis H. Redfield, John H. Johnson. Assessors—Amos P. Granger, John Wilkinson, David S. Colvin. Clerk—Edward B. Wicks. Treasurer—Hiram A. Deming.

1834.—Trustees—B. Davis Noxon, President; Lyman Phillips, Silas Ames, Paschal Thurber, William K. Blair. Assessors—Hiram Putnam, George W. Burnet, Harmon W. Van Buren. Clerk—J. E. Hanchett. Treasurer—Hiram A. Deming.

1835.—Trustees—Stephen W. Cadwell, President; Vivus W. Smith, Elihu Walter, Silas Ames,

Roswell Hinman. Assessors—Lewis H. Redfield, Henry W. Starin, Thomas Bennett. Clerk—Peter Outwater, jr. Treasurer—Hiram Judson.

1836.—Trustees—Pliny Dickinson. President; Thomas B. Fitch, William Jackson, Elihu L. Phillips, James Huff. Assessors—William B. Kirk, David Stafford, jr., Hiram Putnam. Clerk—Levi L. Chapman. Treasurer—Charles B. Hargin.

1837.—Trustees—Elias W. Leavenworth. President; William Jackson, John H. Lathrop, Theodore Wood, Samuel Larned. Assessors—Hiram Putnam, William H. Alexander, Robert Furman. Clerk—H. Nelson Cheney. Treasurer—Edward B. Wicks.

1838.—Trustees—Elias W. Leavenworth. President; Jonathan Baldwin, Robert Furman, Amos P. Granger, Ziba W. Cogswell. Assessors—Pliny Dickinson, Charles A. Baker, John H. Lathrop. Clerk—Samuel D. Day. Treasurer—Edward B. Wicks.

1839.—Trustees—Elias W. Leavenworth, President; Jonathan Baldwin, Robert Furman, Amos P. Granger, Ziba W. Cogswell. Assessors—Pliny Dickinson, Charles A. Baker, John H. Lathrop. Clerk—Samuel D. Day. Treasurer—Edward B. Wicks.

1840.—Trustees—Elias W. Leavenworth, President; Jonathan Baldwin, Paschal Thurber, Gardner

Lawrence, Lucius A. Cheney. Assessors--Jonathan Baldwin, William K. Blair, Charles A. Baker. Clerk—Jasper Smith. Treasurer—Harmon W. Van Buren.

1841.—Trustees—Thomas T. Davis, President; William Barker, Elisha George, Hiram Putnam, Johnson Hall. Assessors—William H. Alexander, William Malcolm, Mather Williams. Clerk-- William M. Clarke. Treasurer--Harmon W. Van Buren.

1842.—Trustees—Henry W. Durnford, President; George Stevens, Joseph Savage, Charles A. Baker, Robert Furman. Assessors—Horace Butts, Ansel Lull, Henry Gifford. Clerk—John K. Barlow. Treasurer—Pliny Dickinson.

1843.—Trustees—Henry Rhoades, President; George Stevens, Alanson Thorp, R. R. Phelps, Smith Ostrom. Assessors—John Newell, William Barker, Horace Butts. Clerk—Richard A. Yoe. Treasurer—Hiram Putnam.

1844.—Trustees—Philo D. Mickles, President; Alexander McKinstry, Horace Butts, Robert Furman, Lucius A. Cheney. Assessors—Joseph Slocum, Charles A. Baker, Jared H. Parker. Clerk— Rodolphus H. Duell. Treasurer—Hiram Putnam.

1845.—Trustees—William Barker, President; Jared H. Parker, Alexander McKinstry, L. A. Cheney, Bradley Cary. Assessors—William B. Kirk,

Charles A. Baker, Joseph Slocum.   Clerk—Caleb
B. Crumb.   Treasurer—Hiram Putnam.

1846.—Trustees—Elias W. Leavenworth, President;
S. V. R. Van Heusen, Hamilton White, William B.
Kirk, Joseph Billings.   Assessors—George Stevens.
Charles A. Baker. William Barker.   Clerk—
Oliver R. W. Lull.   Treasurer—Hiram Putnam.

1847.—Trustees—Elias W. Leavenworth, President:
Alexander McKinstry, Charles Leonard. Henry
Agnew, Perley B. Cleveland.   Assessors—William
Barker, Harmon W. Van Buren, J. H. Parker.
Clerk—Daniel P. Wood.   Treasurer—Hiram
Putnam.

The city officers of Syracuse are as follows:

1848.—Mayor—Harvey Baldwin, Democrat.   Clerk
—Richard A. Yoe.   Treasurer—Perry Burdick.
Aldermen—First ward—Elizur Clark, James
Lynch.   Second ward—John B. Burnet. Alex-
ander McKinstry.   Third ward—Gardner Law-
rence, William H. Alexander.   Fourth ward—
Robert Furman, Henry W. Durnford.

1849.—Mayor—Elias W. Leavenworth, Whig. Clerk
—S. Corning Judd.   Treasurer—Harmon W.
Van Buren.   Aldermen—First ward—James
Lynch, Thomas Feagan, (resigned February 26,
1850.)   John P. Babcock, (appointed by Common
Council to fill vacancy.)   Second ward—Alexan-
der McKinstry, Silas Titus.   Third ward—

Gardner Lawrence, Amos Westcott. Fourth ward—Henry W. Durnford, Edward B. Wicks.

1850.—Mayor—Alfred H. Hovey, Whig. Clerk— LeRoy L. Alexander. Treasurer—Harvey Hathaway. Aldermen—First ward—John P. Babcock, Miles W. Bennett. Second ward—Silas Titus, George W. Herrick. Third ward—Amos Westcott, John W. Barker. Fourth ward—Edward B. Wicks, Henry D. Hatch.

1851.—Mayor—Moses D. Burnet, Loco Foco, (elected but declined to qualify.) Horace Wheaton, (appointed by Common Council.) Clerk—LeRoy L. Alexander. Treasurer—James A. Castle. Aldermen—First ward—Miles W. Bennett, Burr Burton. Second ward—George W. Herrick, James M. Taylor. Third ward—John W. Barker, (removed from ward,) Benjamin L. Higgins (elected to fill vacancy,) Volney Green. Fourth ward—Henry D. Hatch, Charles Pope.

1852.—Mayor—Jason C. Woodruff, Loco Foco. Clerk—LeRoy L. Alexander. Treasurer—Jacob S. Smith. Aldermen—First ward—Burr Burton, Alonzo Crippen. Second ward—Daniel O. Salmon, Harmon Ackerman. Third ward— Volney Green, Addison G. Williams. Fourth ward—Charles Pope, Oliver T. Burt.

1853.—Mayor—Dennis McCarthy, Loco Foco. Clerk —LeRoy L. Alexander. Treasurer—John M. Jaycox. Aldermen—First ward—Alonzo Crippen,

Patrick Cooney. Second ward—Daniel O. Salmon, Alexander McKinstry. Third ward—Addison G. Williams, John A. Clarke. Fourth ward—Oliver T. Burt, George J. Gardner.

1854.—Mayor—Allen Munroe, Whig. Clerk—Carroll E. Smith. Treasurer—S. Hervey Slosson, Aldermen—First ward—Patrick Cooney, Richard Sanger. Second Ward—Peter Ohneth, Jacob Pfohl. Third ward—Alexander McKinstry, Solomon Wands. Fourth ward—Peter Featherly, Francis A. Thayer. Fifth ward—William B. Durkee, Z. Lawrence Beebe. Sixth ward—John A. Clarke, Timothy Hough. Seventh ward—William C. Young, Robert M. Richardson. Eighth ward—George J. Gardner, Tobias Van Dusen.

1855.—Mayor—Lyman Stevens, Republican. Clerk—Carroll E. Smith. Treasurer—S. Hervey Slosson. Aldermen—First ward—Richard Sanger, Timothy R. Porter. Second ward—Jacob Pfohl, Peter Ohneth. Third ward—Solomon Wands, Manly T. Hilliard. Fourth ward—Francis A. Thayer, William Kirkpatrick. Fifth ward—Z. Lawrence Beebe, Vernam C. James. Sixth ward—Timothy Hough, Charles H. Wells. Seventh ward—Robert M. Richardson, Horatio N. White. Eighth ward—Tobias Van Dusen, Elijah M. Ford.

1856.- -Mayor—Charles F. Williston, Democrat. Clerk—Carroll E. Smith. Treasurer—Edgar Marvin. Aldermen—First ward—Timothy R. Porter, Coddington B. Williams. Second ward— Peter Ohneth, Peter Conrad. Third ward—Manly T. Hilliard, Charles Manahan. Fourth ward— William Kirkpatrick, George Sanford. Fifth ward—Vernam C. James, William B. Durkee. Sixth ward—Henry Church, Amos B. Hough. Seventh ward—Horatio N. White, Francis A. Marsh. Eight ward—James L. Bagg, Norman Watson.

1857.—Mayor—Charles F. Williston, Democrat. Clerk—James S. Gillespie. Treasurer—Horace Wheaton. Aldermen—First ward—Coddington B. Williams, Patrick Cooney. Second ward— Peter Conrad, Cornelius L. Alvord. Third ward —Charles Manahan, John Ritchie. Fourth ward —George Sanford, William Kirkpatrick. Fifth ward—John C. Manly, (to fill vacancy), John J. Mowry. Sixth ward—Amos B. Hough, Henry Church. Seventh ward—Francis A. Marsh, John Radigan. Eighth ward—Norman Watson, Samuel J. Lackey.

1858.—Mayor—William Winton, Democrat. Clerk— James S. Gillespie. Treasurer—Horace Wheaton. Aldermen—First ward—Patrick Cooney. Second ward —Frederick Gilbert. Third ward—Charles

Manahan. Fourth ward—James Johnson. Fifth
ward—Abiah P. Doane. Sixth ward—John L.
Cook. Seventh ward—Robert M. Richardson.
Eighth ward—Samuel J. Lackey.

1859.—Mayor—Elias W. Leavenworth, Republican.
Clerk—Edgar S. Mathews. Treasurer—Norman
Otis. Aldermen—First ward—Harvey Hatha-
way. Second ward—Adam Listman. Third
ward—Samuel P. Geer. Fourth ward—Luke
Collins. Fifth ward—David Field. Sixth ward
—Charles P. Clark. Seventh ward—Jason S.
Hoyt. Eighth ward—Austin Myers.

1860.—Mayor—Amos Westcott, Republican. Clerk—
Edgar S. Mathews. Treasurer—John G. K.
Truair. Aldermen—First ward—Harvey Hatha-
way. Second ward—Adam Listman. Third
ward—Samuel P. Geer. Fourth ward—Luke
Collins. Fifth ward—David Field. Sixth ward
—Charles P. Clark. Seventh ward—Horatio N.
White. Eighth ward—Samuel J. Lackey.

1861.—Mayor—Charles Andrews, Republican. Clerk
—Edgar S. Mathews. Treasurer—John G. K.
Truair. Aldermen—First ward—Garrett Doyle.
Second ward—Jacob Pfohl. Third ward—Samuel
P. Geer. Fourth ward—Horatio G. Glen. Fifth
ward—David Field. Sixth ward—Moses Sum-
mers. Seventh ward—Horatio N. White. Eighth
ward—Ira Seymour.

1862.—Mayor—Charles Andrews, Republican.—Clerk
—Edgar S. Mathews. Treasurer—John G. K.
Truair. Aldermen—First ward—Garrett Doyle.
Second ward—Benedict Haberle. Third ward—
Samuel P. Geer. Fourth ward—William Sum-
mers. Fifth ward—Josiah Bettis. Sixth ward—
Charles P. Clark. Seventh ward—Horatio N.
White. Eighth ward—Ira Seymour.

1863.—Mayor—Daniel Bookstaver, Democrat.—Clerk
—Robert M. Beecher. Treasurer—Daniel J. Hal-
sted. Aldermen—First ward—Franklin Ward.
Second ward—Charles Meebold. Third ward—
Francis H. Kennedy. Fourth ward—Luke Col-
lins. Fifth ward—Jacob Pinkerton. Sixth ward
—Francis E. Carroll. Seventh ward—Parley
Bassett. Eighth ward—George J. Gardner.

1864.—Mayor—Archibald C. Powell, Republican.
Clerk—Edward H. Brown. Treasurer—John
G. K. Truair. Aldermen—First ward—Franklin
Ward. Second ward—Charles F. Wischoon.
Third ward—Jacobus Bruyn. Fourth ward—Ho-
ratio G. Glen. Fifth ward—Josiah Bettis. Sixth
ward—Alfred Higgins. Seventh ward—John J.
Crouse. Eighth ward—Philander W. Hudson.

1865.—Mayor—William D. Stewart, Democrat. Clerk
—Edward H. Brown. Treasurer—John G. K.
Truair. Aldermen—First ward—Peter Mackin.
Second ward—Charles F. Wischoon. Third ward—

Jacobus Bruyn. Fourth ward—Charles Stroh. Fifth ward—Anson A. Sweet. Sixth ward— Alfred Higgins. Seventh ward—John J. Crouse. Eighth ward—James Bonner.

1866.—Mayor—William D. Stewart, Democrat. Clerk —Edgar S. Mathews. Treasurer—Moses Summers. Aldermen—First ward—Peter Mackin. Second ward—John Graff. Third ward—Edmund B. Griswold. Fourth ward—Charles Stroh. Fifth ward—David Field. Sixth ward—Alfred Higgins. Seventh ward—Joseph E. Masters. Eighth ward—Robert Hewitt.

1867.—Mayor—William D. Stewart, Democrat. Clerk —Edgar S. Mathews. Treasurer—Charles J. Foote. Aldermen—First ward—Samuel Kent. Second ward—John Graff. Third ward—Jacobus Bruyn. Fourth ward—David Wilcox. Fifth ward—Horatio G. Glen. Sixth ward—Richard W. Jones. Seventh ward—Miles Handwright. Eighth ward—Robert Hewitt.

1868.—Mayor—Charles Andrews, Republican. Clerk —Edgar S. Mathews. Treasurer—Thomas S. Truair. Aldermen—First ward—John McKeever. Second ward—John Hirsch. Third ward—Jacobus Bruyn. Fourth ward—Nicholas Grumbach. Fifth ward—John Stedman. Sixth ward—Richard W. Jones. Seventh ward—Benjamin L. Higgins. Eighth ward—James Pinkerton.

1869. Mayor—Charles P. Clark, Republican. Clerk —Edgar S. Mathews. Treasurer—Thomas S. Truair. Aldermen—First ward—Samuel Kent. Second ward—Peter Miller. Third ward—William H. Austin. Fourth ward—Nicholas Grumbach. Fifth ward—Horatio G. Glen. Sixth ward—Alfred Higgins. Seventh ward—Jacob Levi. Eighth ward—James Pinkerton.

1870.—Mayor—Charles P. Clark, Republican. Clerk —Samuel W. Sherlock. Treasurer—Parley Bassett. Aldermen—First ward—John McGuire. Second ward—Maximilian Blust. Third ward—Martin Smith. Fourth ward—William Phillipson. Fifth ward—Christopher C. Bradley. Sixth ward—Samuel E. Kingsley. Seventh ward—Jacob Levi. Eighth ward—George Draper.

1871.—Mayor—Francis E. Carroll, Democrat. Clerk —Samuel W. Sherlock. Treasurer—Parley Bassett. Aldermen—First ward—John McGuire. Second ward—Jacob Knapp. Third ward—Alfred A. Howlett. Fourth ward—William Phillipson. Fifth ward—Christopher C. Bradley. Sixth ward—Thomas Nesdall. Seventh ward—Jacob Levi. Eighth ward—Thomas G. Bassett.

1872.—Mayor—Francis E. Carroll, Democrat. Clerk —Samuel W. Sherlock. Treasurer—Parley Bassett. Aldermen—First ward—John McGuire. Second ward—John Demong. Third ward—

Richard Clancy. Fourth ward—John Kohl. Fifth
ward—Jacob Pinkerton. Sixth ward—Thomas
Nesdall. Seventh ward—William Cahill. Eighth
ward—E. Austin Barnes.

1873.—Mayor—William J. Wallace, Republican.
Clerk—Samuel W. Sherlock. Treasurer—Parley
Bassett. Aldermen—First ward—John Cawley.
Second ward—John Demong. Third ward—
Richard Clancy. Fourth ward—John Kohl.
Fifth ward—John H. Horton. Sixth ward—John
R. Whitlock. Seventh ward—William Cahill.
Eighth ward—George J. Gardner.

1874.—Mayor—Nathan F. Graves, Democrat. Clerk—
Samuel W. Sherlock. Treasurer—Parley Bassett.
Aldermen—First ward—John Cawley. Second
ward—John Demong. Third ward—Richard
Clancy. Fourth ward—William Kirkpatrick.
Fifth ward—John D. Gray. Sixth ward—John R.
Whitlock. Seventh ward—William Cahill.
Eighth ward—James L. Hill.

1875.—Mayor—George P. Hier, Republican. Clerk—
Lyman C. Dorwin. Treasurer—Albert L. Bridge-
man. Aldermen—First ward—Jeremiah F.
Barnes. Second ward—Adam Filsinger. Third
ward—Austin C. Wood. Fourth ward—Thomas
Ryan. Fifth ward—William Dickinson. Sixth
ward—Alfred Higgins. Seventh ward—Albert
M. Morse. Eighth ward—James L. Hill.

1876.—Mayor—John J. Crouse, Republican. Clerk—
Lyman C. Dorwin. Treasurer—James B. Rae.
Aldermen—First ward—John Harvey. Second
ward—John Demong. Third ward—Timothy
Sullivan. Fourth ward—Thomas Ryan. Fifth
ward—Samuel Taylor. Sixth ward—Alfred Higgins. Seventh ward—Albert M. Morse. Eighth
ward—Riley V. Miller.

1877.—Mayor—James J. Belden, Republican. Clerk
—Lyman C. Dorwin. Treasurer—Stiles M. Rust.
Aldermen—First ward—Jeremiah F. Barnes.
Second ward—John Listman. Third ward—
Timothy Sullivan. Fourth ward—J. Emmet
Wells. Fifth ward—A. Clarke Baum. Sixth
ward—Alfred Higgins. Seventh ward—Albert
M. Morse. Eighth ward—Jacob Crouse.

1878.—Mayor—James J. Belden. Clerk—Lyman C.
Dorwin. Treasurer—Stiles M. Rust. Aldermen
—First ward—John Harvey. Second ward—
Philip Schaefer. Third ward—Timothy Sullivan.
Fourth ward—J. Emmet Wells. Fifth ward—
Pierce B. Brayton. Sixth ward—Alfred Higgins.
Seventh ward—Thomas McCarthy. Eighth
ward—Dennis M. Kennedy.

1879.—Mayor—Irving G. Vann, Republican. Clerk
—Lyman C. Dorwin. Treasurer—Timothy Sul-
livan. Aldermen—First ward—Andrew Martin.
Second ward—Joseph Walier. Third ward—

Anthony S. Webb. Fourth ward—Charles
Schlosser. Fifth ward—Charles Hubbard. Sixth
ward—Daniel Candee. Seventh ward—Dennis
B. Keller. Eighth ward—Luther S. Merrick.

1880.—Mayor—Francis Hendricks, Republican. Clerk
—Lyman C. Dorwin. Treasurer—Timothy Sulli-
van. Aldermen—First ward—Andrew Martin.
Second ward—Joseph Walier. Third ward—
Anthony S. Webb. Fourth ward—Charles Schlos-
ser. Fifth ward—Greene W. Ingalls. Sixth
ward—Daniel Candee. Seventh ward—William
Cahill. Eighth ward—Luther S. Merrick.

1881.—Mayor—Francis Hendricks, Republican. Clerk
—Lyman C. Dorwin. Treasurer—Timothy Sulli-
van. Aldermen—First ward—Frederick Beley.
Second ward—Jacob Eichenlaub. Third ward—
Anthony S. Webb. Fourth ward—James Fine-
gan. Fifth ward—Richard Tremain. Sixth
ward—Willis B. Burns. Seventh ward—John
Bedford. Eighth ward—Luther S. Merrick.

1882.—Mayor—John Demong, Democrat. Clerk—
Lyman C. Dorwin. Treasurer—Timothy Sulli-
van. Aldermen—First ward—Frederick Beley.
Second ward — Jacob Eichenlaub. Third ward
—Anthony S. Webb. Fourth ward—James
Finegan. Fifth ward—Richard Tremain. Sixth
ward—Willis B. Burns. Seventh ward—John
Bedford. Eighth ward—Luther S. Merrick.

1883.—Mayor—Thomas Ryan, Democrat. Clerk—
Lyman C. Dorwin. Treasurer—Charles J. Rae.
Aldermen—First ward—Frederick Beley. Second
ward—Jacob Eichenlaub—Third ward—Frank
Matty. Fourth ward—J. Emmet Wells. Fifth
ward—John C. Keefe. Sixth ward—Charles E.
Candee. Seventh ward—Thomas McManus.
Eighth ward—Luther S. Merrick.

1884.—Mayor—Thomas Ryan, Democrat. Clerk—
Henry W. Bannister. Treasurer—Charles J.
Rae. Aldermen—First ward—Hoyt H. Freeman.
Second ward—Charles Listman. Third ward—
Frank Matty. Fourth ward—Frederick Schwarz.
Fifth ward—William J. Gillett. Sixth ward—
Charles E. Candee. Seventh ward—Thomas
McManus. Eighth ward—James B. Brooks.

1885.—Mayor—Thomas Ryan, Democrat. Clerk—
Henry W. Bannister. Treasurer—Charles J.
Rae. Aldermen—First ward—John Leahey.
Second ward—Charles Listman. Third ward—
James Downey. Fourth ward—Phillip Goettel.
Fifth ward—John G. Glazier. Sixth ward—
Charles E. Candee. Seventh ward—Thomas
McManus. Eighth ward—Terrence D. Wilkin.

1886.—Mayor—Willis B. Burns, Republican. Clerk—
Henry W. Bannister. Treasurer—Michael
Whelan. Aldermen—First ward—John Leahey.
Second ward—Charles Listman. Third ward—

James Downey. Fourth ward—Phillip Goettel.
Fifth ward—John G. Glazier. Sixth ward—
Charles E. Candee. Seventh ward—Thomas
Mc Manus. Eighth ward—Terrence D. Wilkin.

1887.—Mayor—Willis B. Burns, Republican. Clerk
—Henry W. Bannister. Treasurer—Michael
Whelan. Aldermen—First ward—John Leahey.
Second ward—Charles Listman. Third ward—
Patrick Quinlan. Fourth ward—Jacob Galster.
Fifth Ward—Charles C. Lott. Sixth ward—
Charles E. Candee. Seventh ward—Peter E.
Garlick. Eighth ward—Joseph W. Young.
Ninth ward—Frank M. Sweet. Tenth ward—
John P. Shumway. Eleventh ward—John Mc-
Lennan.

1888.—Mayor—William B. Kirk, Democrat. Clerk—
Henry W. Bannister. Treasurer—Michael Whe-
lan. Aldermen—First ward—John Leahey.
Second ward—Peter Snavely. Third ward—
Patrick Quinlan. Fourth ward—John Finegan.
Fifth ward—Charles C. Lott. Sixth ward—
Charles E. Candee. Seventh ward—Peter E.
Garlick. Eighth ward—C. Eugene Seager.
Ninth ward—Frank M. Sweet. Tenth ward—
John Scanlan. Eleventh ward—John McLennan.

1889.—Mayor—William B. Kirk, Democrat. Clerk
—Henry W. Bannister. Treasurer—Benjamin
W. Roscoe. Aldermen—First ward—Thomas

Small. Second ward—Peter Snavely. Third
ward—Frank Matty. Fourth ward—James Finegan. Fifth ward—Terrence D. Wilkin. Sixth
ward—Charles E. Candee. Seventh ward—
Michael D. McAuliffe. Eighth ward—C. Eugene
Seager. Ninth ward—Edward M. Klock. Tenth
ward—John Scanlan. Eleventh ward—John
McLennan.

1890.—Mayor—William Cowie, Republican. Clerk
—Henry F. Stephens. Treasurer—Benjamin W
Roscoe. Aldermen—First ward—Thomas Small.
Second ward—Andrew Zinsmeister. Third ward—
Frank Matty. Fourth ward—Benjamin Stephen-
son. Fifth ward—Terrence D. Wilkin. Sixth
ward—Charles E. Candee. Seventh ward—
Michael D. McAuliffe. Eighth ward—Charles
F. Ayling. Ninth ward—Edward M. Klock.
Tenth ward—Michael O'Neill. Eleventh ward—
John McLennan.

1891.—Mayor—William Cowie, Republican. Clerk
—Henry F. Stephens. Treasurer—Benjamin W.
Roscoe. Aldermen—First ward—John Leahey.
Second ward—Andrew Zinsmeister. Third ward—
Frank Matty. Fourth ward—Benjamin Stephen-
son. Fifth ward—Peter J. Mack. Sixth ward
—Charles E. Candee. Seventh ward—John J.
Murray. Eighth ward—Thomas Merriam. Ninth
ward—Philip G. Brown. Tenth ward—Thomas

McCarthy. Eleventh ward—Fred A. M. Ball. Twelfth ward—Edward C. Smith. Thirteenth ward—Leonard S. Hamson. Fourteenth ward—John S. Carter.

1892.—Mayor—Jacob Amos, Republican. Clerk—Henry F. Stephens. Treasurer—Patrick R. Quinlan. Aldermen—First ward—John Leahey. Second ward—Andrew Zinsmeister. Third ward—Frank Matty. Fourth ward—Benjamin Stephenson. Fifth ward—Peter J. Mack. Sixth ward—Robert C. McClure. Seventh ward—John J. Murray—Eighth ward—Eugene J. Mack. Ninth ward—Philip G. Brown. Tenth ward—William J. Nairn. Eleventh ward—Fred A. M. Ball. Twelfth ward—Jay B. Kline. Thirteenth ward—Leonard S. Hamson. Fourteenth ward—John A. Tholens.

1893.—Mayor—Jacob Amos, Republican. Clerk—Henry F. Stephens. Treasurer—Patrick R. Quinlan. Aldermen—First ward—John Leahey. Second ward—Andrew Zinsmeister. Third ward—Frank Matty. Fourth ward—Benjamin Stephenson. Fifth ward—Peter J. Mack. Sixth ward—Robert C. McClure. Seventh ward—George Freeman. Eighth ward—Eugene J. Mack. Ninth ward—George A. Ball. Tenth ward—William J. Nairn. Eleventh ward—Robert Ballard. Twelfth ward—Jay B. Kline. Thir-

teenth ward—Leonard S. Hamson. Fourteenth
ward—John A. Tholens. Fifteenth ward—John
Reagan. Sixteenth ward—Frederick A. Schuck.
Seventeenth ward—Patrick J. McMahon. Eight-
eenth ward—Otto A. Thomas. Nineteenth ward
—John J. Murray.